Mastering StaffPad

by Steve Barden

DIGITAL MUSIC NOTATION FOR THE MODERN COMPOSER

I0808634

ISBN: 978-1-57424-393-2
SAN 683-8022

CENTERSTREAM

P.O. Box 17878 - Anaheim Hills, CA 92817

www.centerstream-usa.com | centerstrm@aol.com | 714-779-9390

For Finley and Charlotte

Table of Contents

Foreword

I've always wanted to write music. As soon as I was old enough, I moved to London to pursue a career in the music industry. I was fortunate enough to work with talented people, and I was struck by how often I'd see pencil and paper on very high profile projects. I could see why - it's quick, simple, reliable and flexible. Of course, as a young newcomer to the industry I could also see that within a modern workflow, it's also hopelessly inefficient. Those static pencil markings can't be previewed without sequencing or distributed without typesetting and printing. Keeping these separate from the composition process turns the fast-paced, agile workflow we expect today into a slow, expensive, cumbersome chore - one that I was becoming increasingly jaded with.

In 2008, I began thinking about ways to streamline the entire process, from the first idea to the final performance. Whilst working with the esteemed orchestrator Nicholas Dodd, I realised all of the technical obstacles could be overcome by simply focusing on the music itself. Notation is the written language of music, so it makes perfect sense to work entirely within that form. Notation needed to be rebooted for the 21st century - to combine the best of the old and the new. The vision was to create virtual manuscript paper - a digital "staff pad" - that you could write on with fluency, edit with efficiency, hear back with realism, and share with simplicity. Every musician in the room should be able to see the latest version of this score, with their part rendered just for them. This would be the most direct form of composer-to-musician collaboration possible, in the most universal and simplest form.

Across the Atlantic, Matthew Tesch - an immensely talented developer and musician - had been dreaming of a similar system. I was incredibly fortunate to find Matt; our skillsets were complementary, our vision was clear, and our goals were aligned. We built a small team, and set to work creating a fully fledged, pen-first composition tool for the latest tablet devices. The first version of StaffPad was released in 2015. The full vision of realtime synchronised scores would take us another 4 years. However, at the start of 2020, we released StaffPad and StaffPad Reader, for iPad and Windows, featuring realistic playback and the ability to share the realtime score to an entire orchestra with one touch. The full vision was complete... nearly.

Of course, we're not done yet! StaffPad is constantly evolving and improving, driven by our key goal: to simplify the process of making music.

Steve has done an excellent job of writing a thorough and clear reference guide for StaffPad, including valuable insight into the creative process along the way. This is a fantastic resource for beginners and professionals alike.

Whatever your skill level, I hope you enjoy creating music with StaffPad!

David William Hearn
StaffPad Creator
London, England
May 2020

Introduction

I must say, I am smitten.

It's not often that one can say they've fallen in love with a piece of computer software. But that's how I feel about StaffPad. I know, you'll say it's just infatuation now, but I'm pretty sure this is *"the one"*.

I'm old fashioned in a way. I like writing music with a pencil and paper. Don't get me wrong, I *love* modern technology. I love my DAW, and my sample libraries, and all the digital tools that go along with it. I wouldn't want to go back to the "old days" of creating music. But I can't get over writing with a pencil and paper.

To survive in life, you must accept newer technologies and give up the old, archaic ways of doing things. Sure, I could dig a hole with my bare hands, but wouldn't it be simpler with a shovel? Of course, it would. And faster!

The job of "music copyist" is all but an ancient profession. Now, music parts for each individual musician is computer generated - extracted - from the full score of a digital work. Often, the music orchestrator inputs the music into a program such as Finale or Sibelius, then pushes a button to print out individual parts. Gone are the days of writing the individual parts on onion skin paper in ink to be mimeographed for each musician. And if the score were not already transposed by the orchestrator, the copyist would have to manually transpose the parts. Yikes! That sounds incredibly prone to error.

Over the years, I've tried most of the music notation programs. Finale was first introduced in 1988. It had basic functionality and was very buggy. But hey, you gotta start somewhere. A few years later, 1993, Sibelius was introduced. Along the way numerous other music notation software programs came and went, but none were considered suitable for professionals as well as the two big boys: Finale and Sibelius.

Printing music for mass consumption, commonly referred to as "sheet music", traditionally used a process known as "engraving". This process was essentially the same as printing words for books and newspapers. A typesetter would load a machine with individual notes and letters and other musical symbols. Later, specialized versions of a musical typewriter allowed these pages to be created at a much quicker pace.

We still use the term "engraving" even though we no longer use those types of machines to print music. In comparison, we also still refer to "horsepower" to quantify the strength of an automobile's engine. I don't think anybody has measured a car's power to that of a bunch of horses in quite a long time!

Why StaffPad?

So why StaffPad? Why now? What makes StaffPad such an amazing program? I'll tell you why: the pencil.

Using the computer keyboard and mouse to enter music is tedious. It's not intuitive. It breaks the flow of creativity. You must first tell the program the value of what you want to enter: quarter, eighth, sixteenth, etc. Then specify if it should be a musical note or a rest. Finally, enter the note. But if you want to beam the notes together you must specify *that* by selecting a group of notes. And so on, and so on...

Sure, you can build up muscle memory and memorize shortcut keys to speed up the process, but this seems counter-intuitive! I always knew that if I could just write the notes with a pencil tool of some sort, I could move a lot quicker.

I've been waiting for a program like this for 30 years. And now it's here. For me, this is the only way to create music.

But couldn't I just play the notes with my MIDI keyboard into my DAW? Sure. I've been doing it that way for years. But what has always been lacking in that approach is the visual representation of what the score looks like. A violin part might require several tracks just to accommodate all the articulations required for the score. With musical notation, I can glance at a score from top to bottom and see how each section is working with the rest of the orchestra; where it needs counter melody; where it's too cluttered or where it's too sparse.

With StaffPad I can write notes like I would on paper and keep my left brain, the technical side, separate from the work of my right brain, the creative side. It's a natural flow and keeps things moving.

The History of StaffPad

David William Hearn is the founder of StaffPad. David is a composer, arranger, orchestrator, and music producer based in London. Along with Alex Wallbank, they co-created the Kontakt-based sample library, Cinematic Studio Strings.

As an arranger, David experienced firsthand the difficulties of composing music first in the sequencer (DAW), then having to lay out playable parts for the musicians in the Sibelius music engraving program. The disruption of workflow and creativity was apparent. Along with the many technological roadblocks that inevitably come when working with modern technology, David knew there must be a better way. Focusing on things like CC 1 and CC 11 data to sculpt the music and make it breathe life into a composition, a composer falls into the trap of giving more attention to the technology rather than the actual art of composing music.

> *If you know how to write music, you're already using the app; there's no learning curve.*

David joined forces with developer Matthew Tesch and in 2015 released the first version of StaffPad for the Microsoft Surface 3 tablet. Although the Apple iPad tablet had a larger market share than the Surface, there were some initial technological limitations that would delay the release of an iPad version for the next five years.

In early 2020, StaffPad for the iPad was finally released. In addition, many third-party sample libraries were made available to rival sounds traditionally only available from a DAW. The StaffPad app is constantly evolving and becoming more powerful and fun every day!

What is StaffPad?

Let's talk about what StaffPad is, and what it *isn't*.

First and foremost, StaffPad is a composition tool, but is also a very cool music notation tool. As a composition tool StaffPad will play back your composition with full orchestral sounds so you will get immediate feedback about how your composition sounds. The stock sounds that come with StaffPad are pretty amazing! Compared to other notation programs these stock sounds are very workable. You could probably be very happy working with these sounds alone. On the other hand, StaffPad has partnered with several sample library companies such as Cinesamples, Orchestral Tools, Spitfire, and others to provide versions of their most popular libraries to be incorporated into your compositions as In-App Purchases.

What StaffPad *isn't* is a full-fledged music engraving program such as Finale or Sibelius. There are numerous styles of notation that fall out of the scope of StaffPad's mission: to provide the most common types of music notation for everyday music scores. If you look at the capabilities of programs like Finale and Sibelius, they fall into the **80/20 Rule**: 80% of what you'll use on a regular basis will utilize only 20% of the program's full capabilities.

StaffPad is also not a DAW. In other words, you shouldn't expect to create broadcast-quality audio for film, television, or video games. Why? The app lacks some important mixing capabilities that you would find in your DAW: bus channels, channel inserts, sends and returns, third party VSTs such as reverb and compression, etc. Don't get me wrong, the sampled instruments sound amazing! But without full control over mixing and mastering you will come up short as a music producer.

StaffPad does, however, give you the ability to export each instrument as a separate stem in order for you to work with these components inside your DAW. StaffPad is not trying to be a closed system. It plays nicely with others.

About this Book

Mastering StaffPad: Digital Music Notation for the Modern Composer is a complete reference manual. In it you will find detailed descriptions of every feature in the app with examples of how to use them. Where differences occur between the Surface and iPad, those will be highlighted.

The Apple logo will appear when talking about something specific to the iPad.

The Microsoft logo will appear when talking about something specific to Microsoft devices (e.g. Surface Pro).

A lightbulb will appear when an important tip is presented.

There is also a section on best practices for music notation and tips on how to improve your workflow with the app. Finally, at the end of the book you will find a complete glossary of terms used in music notation as well as the most commonly used terms in French, German, and Italian.

I hope you will find StaffPad as useful and fun as I have. And maybe after using the app for a while, you too, will become smitten!

Regarding Illustrations

EDITOR'S NOTE: Throughout the book are hundreds of illustrations to help clarify how to use the app. These illustrations are 100% real screenshots taken from the app, along with the occasional annotation.

Because the app uses dark backgrounds for many of the pages within, this presented a problem when preparing this book. The book features no color illustrations or text, only black and white. As a result, many of the images were deemed too dense and somewhat unreadable - the smaller the details, the more difficult it was to read clearly.

The illustrations are the focal point of the book and it was important that all information conveyed is clear and readable, therefore, we have inverted the coloring from white-on-black to black-on-white on selected images. This is only being done to help you, the reader. It is not meant to suggest that's what StaffPad looks like. For example, ...

will become

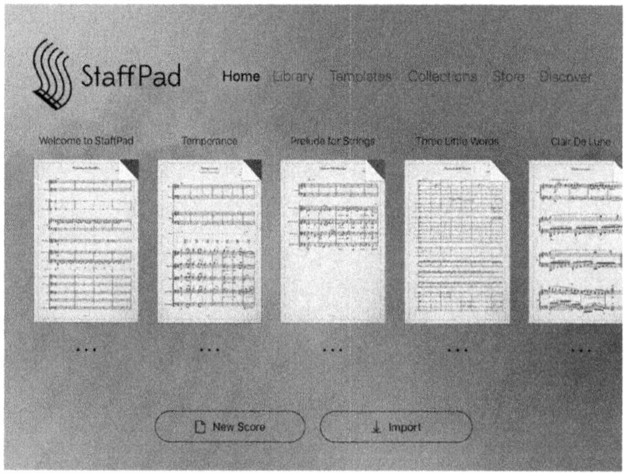

will become

Chapter 1
StaffPad Features

As StaffPad creator David William Hearn stated, *"If you know how to write music, you're already using the app."*. This couldn't be truer. Since the app is designed around writing music with a pencil, entering music notes, rests, ties, slurs, dynamics, etc., it is the most intuitive music writing app available. In fact, writing with the pencil is the *only way* to write music in StaffPad. There is no other way. You don't have a choice of tapping onto a virtual piano or connecting a MIDI keyboard to enter data. You must use the pencil. But that's the whole point of StaffPad and its greatest strength.

Handwriting Recognition

StaffPad utilizes a proprietary handwriting recognition engine. It is not an off-the-shelf OCR tool. It is designed specifically to understand music notation. It also understands *intent* based on musical context. So even if you write something that's not quite right, there's a good chance StaffPad can interpret your thoughts correctly.

Yes, there is a slight learning curve. You can't scribble nonsense on the page and expect StaffPad to understand your intent based on what you are thinking in your head. Maybe your pharmacist can decode a prescription from your doctor's unintelligible handwriting, but StaffPad needs you to be a little bit more precise.

Think of it as when you were first learning penmanship as a child. You were forced to practice and practice until you could clearly differentiate the letters in the alphabet. Of course, everyone has a style to their handwriting. The same goes for music notation. You must make a concerted effort to write letters (notes) and punctuation (rests and dynamics) that can be read by your teacher (StaffPad).

This means learning how big a note head should be. Not too big. Not too small. Just right. Whether it sits on a space between two lines or sits *on* the line - the size must remain constant. StaffPad will do its best to understand what you're trying to say. You'll be given a lot of leeway.

Editing Notation

We all make mistakes. If you were writing on paper with an ink pen (not a pencil), correcting your mistake would be a headache. Not so with StaffPad. Erasing notes, changing note pitch, changing note values, changing *anything* in StaffPad is effortless. Cutting and pasting individual notes or entire bars of music is extremely easy. Have a repeating ostinato pattern you need to extend to 40 measures? Piece of cake.

The user interface for editing in StaffPad is extraordinarily well thought out. It is the easiest user interface I've ever experienced in a music notation program. The key to its ease of use is, once again, the pencil. Just as it is simple to enter notes by writing naturally, it's just as easy to edit notes with the pencil. No more breaking your thought process looking for the shortcut command to handle some basic editing feature.

Learn more about editing in *Chapter 4 - Music Input*.

The Power of Text

Text usage in music notation is largely used for lyrics, tempo descriptions (“adagio”, “allegrissimo”, etc.), and the like. With StaffPad, text will be interpreted based on the context of where it is placed. For example, for string instruments, entering “*pizz*” above the note tells the musician to pluck the string instead of bowing it. But it will also instruct StaffPad to play the sound with a pizzicato sample. Think of it like keyswitching in a DAW to get a different articulation.

Entering a number above the staff, for example, “140”, will alert StaffPad that you intend to set a new tempo. It will automatically give you choices of how to interpret the tempo: quarter note = 140; eighth note = 140; etc.

Of course, entering a dynamic under the staff such as *mf*, *fff*, etc. will convert the text into the proper dynamic marking font as well as instruct the playback engine how loud to play the part.

Learn more about using text in *Chapter 5 - Text*.

Performance Symbols

As a secondary method of adding performance instructions, StaffPad offers a toolbar of useful articulations such as tremolo, mute, grace notes, octave lines, and more. By selecting an articulation from the symbols palette, the pencil will be used to simply draw where that symbol will be used. For example, adding a crescendo is as easy as selecting the hairpin symbol and dragging the pencil from the note where the crescendo begins and lifting the pencil where it will finish. This is an amazingly fast method for adding life to a performance without losing the flow of composing.

Drawing up and down bow symbols for strings could not be easier. Just a flick of the wrist to indicate an up- or down-bow. Drawing these manually would normally take a ridiculous amount of time.

Learn more about symbols in *Chapter 6 - Symbols*.

Chords

Chords are often thought of as simple text symbols for lead sheets and jazz charts. The chords feature in StaffPad has added value in addition to the traditional chord symbol usage.

You can type in the name of the chord you wish to display, but you can also utilize the chord analysis feature and let StaffPad determine what the harmony is based on the notes used in your music! That is a great learning aid, especially when dealing with complex harmony.

Learn more about chords in *Chapter 7 - Chords.*

Selecting Things

Selections will be made when you need to modify, copy, delete, and paste items. Selections are largely made at the measure-level, but individual notes can also be selected by using the lasso tool.

Additional usage of selections includes changing stem direction and transposing notes. But not just notes are selectable: text, rehearsal mark, articulations, dynamics...pretty much anything you've created can be selected and moved, deleted, or modified.

Learn more about selection features in *Chapter 8 - Selections.*

Playback

Playback is the funnest part of using StaffPad. Immediate self-gratification comes from hearing the notes you've written played back with sounds from the instruments you wrote them for!

Even though StaffPad is not a DAW, the automation layer provides the ability to further enhance the performance by being able to modify CC 11 Expression data, as well as volume, pan, and tempo.

Tempo maps can be created or imported from a MIDI file. Bar numbers can be customized so you don't always have to have Bar 1 as the first measure.

You can also isolate instruments by soloing the part(s) or mute any instrument you don't want to hear. This ability also aids in generating alternate mixes when exporting audio and don't want to export stems for editing in a DAW.

Learn more about playback in *Chapter 9 - Playback.*

Sample Library Add-ons

Playing back the music is fantastic in StaffPad because of the included stock instruments. Without having to manually assign an instrument staff to a sound library instrument, you will instantly hear some quality sampled orchestral instruments.

StaffPad has partnered with several high-end sample library companies such as CineSamples, Orchestral Tools, and Spitfire to offer you the option of adding additional sounds to your compositions. These libraries are customized versions of popular libraries that have Kontakt-based counterparts in the DAW world. At a fraction of the cost of these Kontakt versions, you can add these incredible sound libraries to your musical palette.

These libraries have been customized to work with StaffPad's all new proprietary sample engine. The instruments contain a single microphone position to reduce storage requirements on the mobile device as well as simplifying the mixing of instruments in your composition.

These libraries are purchased through the app's eco-system whether that be through Microsoft or Apple.

Learn more about third party add-ons in *Chapter 12 - Store.*

Sharing Your Work

Once you've completed your masterpiece you can share your work in several ways:

- Export the audio as AAC, WAV, MP3 full mixes, or WAV stem files.
- Print the score to a printer
- Print the score as a PDF file
- Print the full score and/or individual instrument parts
- Export the score as a MusicXML file
- Export the score as a MIDI file
- Generate a template based on the layout of the score
- Export the score in its native StaffPad file format

Once you've exported to MusicXML or MIDI file format, you can import it into your DAW to further customize the sound or assign higher-end sound libraries than are available to you in StaffPad, or import into a music engraving program such as Finale or Sibelius.

StaffPad is very flexible in helping you get the best result from your work.

Learn more about sharing in *Chapter 11 - Sharing.*

Chapter 2
Music Notation Basics

Music is a language, in fact, it is a universal language. Music notation is its written counterpart. It is how for centuries we've communicated the intention of sound. It's how we've documented melody, harmony, and rhythm.

You may not come from a background of knowing music notation. It's really not required that you know music notation to use StaffPad. You could just poke around and enter some notes and playback what you've written to hear the result. That in itself is educational. Experimentation is encouraged.

Music education in schools at an early age is not what it once was. Before the 1970s it was almost certain that a basic introduction to music was taught in schools. Even if a student didn't pursue music in any formal sense after that, a curious student may have picked up a guitar and started jamming in a garage band. That curiosity might have eventually led to the need for more formal instruction in music.

Today, any curious student can learn a University's worth of material from YouTube, or any other number of online education services. No matter where your education lies, StaffPad is just plain fun, so come on, let's learn about music!

This chapter is not intended to be a complete resource of music notation or music theory. It is intended to point out the basic structure of the language and help you understand what you're looking at after StaffPad finishes transforming your music into proper music notation.

If you are already an expert on music notation practices, feel free to skip this chapter entirely. Or you may use it as a refresher course in case you've forgotten anything.

The Staff

The modern musical staff consists of five lines. Within those five lines are four spaces. Musical notes will either sit on a line or a space.

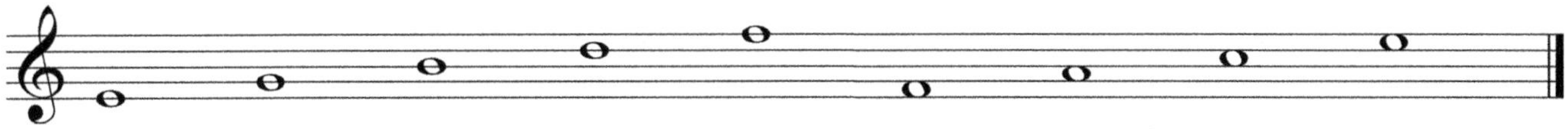

Notes are named alphabetically from A to G. It's easier to visualize the notes on a piano where the note sequence will repeat many times from very low to very high notes. The note in the very middle of the piano keyboard is C, and because it's in the middle of the keyboard it's referred to as "Middle C".

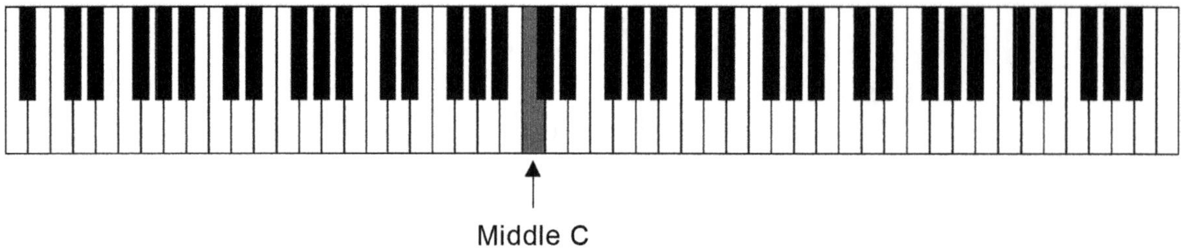

Notes ascend and descend the keyboard alphabetically. Ascending, once it reaches the last letter (G), it begins again with A. The same goes for descending, once you reach A, you start again with G.

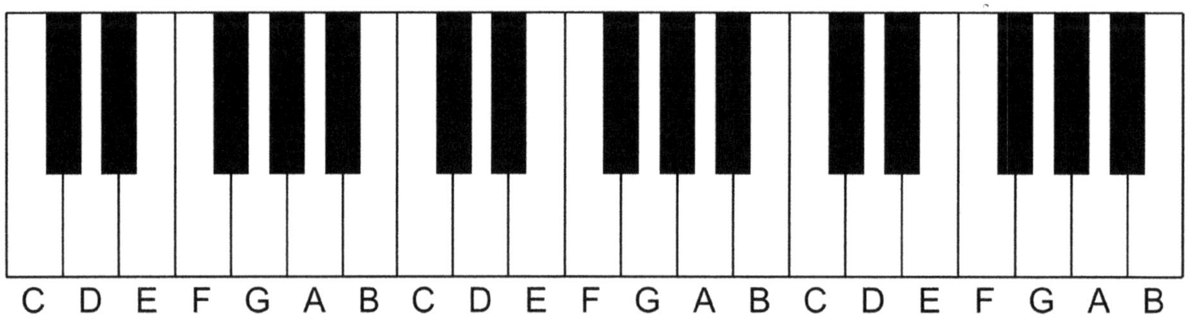

The alphabetic letters represent the white keys only. The black keys are the sharp and flat notes. The black key between C and D is C# (C-sharp), between D and E is D#. The "#" symbol means "sharp".

Ascending notes are typically spelled as sharp notes. Descending notes are spelled as flat notes. For example, the black note between D and C (going downward in pitch) would be called D*b* (D-flat). The small "*b*" is the symbol for "flat".

In other words, the black keys can be referenced with two different values: C# is the same note as D*b*. Confused yet? Don't worry, it'll get easier.

When we get into key signatures, you'll see why we would always refer to that note as C# and not D*b*, or always refer to the note as D*b* and not C#. There is logic behind this, trust me.

Now, back to the staff. Every key on the piano keyboard will be represented by a written note. That note will either sit on a line or on a space. If it is a white-key note you will just see the note unadorned. But if it's a black-key note - a sharp or flat - you will see the note written with the # or *b* symbol next to it.

Notes that sit on the lines are named E-G-B-D-F. A helpful mnemonic is "**E**very **G**ood **B**oy **D**oes **F**ine". Notes that sit on the spaces are named F-A-C-E and spell out an easy to remember word.

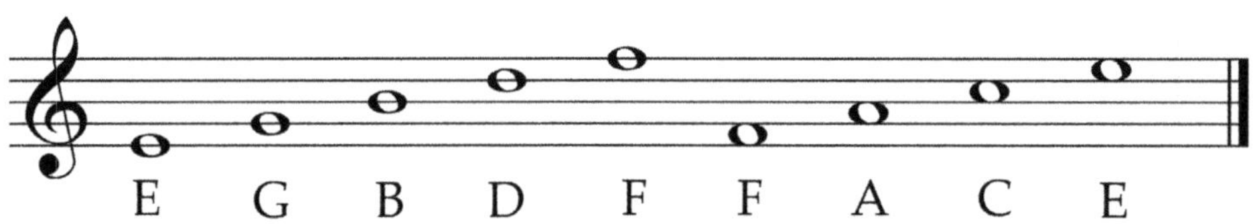

Remember, these are all notes on the white keys of the piano. To place them on a black key we will have to add a sharp (#) or flat (*b*) symbol next to it.

This sequence - a chromatic scale - would include every note starting with Middle-C: C, C#, D, D#, E, F, F#, G, G#, A, A#, B, C. This last C would be the "C above middle-C". Middle-C is commonly used as a reference point to any pitch.

Key Signatures

A key signature defines what notes are considered natural to that key. Any other note would be considered an "accidental". For example, the simplest key to understand is C Major. That is a major key (as opposed to a minor key) that is made up of a sequence of notes: C, D, E, F, G, A, B.

These seven notes make up the C Major scale. You may know this sequence by hearing it sung as "*Do-re-mi-fa-sol-la-ti-do*". In the *Sound of Music,* Julie Andrews sang, "Doe, a deer, a female deer...".

A major scale is made up of a sequence of notes with whole- and half-step intervals. An interval is the distance from one note to the next. Looking at the piano keyboard, C to D is a whole step interval. C to C# is a half-step interval. A major scale is a series of whole- and half-step intervals that follow this pattern:

Whole, whole, half [C (whole step to) D (whole step to) E (half step to) F]

Whole, whole, whole, half [(whole step from F to) G (whole step to) A (whole step to) B (half step to) C]

Whew! That seems complicated but it's not. Follow along with the notes on the piano and you'll see the relationship for these intervals.

This interval relationship is the same for all major keys. Start on any note and follow the interval pattern to complete the scale. For example, a D Major scale would be D-E-F#-G-A-B-C#-D.

An E*b* Major scale would be E*b*-F-G-A*b*-B*b*-C-D-E*b*.

Wait. Why did we just switch to flats instead of sharps? Why isn't it E*b*-F-G-G#-A#-C-D-E*b*? The reason is that each note in the scale needs to have a unique letter of the alphabet. You'll never see G and G# together in the same key. We must instead refer to G# as A*b*.

When writing music in a specific key, we can specify a key signature that defines how notes will be played. For example, in the key of E*b*, we saw that the E*b* Major scale contains the black key notes E*b*, A*b*, and B*b*. All other notes in the key are natural (neither sharp nor flat). We indicate this by using a key signature legend at the beginning of every stave:

Here, there is a flat symbol on the B*b*, the E*b*, and the A*b* notes. So, every time you see one of those notes you know you are supposed to play them as flats, regardless of the octave.

But why are the flats in this crazy order? Why aren't they in alphabetical order? It's because they follow the "circle of fifths". The chart below identifies the circle, but the theory behind it is just slightly beyond the scope of this tutorial. I encourage you to turn to a music theory book if you are interested in learning more about this.

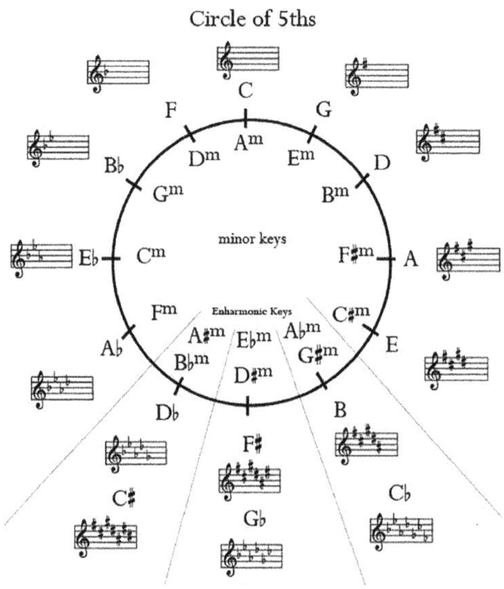

Clefs

Up to now, we've only shown you notes that reside using the treble clef:

It is sometimes called the "G" clef as the bottom of the clef encircles the G staff line:

Other clefs used commonly are the treble, bass, alto, and tenor clefs:

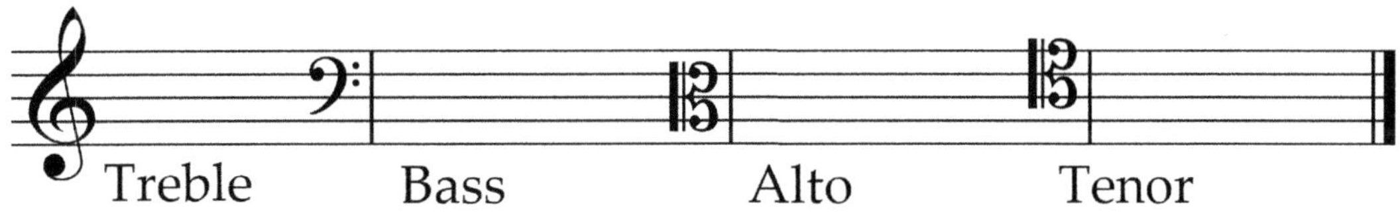

The reason for the various clefs is not to confuse you no matter how arbitrary it may seem. Clefs were created to simplify the readability of notes. Once a note goes higher or lower than the lines on the staff, you must extend the staff by using "ledger lines".

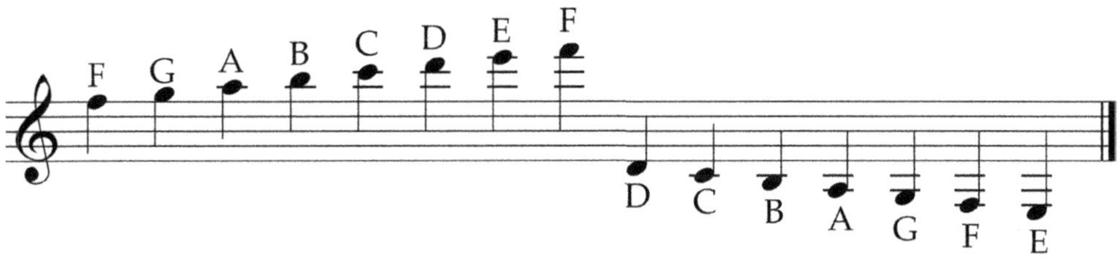

Following the same sequence of alphabetic letters, notes continue upward or downward by adding additional lines and spaces. The problem with this approach is with instruments that sound considerably lower (or higher) than the notes of the treble clef. That's where the additional clefs come in. Consider a tuba playing the lowest C note on the piano. To write that note on the treble clef would require eight ledger lines below it! It would be almost impossible for any musician to sight read that.

Bass Clef

Bass clef is simply a continuation of the treble clef, using middle-C as the dividing point between the two clefs.

The bass clef is also known as the "F" clef as the two dots surround the note F.

Alto and Tenor Clefs

Alto and tenor clefs come in handy for the same reason as the bass clef solves the problem of too many ledger lines in the treble clef. The viola uses the alto clef for that very reason: it's range would require too many ledger lines, however, neither treble clef nor bass clef alone would suffice. Either of those choices would still require many ledger lines.

The unique thing about this clef is that it is *moveable*. Wherever the center point is for the clef, that represents middle-C. Thus, this clef is also known as the "C" clef as it defines where middle-C is. The alto clef has middle-C sitting on the middle line. The tenor clef has middle-C sitting on the fourth line (counting from the bottom).

The moveable C clef may be found in choral work. Middle-C is shown for each voice in a choir:

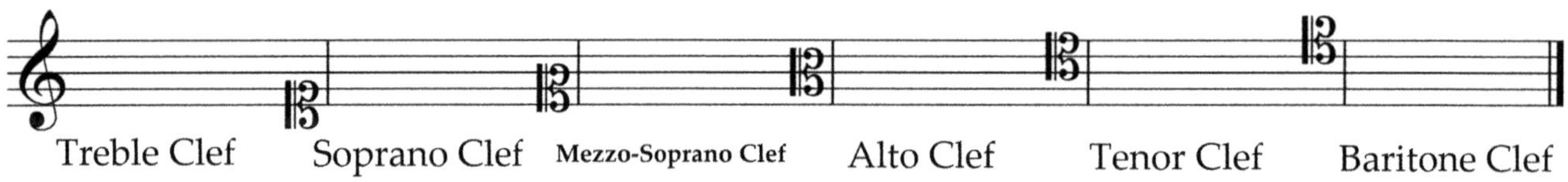

Stems

Normal stem direction is based on where the notes lie. Notes on the middle line (regardless of clef) and upward will have stems pointing down. Anything below the middle line are stems up. This improves readability of the music.

Exceptions occur when using divisi (dividing the parts).

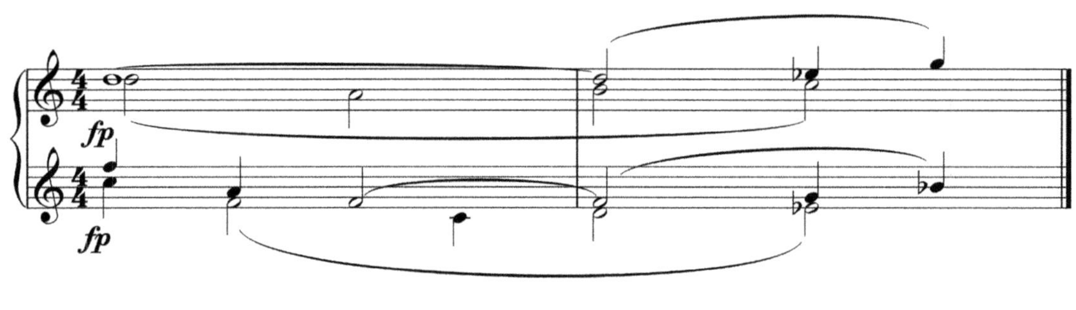

Time Signatures

A time signature defines how many beats there will be in each measure. What is a beat? That's specified by the denominator.

The number on the top - the numerator - indicates how many beats per measure. The first time signature, 4/4 means 4 beats per measure. The bottom number - the denominator - indicates that a quarter note gets one beat.

A time signature of 4/4 is so common that the time signature "C" means "common time".

The next example, 2/2, indicates two beats per measure and a half note gets one beat. It's the same as 4/4 but cut in half. This is also known as "cut time". This is indicated by the abbreviated "C" with a vertical line through it.

Other often-used time signatures are 2/4 (two beats per measure with a quarter note getting one beat), 3/4 (three beats per measure with a quarter note getting one beat), and 6/8 (six beats per measure with an eighth note getting one beat)

Note Values

The length of time a note will sound is represented by note types that have mathematical relationships to one another. The basic sub-division is the quarter note valued at one beat.

Note	American Name	British Name	Value	Dotted Value
𝅝	whole note	semibreve	4 beats	6 beats
𝅗𝅥	half note	minim	2 beats	3 beats
♩	quarter note	crotchet	1 beat	1 1/2 beats
♪	eighth note	quaver	1/2 beat	3/4 beat
𝅘𝅥𝅯	sixteenth note	semiquaver	1/4 beat	3/8 beat
𝅘𝅥𝅰	thirty second note	demisemiquaver	1/8 beat	3/16 beat

The half note is twice as long as two beats (two quarter notes), the whole note four times as long, an eighth note half as long, a sixteenth note one fourth as long, and the thirty second note one eighth as long as a quarter note.

With a time signature of 4/4, four full beats must be accounted for in each bar whether by notes and/or rests. Four quarter notes would fill out the bar as would two half notes, or one half note and two quarter notes. The combinations are endless. If they mathematically add up, then you've succeeded.

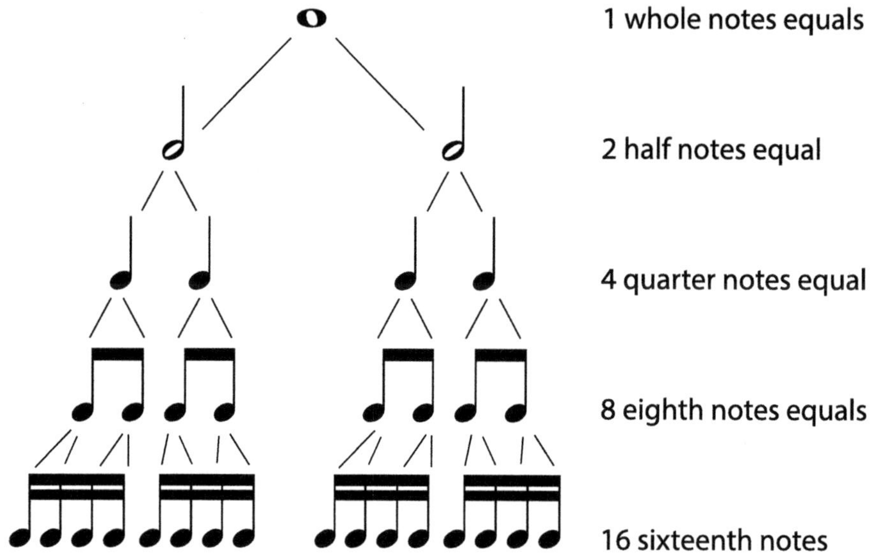

Bar Lines

Bar lines are the vertical lines that separate one bar from the next. Each bar should be filled with a mathematically correct number of notes and/or rests. There are a few bar line styles that help define the structure of the music.

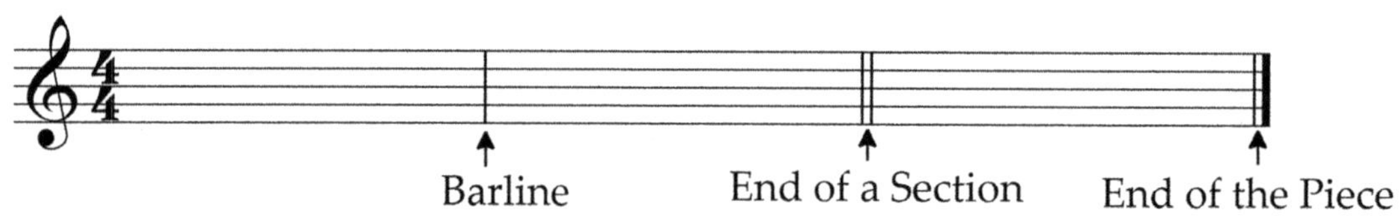

A single bar line is the normal bar line. A double bar line represents the end of a section. What follows is a new section of music. A double bar line with a heavy line indicates the end of the piece. There will only be a single end bar line in any piece of music.

Repeats

Repetition is important and writing the exact same music over and over is tedious and unnecessary. The repeat bar line resembles the end bar line, but with two dots.

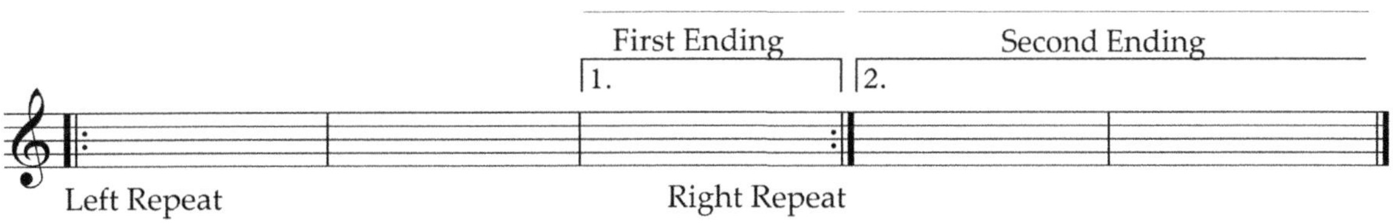

Following the example above, you would play bars one, two, and three. In the third bar you see the repeat bar line. Also, in the third bar you see a "first ending" mark. You will repeat back to bar one because there is a "repeat from" bar line (if there is no "repeat from" bar line you would go back to the beginning of the piece).

Once again you will play bars one and two. But instead of playing bar three you will skip over it as it was the "first ending". Now you jump to bar four, the "second ending" and continue.

Expressions and Articulations

Music comes to life when adding expression to the notes. The only way for the composer to convey that information to the musician is by adding articulation marks to the notes.

Slurring notes designates that the notes be played smoothly, connecting one note to the next with as little separation as possible. A long curved line over the notes that will be slurred, also known as "legato" playing:

Staccato notes are to be played shorter than the note value indicates. A small dot over the note indicates that it should be played shorter than the written value. For example, a staccato quarter note will likely be played as if it were an eighth note:

Additional performance marks include:

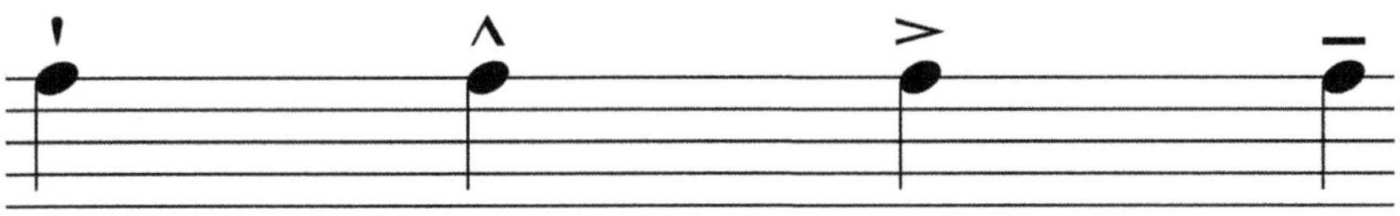

Staccatissimo: play the note even shorter than staccato

Martellato: strong accent

Marcato: normal accent

Tenuto: long accent

Dynamics

Dynamics specify how loud or how soft the music should be played. The following marks are used:

ppp - Pianisissimo (quietest)

pp - Pianissimo (very quiet)

p - Piano (quiet)

mp - Mezzo Piano (moderately quiet)

mf - Mezzo Forte (moderately loud)

f - Forte (loud)

ff - Fortissimo (very loud)

fff - Fortisissimo (loudest)

sfz - Sforzando (suddenly, with force)

The music can gradually grow louder or softer by specifying "*cresc*" (crescendo) or "*decresc*" (decrescendo). "*dim*" (diminuendo) is the same as decrescendo. Alternatively, the hairpin symbol can be used:

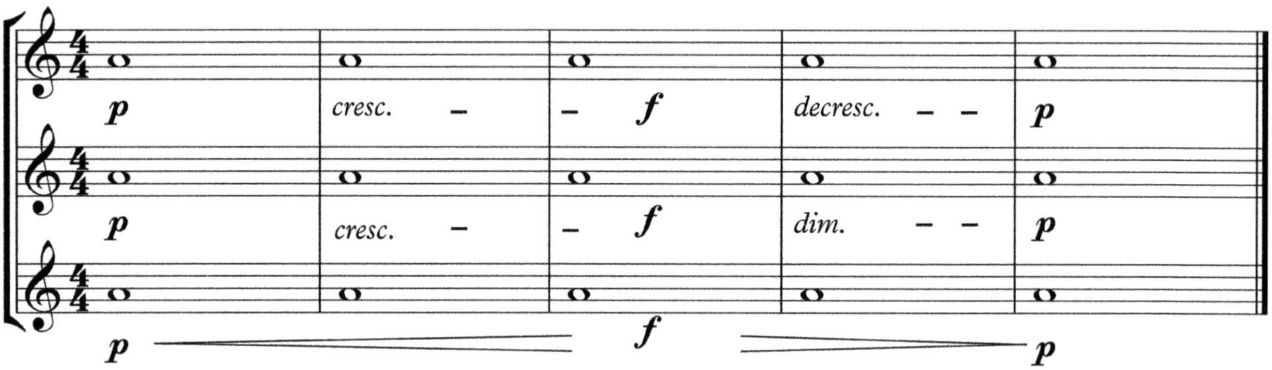

Recap

This has by no means been a comprehensive tutorial on music theory and notation. You are encouraged to seek out additional texts on the subject. Anything more than this here would be beyond the scope of this book.

Chapter 3
Where to Begin

Device Requirements

StaffPad is designed to be used on devices that support a digital pencil. It must also support finger touches. StaffPad is smart enough to be able to distinguish between the two types of touches. The pencil is necessary for accuracy such as when writing music. Standard finger touches are used for selections and navigation.

StaffPad is not designed to work with MIDI keyboards. QWERTY computer keyboards connected via Bluetooth can be used for navigation shortcuts. The workflow of the app is designed strictly around the pencil and finger touches. The focus of the app is all about "*writing down your ideas quickly and easily*".

StaffPad recommends the iPad Pro 12.9" or Microsoft Surface Pro 7. However, it will work on a wide range of iPads and pen/touch capable Windows devices, including the following:

- iPad Air (3rd generation)
- iPad mini (5th generation)
- iPad Pro 12.9-inch (1st or 2nd generation)
- iPad Pro 10.5-inch
- iPad Pro 9.7-inch
- iPad (6th generation)
- iPad (7th generation)
- iPad Pro 11-inch*
- iPad Pro 12.9-inch (3rd generation, 4th generation) *

*requires Apple Pencil 2nd Generation

- Microsoft Surface Pro (all models)
- Microsoft Surface Book (all models)
- Microsoft Surface Pro X
- Microsoft Surface Laptop
- Microsoft Surface Studio
- Microsoft Surface Hub
- Microsoft Surface Go
- Microsoft Surface 3

StaffPad for iPad requires an Apple Pencil to write music. The Logitech Crayon is not supported.

StaffPad for Windows 10 requires a device that supports active pen and touch.

StaffPad Reader is compatible with all iPad and Windows 10 devices and does not require a Pencil/Pen.

Keyboard Shortcuts

Microsoft devices utilize a keyboard more frequently than iOS devices. Here is a list of useful shortcuts used throughout the app.

Welcome Page:

- Just start typing on the home tab to search the library
- Ctrl+N = New Score
- Ctrl+I = Import Score
- Alt+S = Show settings/info pane

Standard:

- Ctrl+Z = Undo
- Ctrl+Y = Redo
- Ctrl+X/C/V = Cut/Copy/Paste
- Ctrl+S = Save
- Ctrl+P = Print
- Ctrl+A = Select All
- Ctrl+D = Deselect All
- Ctrl+W = Close Score
- Ctrl+Q = Save and Quit

Playback:

- Spacebar = Toggle Play/Pause
- , = Rewind 1 bar
- . = Ffward 1 bar
- 0 = Return to the beginning of the score
- Number keys 1-8 = Jump to rehearsal marks
- 9 = Jump to end of score
- M = Mute Staff (under Pen cursor)
- S = Solo Staff (under Pen cursor)
- C = Toggle Click/Metronome
- Shift+S = unsolo all
- Shift+M = unmute all

General:

- I = Instruments control
- V = Versions control
- E = "Latch" Eraser
- Shift + E = Permanently toggle Eraser
- A = Show Automation Layer
- P = Open Symbols Palette
- F = Follow Score
- D = Show mark-up tools
- T = Insert Text (under cursor)
- H = Hairpin tool
- G = Glissando tool
- O = Octave up/down tool
- R = Rehearsal Mark
- X = X Notehead tool
- Shift+C = Change clef
- Shift+B = Change bar line
- Shift+K = Change key signature
- Shift+T = Change Time Signature
- Escape key = Cancel all tools
- Alt key = temporarily show the automation layer
- Shift 1/2/3/4 = select Voice 1/2/3/4

Selections:

- Ctrl+Click = select bar/expand selection
- Ctrl+D = deselect all
- Right mouse button draw = lasso select
- Ctrl+Up arrow = transpose up an octave
- Ctrl+Down arrow = transpose down an octave
- Delete key = delete selection

Keyboard Shortcuts

Using a Bluetooth keyboard connected to your iPad you will have access to a few shortcuts, but not as many as with Microsoft. Hold down the CMD key for a couple of seconds and a help screen will appear:

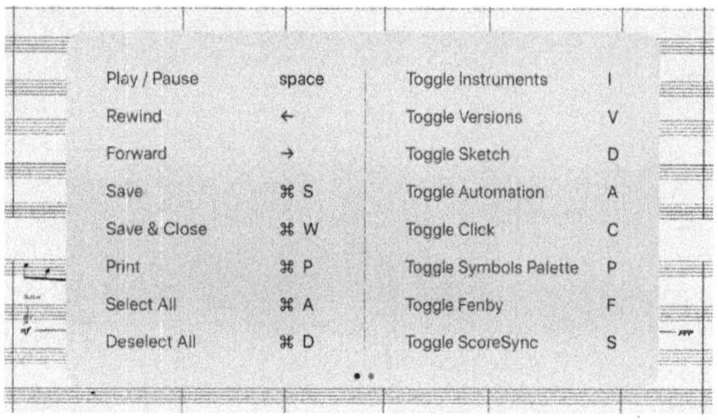

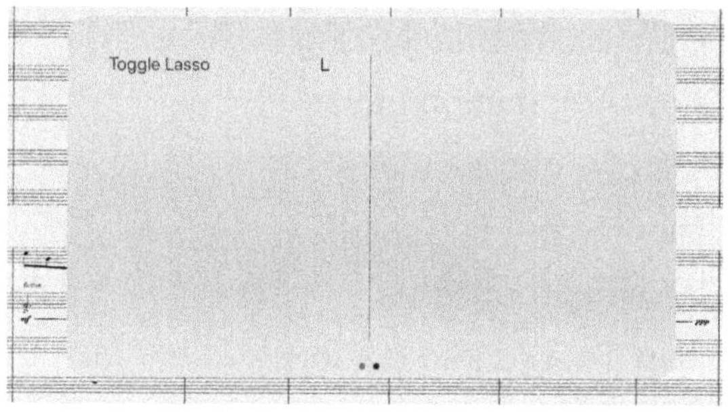

Sketch ("D") is another name for Markup which allows you to scribble annotations or *sketch* your composition without entering any actual notes. Click ("C") is for metronome activation.

The Welcome Page

When the app starts you will be taken to the Welcome Page. From here you can:

- Begin a new score
- Continue working on an existing score
- Import a score from StaffPad, MusicXML, or MIDI file formats
- Purchase sound libraries from the store
- Watch tutorial videos
- Modify app settings and other utility functions

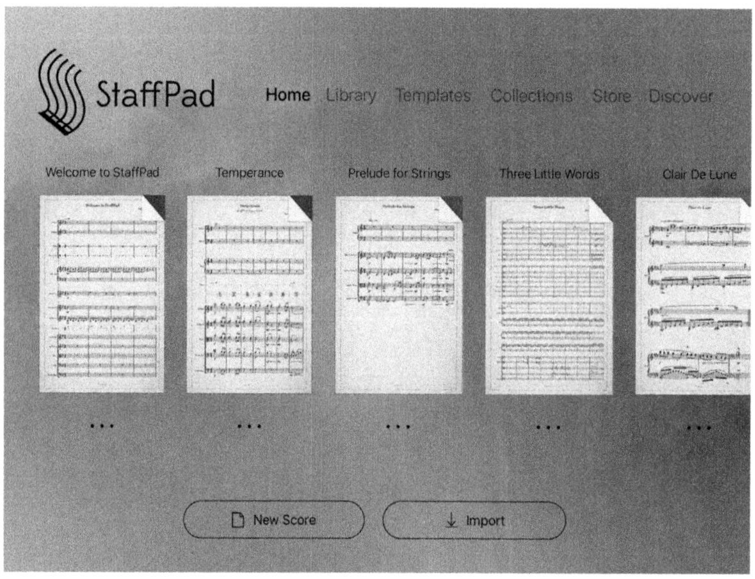

The top of the page is a menu of pages for score organization and more. They include **Home**, **Library**, **Templates**, **Collections**, **Store**, and **Discover**. If you are looking at this page on your device in portrait mode, you may not see all the items. You can scroll the list left or right to reveal the hidden items. Briefly, these pages include:

- **Home** - the home page will display a list of your six most recent scores you've worked on. The thumbnail image will display a tiny representation of the first page of your score.
- **Library** - the library contains all of your scores listed alphabetically.
- **Templates** - scores (usually blank) with pre-defined groupings of instruments.
- **Collections** - organizational folders for categorizing related scores
- **Store** - online store for purchasing third party sample libraries
- **Discover** - video tutorials and help guide

See *Chapter 10 - Score Management* for more details.

New Score

To begin a new score, you have a couple of options:

- Create a blank score where you get to choose the instruments to include
- Create a new score based on a template of pre-defined instruments

To create an empty score with no instruments, select:

Score Details

The name of the new score will be "Untitled Score" and the composer's name will be "Unknown Composer". If you are a Microsoft user and have elected to allow StaffPad to access your Microsoft Account Information, the app will pre-fill the composer's name with your name.

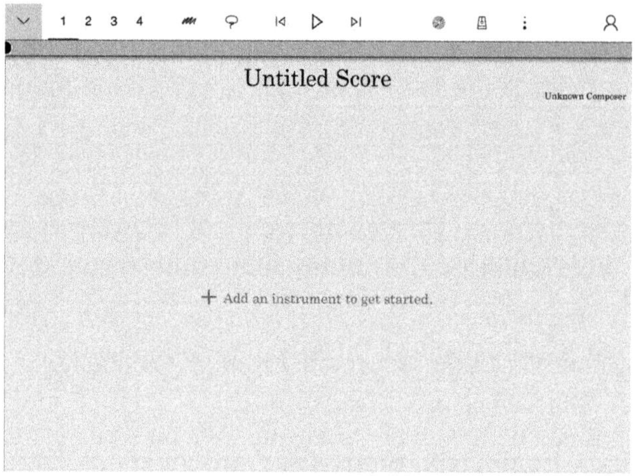

Change the title of the score from "Untitled Score" by tapping anywhere on the title. When you are finished with the title, tap Return and the cursor will appear on a second line where you may enter a subtitle. You may also leave it blank by tapping Return a second time without entering anything.

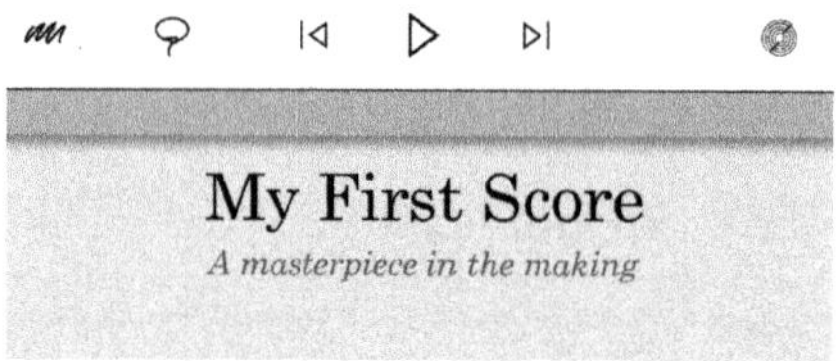

Change the name of the composer to your name (or anyone else's) by tapping anywhere in the composer name field. As with the score title, when you are finished with the title, tap Return and the cursor will appear on a second line where you may enter a subtitle. You may also leave it blank by tapping Return a second time without entering anything.

If at any time you wish to change this information you may follow these same steps again when you open the score, or from the Welcome page. See ***Chapter 10 - Score Management*** for details.

Key, Time Signature, and Tempo

A brand-new score will default to the key of C with a time signature of 4/4. And although the tempo is not displayed, a default tempo of 120 bpm is set until you change it.

Details on setting the key and time signature are found in *Chapter 4 - Music Input* and changing the tempo will be found in ***Chapter 5* – *Text*** and ***Chapter 9* – *Playback***.

Adding Instruments

Now comes the fun part, adding instruments. Tap the big button in the middle of the page:

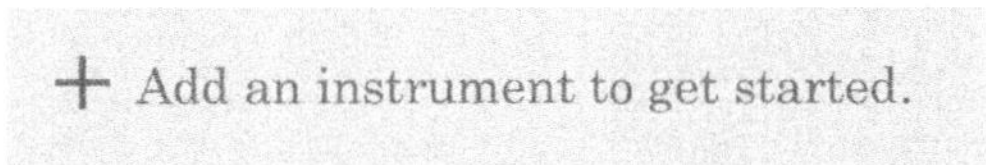

Later on, you can always get back to this page to modify your list of instruments by tapping the **Instruments** button on the Command Bar:

From here you will be taken to the **Staffs** selection page:

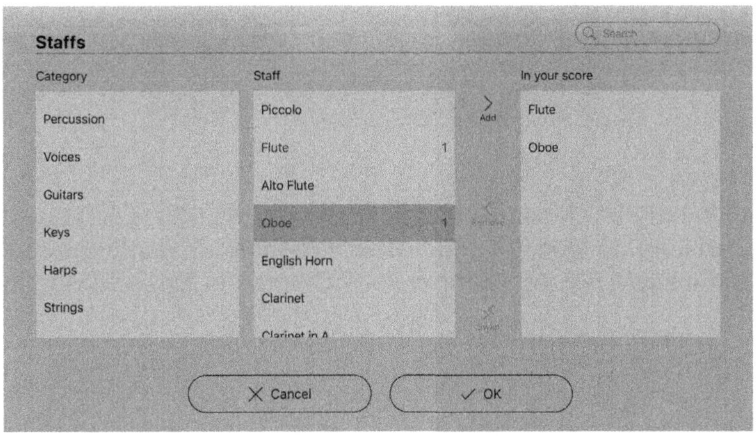

Scroll through the Category column on the left to find Woodwinds, Brass, Percussion, Strings, etc. The categories are not in alphabetical order, but rather *score* order - the order in which the sections will appear on the score page.

Add

After choosing an orchestral section (a category), choose from a list of instruments from the center column, **Staff**. Tap on a selected instrument and tap the Add button:

That new instrument will now be part of your score and will be listed in the right column **In Your Score**. In addition, every instrument you add will be positioned in the right column in *score order* just like the Category column. You are not limited to a single instrument of any kind. You could create a custom orchestra featuring 12 tubas and 3 xylophones if you wanted!

Most instruments require only a single staff, but instruments such as the piano, celesta, and harp will be given a double staff, known as the Grand Staff.

Search

As your list of instruments grow you may find it difficult to locate a particular instrument to add. Use the Search field to locate the instrument:

With each letter you type in the search field, the result list will be refined until you locate the instrument you are searching for. For example, if you type "CL" the search results will contain everything that includes that combination of letters. You will see Clarinet, Clarinet in A, Clarinet in Eb, and Bass Clarinet.

Remove

If you change your mind and wish to remove that instrument from your score, select that instrument from the **In Your Score** column and tap the Remove button:

IMPORTANT: If you've already added music to that staff, all your data will be lost.

Swap

The Swap button allows you to replace one instrument with another with one simple tap. For example, let's say you meant to add a Clarinet but accidently added a Bass Guitar.

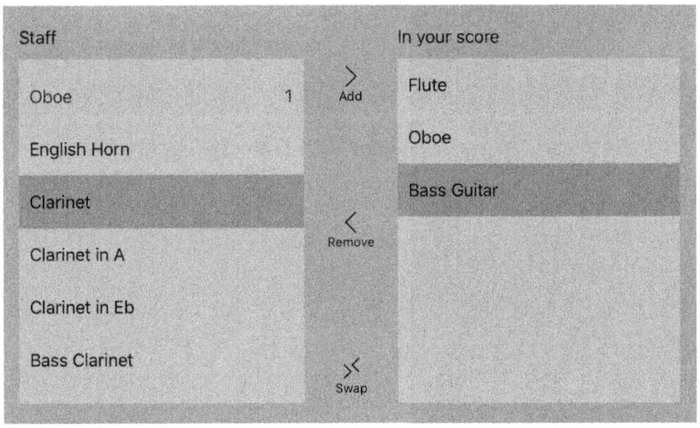

Select the instrument in the right column you wish to get rid of, select the instrument from the center column you wish to replace it with and tap the Swap button:

You could also achieve the same result in multiple steps by first removing the Bass Guitar, then adding the Clarinet.

Ordering Your Instruments

You may set your own custom order of the instruments if you don't want to adhere to the traditional orchestral score order. So, if you wanted to have a bassoon sitting between the violas and the cellos you could do that.

Apple users can tap-and-hold an instrument in the **In Your Score** column with their finger and slide it up or down to its new position.

Microsoft users will select an instrument and tap the **Move Up** and **Move Down** buttons to change its position.

Finish

When you are happy with your selections, tap the OK button:

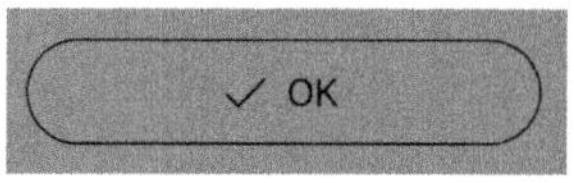

Otherwise, tap the Cancel button and all your changes will be abandoned:

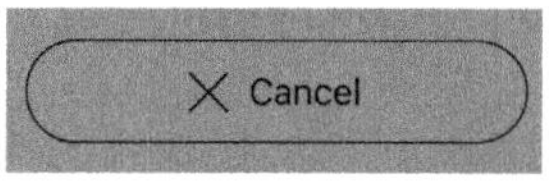

Toolbars

StaffPad provides three different types of toolbars: Toolbar, Command Bar, and Selection Bar. Each of these toolbars occupy the very top of the screen when you are working on your score.

Toolbar

When starting or opening a score you will initially see the Toolbar:

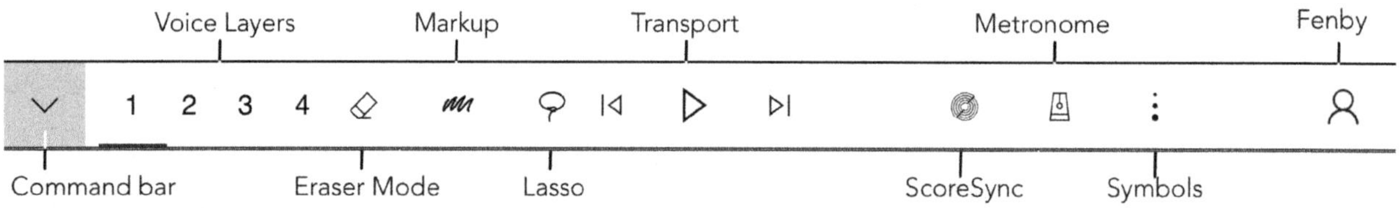

The Toolbar contains items that will be the most frequently used during an editing session:

The down-pointing chevron will open either the Command Bar or the Selection Bar (see below). If you have made a section of any kind then the Selection Bar will be shown, otherwise you will see the Command Bar.

Voice Layers. The Voice Layers feature provides up to four distinct instrument voicings. See ***Chapter 4 - Music Input*** for details.

Eraser Mode. This will set the drawing mode to eraser mode until it is deselected. This is an alternative method to the pressure method of the pencil. Using the pressure method, eraser mode will turn off as soon as the pencil is lifted from the screen. See ***Chapter 4 - Music Input*** for details.

Markup. Also known as "sketch" tools, these are special drawing tools for making annotations on the score which can be public or private. If public, the annotations will be visible from the StaffPad Reader. See ***Chapter 4 - Music Input*** and ***Chapter 14 - StaffPad Reader*** for details.

Lasso. The Lasso tool allows you to select individual notes, dynamic markings, and many other individual items for manipulation. This is a finer control than normal selection of everything contained within a measure (or range of measures). See ***Chapter 4 - Music Input*** for details.

Transport. The transport controls playback of your score. The forward and back buttons control moving through the score one measure at a time, or to the beginning or end of the piece. See ***Chapter 9 - Playback*** for details.

ScoreSync. The ScoreSync button controls the connection between the StaffPad app and remote devices using the **StaffPad Reader** app over Wi-Fi. See ***Chapter 14 - StaffPad Reader*** for details.

Metronome. Enables an audible click track that will sound during playback. StaffPad uses the famous UREI metronome click based on the UREI 964 Digital Metronome.

Symbols. Reveals the symbols palette for adding articulations and other performance marks to the score. See ***Chapter 6 - Symbols*** for details.

Fenby. Fenby is the voice-activated virtual assistant capable of automating simple tasks such as setting the tempo, adding instruments, or changing the time signature. See below for more information.

Command Bar

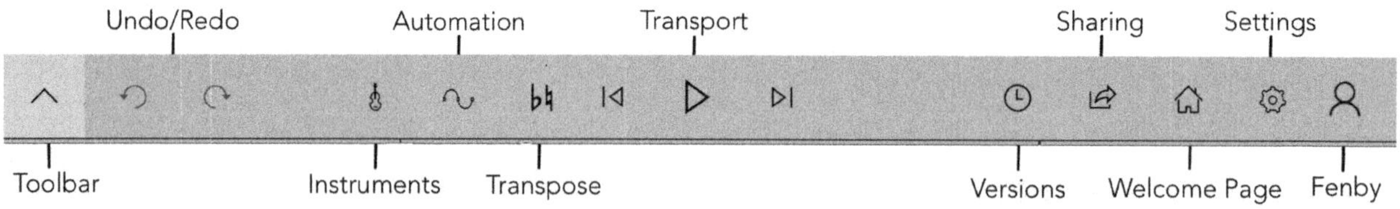

As you tap on the down-pointing chevron in the Toolbar a new toolbar will drop down from the top of the screen, the **Command Bar**. Here you will find additional tools that are needed less frequently than those found in the main Toolbar.

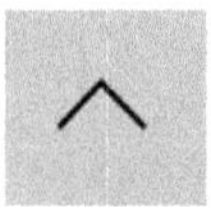

The up-pointing chevron will return to the Toolbar (see above).

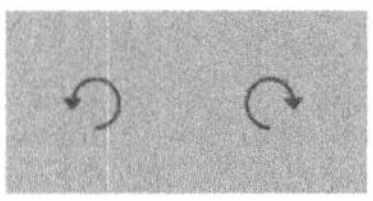

Undo and Redo. Undo will reverse every action taken during the current session. An undo action can be reinstated with Redo.

Instruments. Opens the **Staffs** selection page. Refer to the *Adding Instruments* section above.

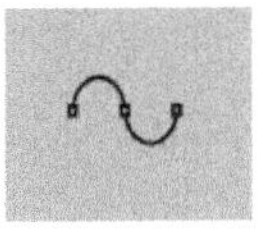

Automation Layer. Allows you to "draw" controller data for Expression (CC 11), Volume, and Pan in a way similar to editing controller data in a DAW. See ***Chapter 9 - Playback*** for details.

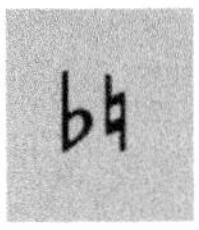

Transpose. Toggles the written transposition of the score between "C Score" and transposed. If you're not comfortable in writing an instrument such as Bb Trumpet in its transposed key, you can write in a non-transposed key and switch when it's time to print the part for the player. See ***Chapter 4 - Music Input*** for details.

Transport. The transport controls playback of your score. The forward and back buttons control moving through the score one measure at a time, or to the beginning or end of the piece. See ***Chapter 9 - Playback*** for details.

Versions. Create alternate versions of your score. Versions are stored together in the same file rather than saving as a new and separate file. You can switch back and forth with ease. See ***Chapter 10 - Score Management*** for details.

Sharing. Print, export as audio, create PDF, and save as a template are some of the many ways to share your score. See ***Chapter 11 - Sharing*** for details.

Home. Return to the Welcome page to select a different score, create a new one, or visit the Store.

Settings. Access the Settings panel to set up global settings used by all scores. See ***Chapter 10 - Score Management*** for details.

Fenby. Fenby is the voice-activated virtual assistant capable of automating simple tasks such as setting the tempo, adding instruments, or changing the time signature. See below for more information.

Selection Bar

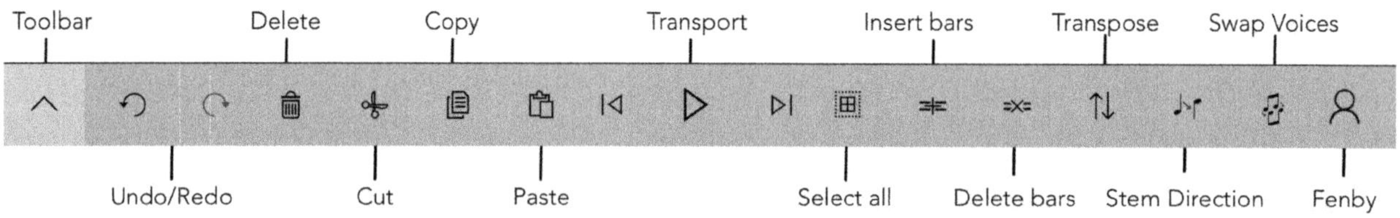

The Selection Bar will appear instead of the Command Bar whenever a selection of any kind is made. Not all options will be visible until they are needed. For example, the Paste button will not be available until there is something in the clipboard to paste.

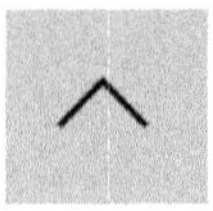

The up-pointing chevron will return to the Toolbar (see above).

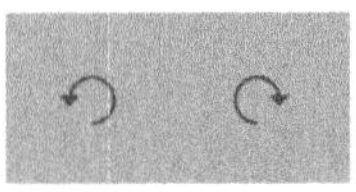

Undo and Redo. Undo will reverse every action taken during the current session. An undo action can be reinstated with Redo.

Delete. Selected items will be deleted and *not* placed on the clipboard.

Cut. Selected items will be deleted (cut) and placed on the clipboard to be pasted elsewhere.

Copy. Selected items will be copied and placed on the clipboard.

Paste. The contents of the clipboard will be pasted into the currently selected measure.

Transport. The transport controls playback of your score. The forward and back buttons control moving through the score one measure at a time, or to the beginning or end of the piece. See ***Chapter 9 - Playback*** for details.

Select All. The entire score will be selected. In order to use this function, you must first select at least one measure.

Insert Bars. You determine how many bars you will be inserting by selecting *that* number of bars. The existing bars will move to the right by that many measures.

Select how many bars to insert.

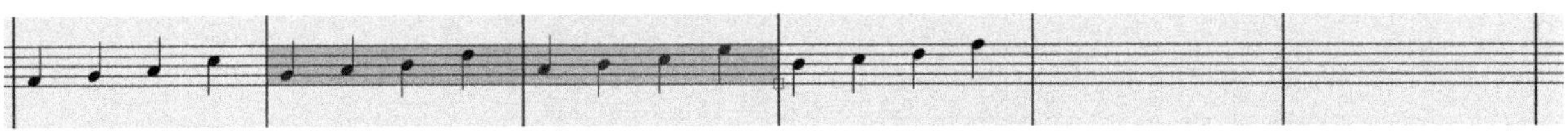

After inserting bars.

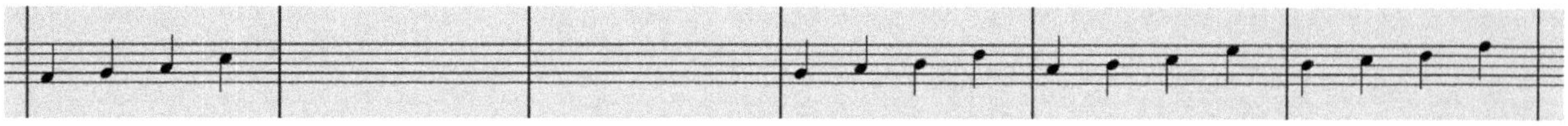

Delete Bars. Similarly, select the number of bars you wish to remove. All measures to the right of the selection will be moved to the left by that number of bars.

Select bars to delete.

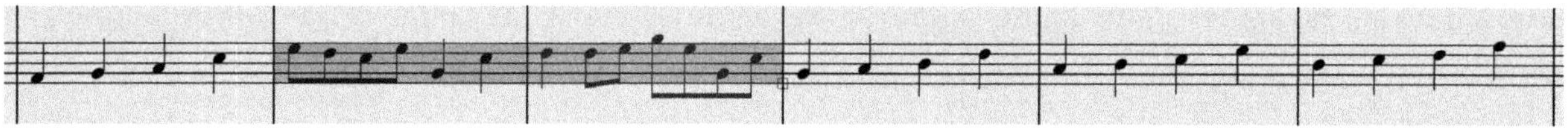

After deleting bars.

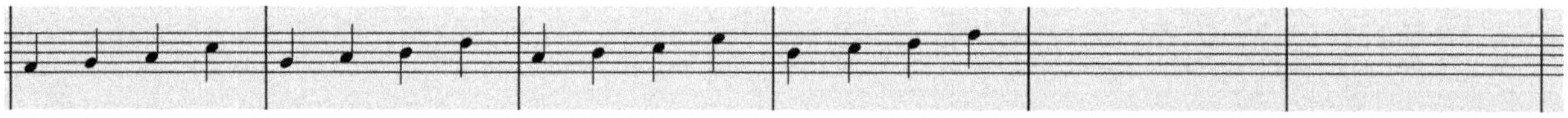

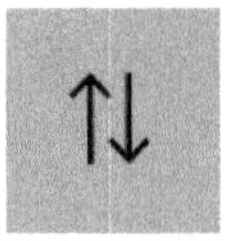

Transpose. Transpose the selected notes up or down from any interval up to a 15th (two octaves). Intervals may be designated as diminished, minor, perfect, major, and augmented. You can also have StaffPad change the key signature. This may make sense to do so depending on the interval selected.

Initially, only the selected measure(s) are transposed. If you don't close the dialog and tap OK again, the *entire staff* will be transposed using the currently value selected.

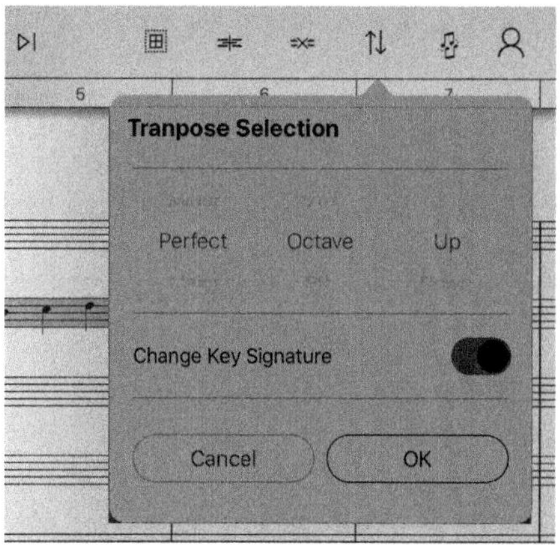

Stem Direction. Reverses the direction of whatever stems are selected. Especially useful when beaming notes that are currently flagged. Use the **lasso** tool to select a single note. See ***Chapter 8 - Selections*** for more info on using the lasso tool and ***Chapter 13 - Writing Tips*** (Tip #3 Beaming Trouble).

Before changing the stem direction of multi-voice notes.

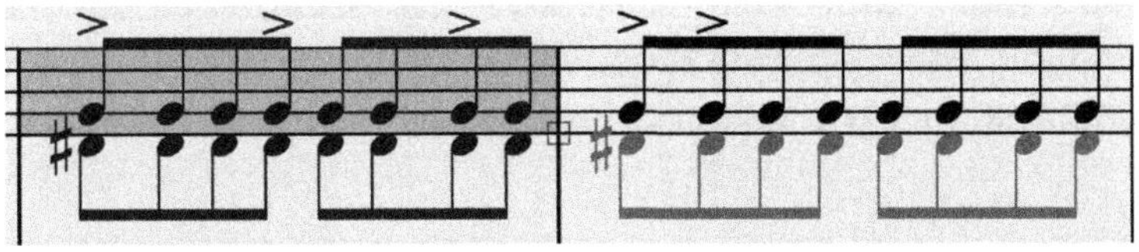

After changing stem direction.

Swap Voices. As the name implies, whatever notes are associated with one voice will be swapped with those of another voice. In the example below, the note G (stems up) are in voice layer one and the note D# (stems down) are in voice layer two. See ***Chapter 4 - Music Input*** for details on using multiple voices.

Before swapping voices.

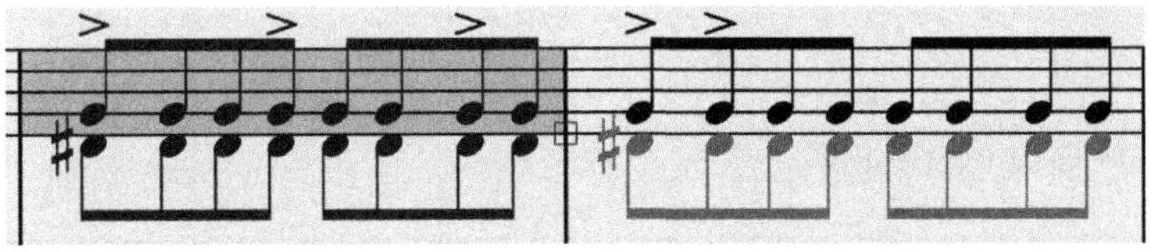

After swapping voices. Voice stem directions remain the same.

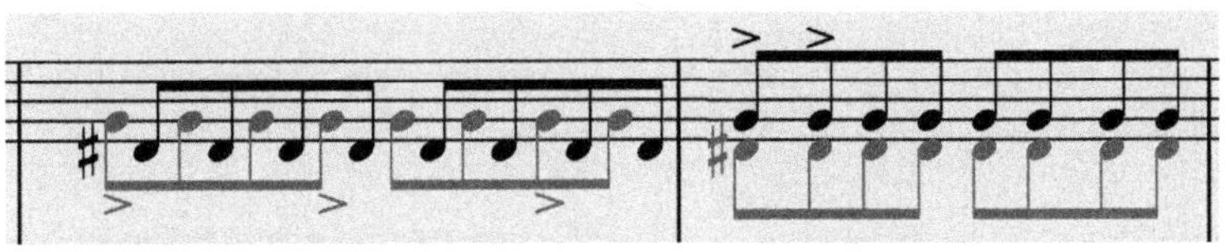

Fenby. Fenby is the voice-activated virtual assistant capable of automating simple tasks such as setting the tempo, adding instruments, or changing the time signature. See below for more information.

Portrait Mode

The previous examples have shown StaffPad in its common Landscape display orientation. Occasionally you may wish to rotate the device into Portrait orientation. When that happens, the Toolbar will always be visible on the top and either the Command Bar or Selection bar will be visible directly below it.

Toolbar / Command Bar

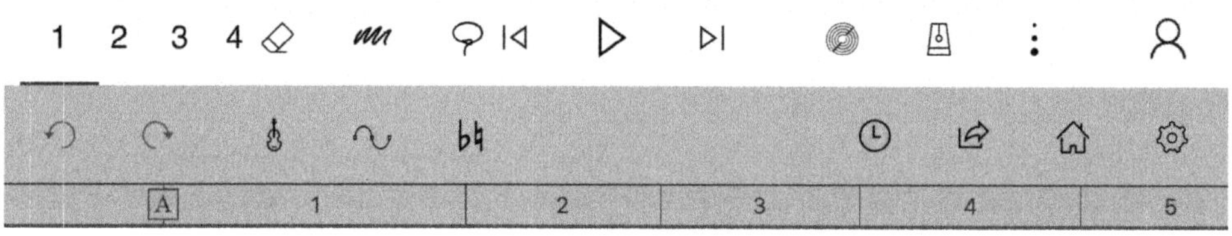

Toolbar / Selection Bar

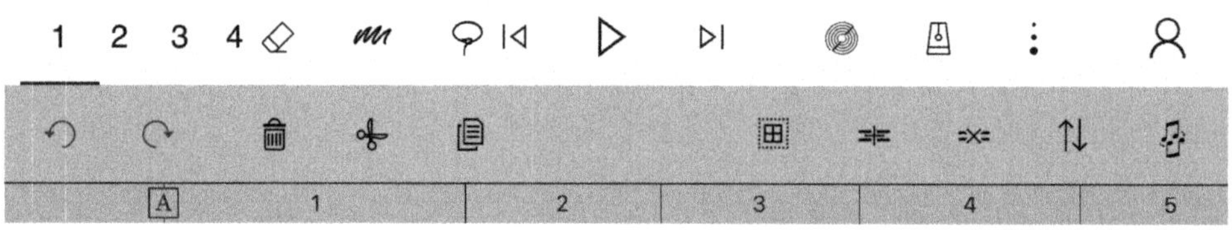

Fenby

Fenby is a voice activated composer assistant. Please note that this feature is still a work in progress and currently only available to accept commands in English.

You must grant permission to use the device's microphone to access Fenby. Fenby is named after Eric Fenby, a British amanuensis and composer.

Tap the Fenby icon in the upper right-hand corner of the toolbar to activate Fenby. Fenby will listen to voice commands. While waiting for you to speak, he will move his eyes back and forth and nod his head. Very cute.

You can speak conversational English and it will understand quite a bit. You can say things like:

"Go to bar 20"

"Set tempo to 80 bpm"

"Change to 3-4 at bar 2" (changes to 3/4 time)

"Add strings" (adds violins 1, violins 2, viola, and cello)

"Change viola to treble clef"

As this is a work-in-progress, what Fenby doesn't recognize today will likely be improved on in future versions.

Chapter 4
Music Input

How to Write Notation in StaffPad

Writing music notation in StaffPad is the *entire point* of StaffPad! Hopefully, you've already experienced writing music notation on paper (real paper - not the digital kind) so you already have an idea of what notes and rests look like. If you need a refresher, look at ***Chapter 2 - Music Notation Basics.***

Writing Notes

In general, how you wrote on paper in the analog world is pretty much the same as it is while using StaffPad. Fortunately, there are also some shortcuts to speed up the process of writing. First, you won't need to neatly draw cute little ovals at a 45-degree angle, spending time filling in the black dots.

For starters, let's write a quarter note. You don't have to draw an oval; a simple slash will do. The slash should be at approximately a 45-degree angle. Then draw a vertical line for the stem. You can do this in one continuous stroke or two. The note head and the stem do not have to touch, but they need to align vertically:

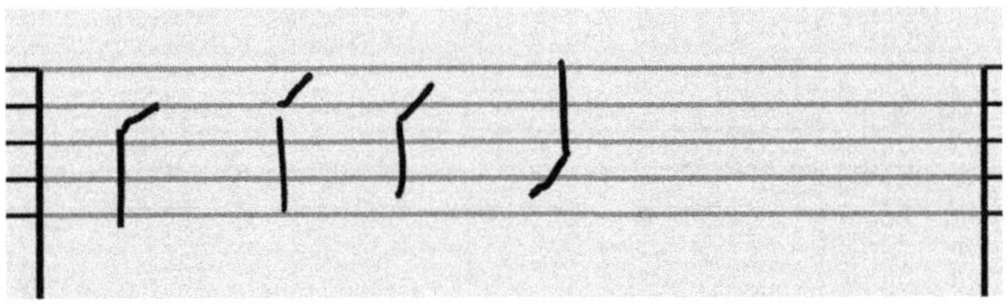

Notice how sloppy this appears to be. Don't worry, StaffPad understood what I was trying to write, and this is the result:

StaffPad utilizes "palm rejection" which understands that you are resting the palm of your hand on the screen. It won't confuse it for a touch or swipe gesture. However, if you're left-handed like me you may still see some issues - especially on a smaller tablet - where your palm touches the toolbar at the top. This *will* trigger a touch gesture and think you're trying to do something up there.

For me, the solution was purchasing an "artist glove". It covers the butt of your hand and the two fingers you normally wouldn't use to interact with when writing.

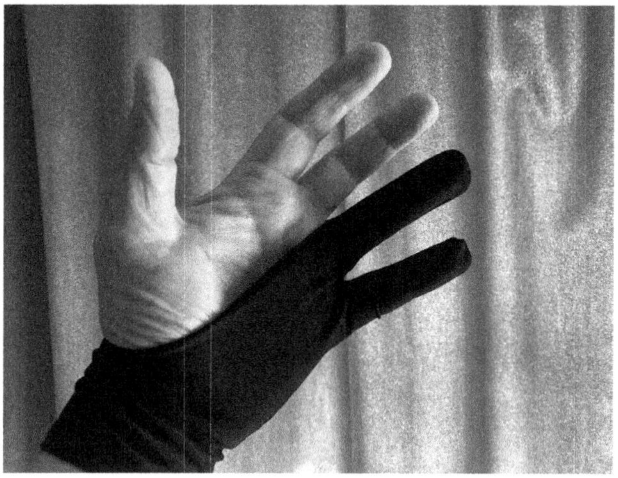 

Whole and half notes start with a circle. It should be more round than oval.

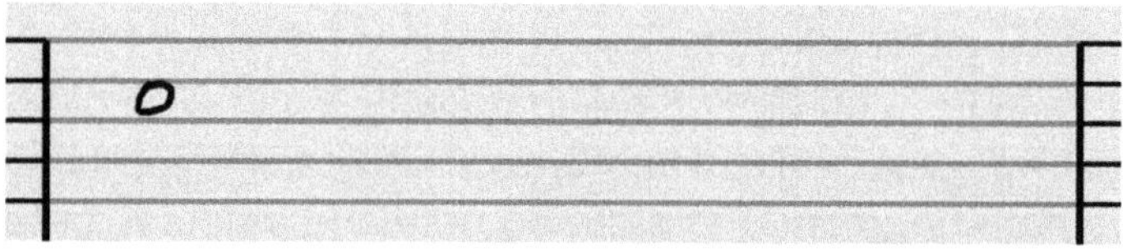

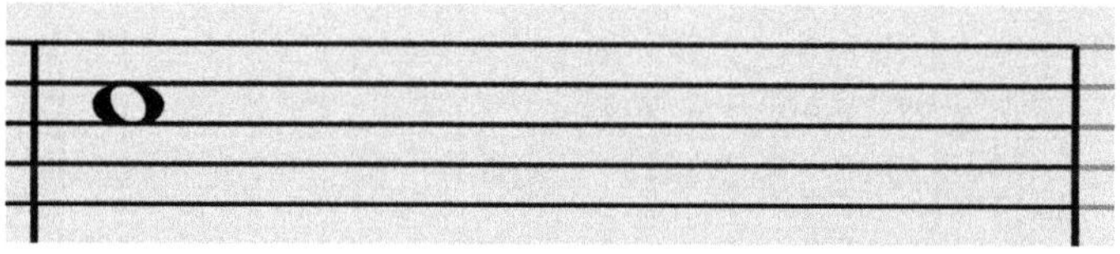

To turn a whole note into a half note, draw a stem.

Drawing eighth notes and sixteenth notes are also simple. Begin just like you are writing a quarter note and add a flag - an angled line:

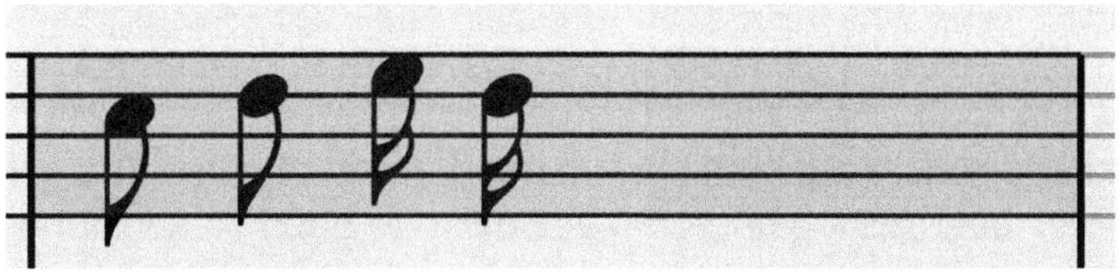

Draw two flags for sixteenths, three flags for thirty seconds, etc. up to five flags for 128th notes.

If you prefer beamed notes instead of flags, start by drawing quarter notes and connect the bottom of the stems with another line.

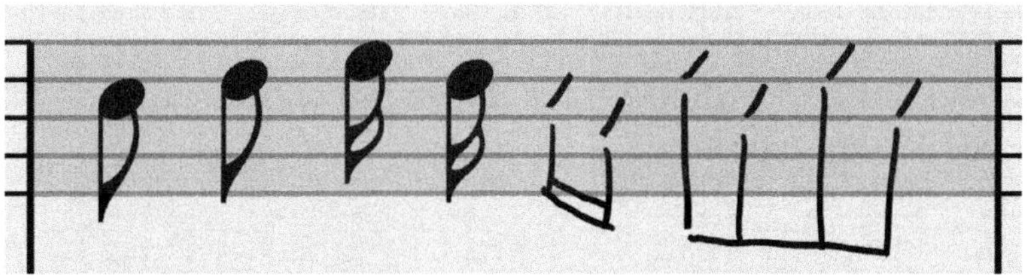

If the bar is getting crowded with notes you can drag the bar line with the pencil and move it to the right to make more space.

If you're drawing notes and not seeing them converted to notation yet, that's because you need to tap outside of the measure first. There's a very good reason for this:

Some music writing programs begin converting almost as soon as you write something. This can be good and bad. It's good because you see the result right away. It's bad because you may not be done drawing. Writing music is a multi-step process. Writing a group of four beamed eighth notes, for example, would require several steps: draw the note heads, draw the stems, draw the beams. But what if any of the notes require accidentals (sharps and flats)? That's an additional step. Adding articulation markings such as staccato dots requires additional steps.

StaffPad's philosophy is to treat music writing just like writing on paper. Once you've completed entering everything you need in a measure, you move on to the next measure. The moment you touch the pencil on a different measure, StaffPad knows you're done with the previous measure and will finally render it to proper music notation.

Inserting Notes

StaffPad allows you to add additional notes within a beamed group of notes at any time. Here is an example of a group of two eighth notes beamed together, but you'd like to add two additional notes to make it a group of sixteenth notes.

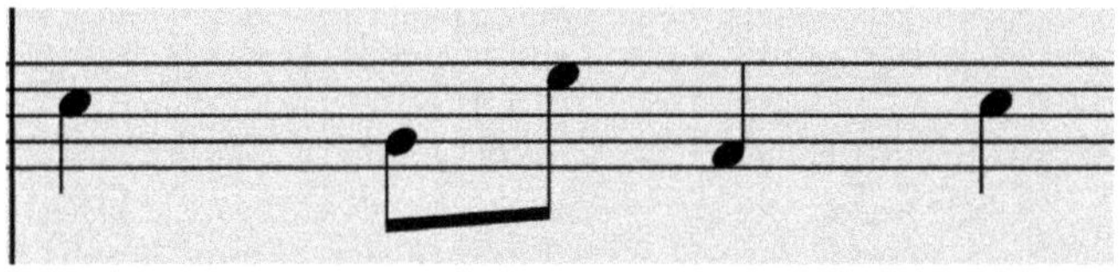

Draw the new notes within the group of beamed notes. Move the original notes to the left or right if you need to make more room to insert the new notes.

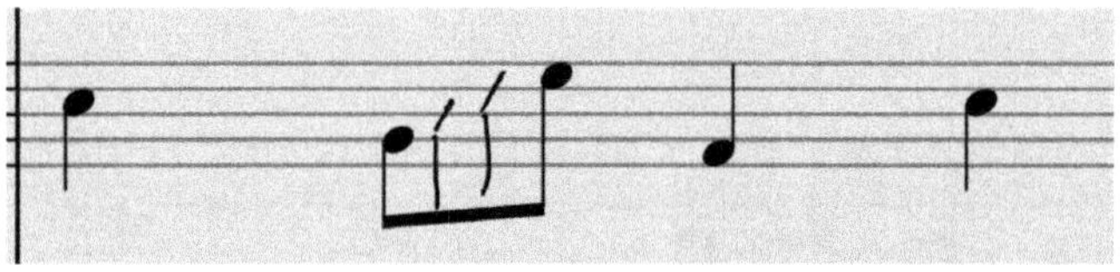

The newly inserted notes are also eighth notes because of the current beaming value which causes the bar to be *overfilled* (see below for more info on Overfilled bars).

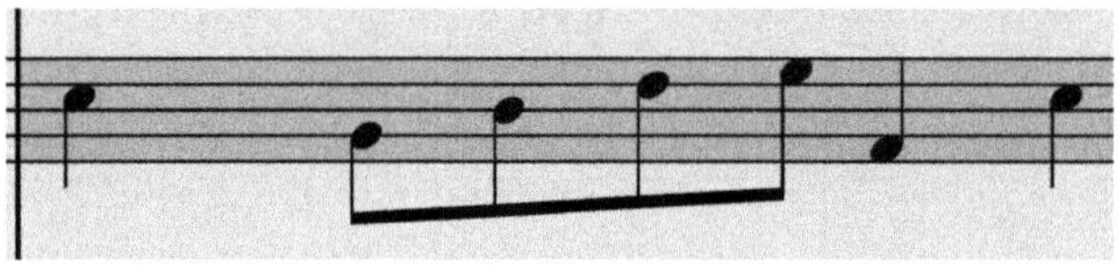

Draw a second beam to turn the group into sixteenth notes.

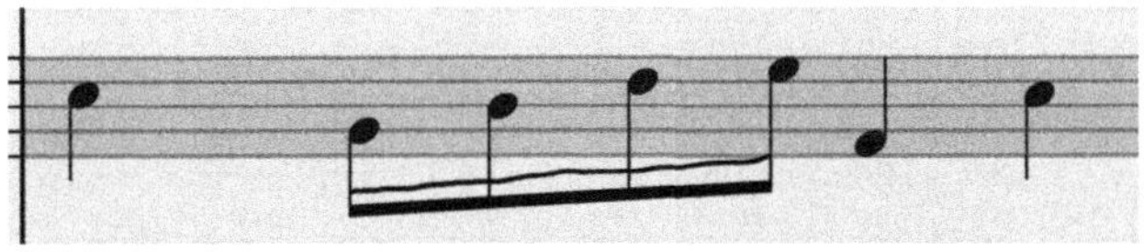

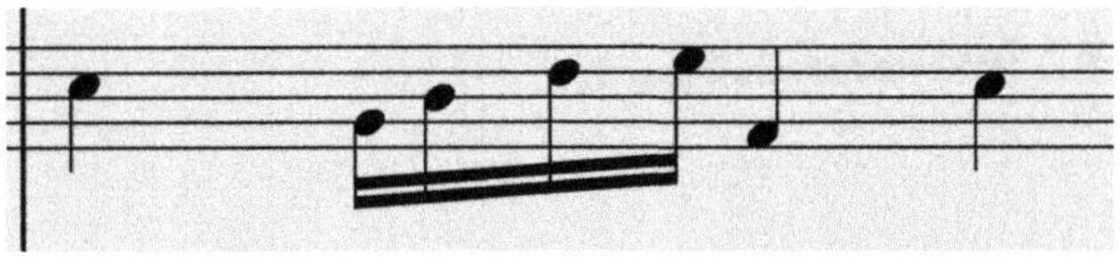

Writing Rests

Rests are as important as notes in music notation. Rests fill out the mathematical requirements of writing a complete bar of music. For every note value there is an equivalent rest: Quarter, eighth, sixteenth, etc.

One striking difference between notes and rests: Notes can be beamed together to form logical groupings, rests cannot. A grouping of four eighth notes beamed together would be represented as rests by several possibilities:

Four eighth note rests.

Two quarter note rests.

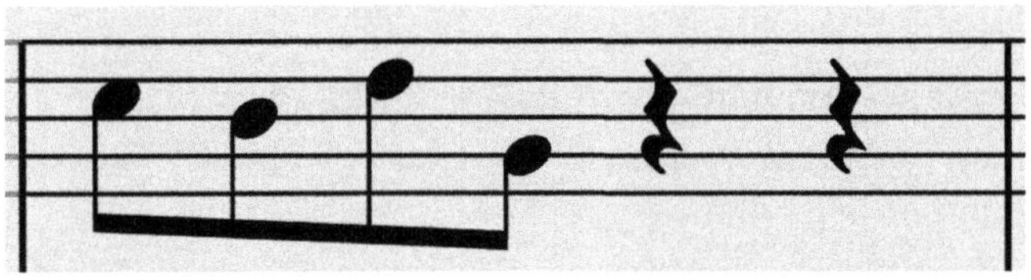

One half note rest.

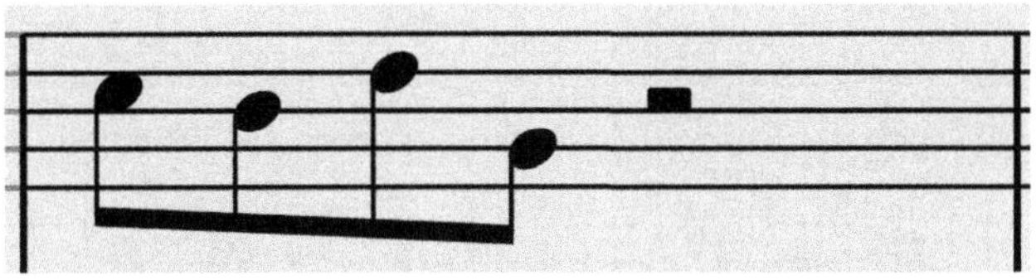

In each example the rest values are mathematically correct.

So how do we write rests in StaffPad? A **quarter** rest can be drawn as a standard quarter rest (the letter Z with a C underneath it) or as the letter S (a unique shortcut in StaffPad):

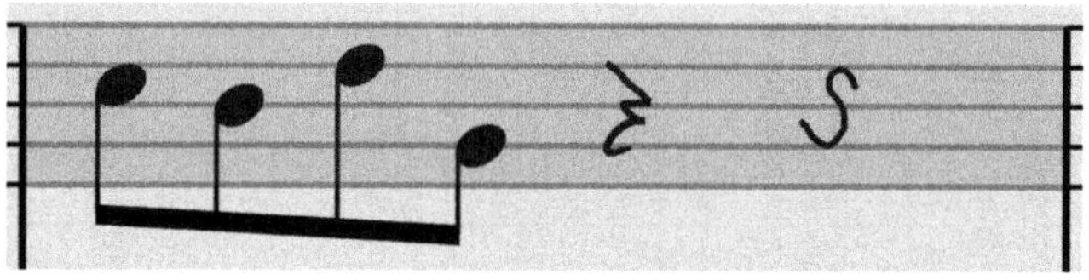

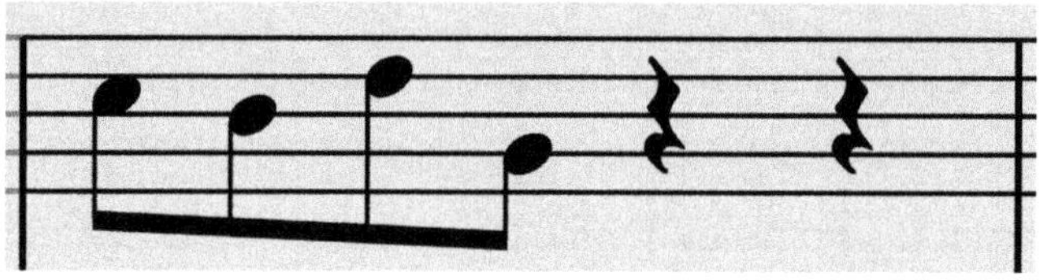

An **eighth** rest is drawn resembling the number 7:

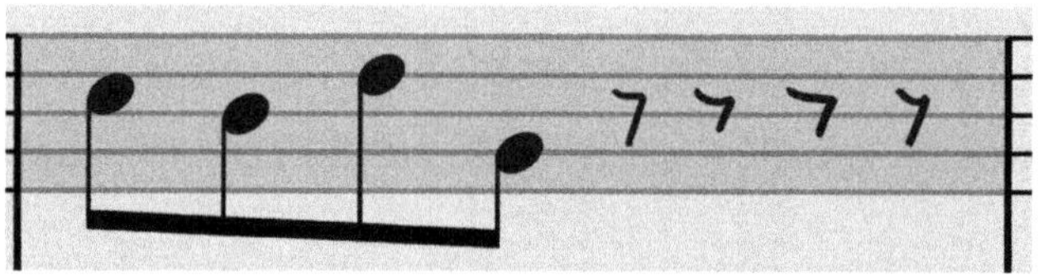

A **sixteenth** (or thirty second) rest begins with the number 7 plus a flag:

A **half** rest is a short horizontal line that sits just above a staff line:

A **whole** rest is a short horizontal line that sits just below a staff line:

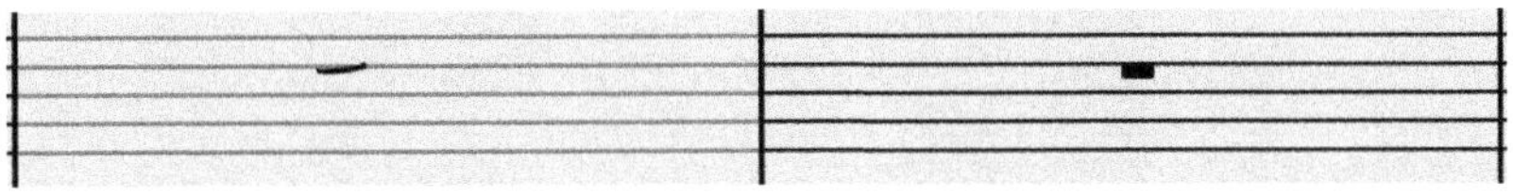

Active Bars

Once you touch the pencil to a measure and begin writing - even if it's an accidental scribble - StaffPad considers it the *active bar*. You will not need to select a bar before you begin writing - just start writing! You will know the bar is active because the staff lines have turned **green**. It will remain the active bar until you tap away. Once you tap away your previous active bar will be rendered...

...or attempt to be rendered! StaffPad will do its best to understand what you've written. It's possible you've written something StaffPad can't figure out. In that case, your original drawing will remain unrendered. It may have rendered everything else. You need to look at what you wrote and try to fix it.

When StaffPad can't understand something, it will turn the active bar's staff lines from **green**...

... to **orange**. It's now up to you to correct this. First, you'll need to erase the culprit and start again.

You are not required to finish a bar completely before moving on. You can always come back and add additional notes, rests, ties, slurs, etc. When you are done adding the new stuff, just tap away and the new items will be rendered once again.

Pending Bars

In the above example, the staff line color has become **orange** because there is unfinished business. The last note was unrecognized and therefore this bar is still **pending**.

StaffPad encourages you to continue with the flow of writing music and not be bogged down with correcting your work right away. The creative flow is more important than the technical elements.

To highlight which bars are still *pending*, StaffPad will set the staff lines to the color orange. This way you can go back later and finish the bar and make any necessary corrections.

Problem Bars

The developers at StaffPad are constantly working to improve handwriting recognition. To aid in their quest they have included a feature to allow you to upload the bar in question so they can analyze and improve the recognition logic.

Simply tap on any orange pending bar and you will be given the option to **Report Bar** by tapping on the **Upload** button. That's it! It will be reported to the StaffPad developers.

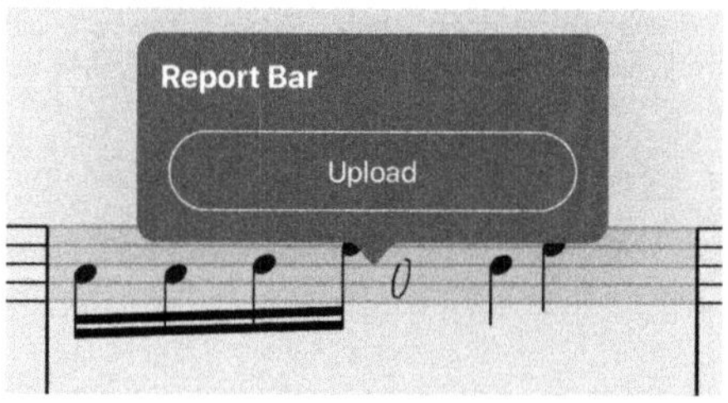

Underfilled and Overfilled Bars

StaffPad expects you to completely fill a bar with notes and/or rests. It won't make any assumptions about what should be there if you leave anything out. Mathematically, this combination of notes and rests need to equal the time signature you've specified. If you have an insufficient amount your bar will be *underfilled*. Conversely, if you have too many notes or rests the bar will be considered *overfilled*.

Here is a 4/4 bar that only has three beats. StaffPad will change the background color of the underfilled bar to gray to let you know that you need to add more notes or rests to complete the bar.

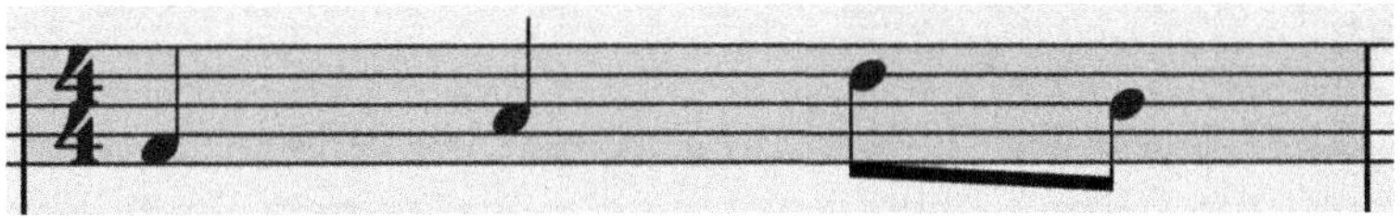

The only time an underfilled bar will be considered correct is if the bar is a *pickup bar*. See ***Pickup Bars*** below for details.

This is also a 4/4 bar but there are five beats of music in it. StaffPad will change the background color of the overfilled bar to red. You could either change the time signature to 5/4 to accommodate the notes or remove the appropriate number of notes to make it fit.

Erasing

We all make mistakes when writing music. StaffPad makes it super easy to make changes. That's the fun of writing in digital ink. For simple, quick erasures it's often quicker to trigger the pencil's eraser mode. How you do this depends on the type of pencil and device you're using.

For Apple pencils, add slightly more pressure with the pencil on the screen to turn on eraser mode. Once eraser mode is on, you can return to normal pressure. Slide the pencil around to erase items. There is no visual indicator that you are in eraser mode except that things will start disappearing! If you lift the pencil off the screen, eraser mode will end.

If you are using a newer iPad that takes advantage of the Pencil 2, you can assign a double-tap gesture to the pencil to activate eraser mode. See ***Chapter 10 - Score Management*** for details on how to set this up in Settings.

For extended erasing activity, turn on Eraser mode by tapping the Eraser button on the Toolbar. With this mode you can lift the pencil off the screen and eraser mode will not terminate. This is the mode that is triggered with the double-tap of the Pencil 2.

Most Windows pens have an eraser tip on the back of the pen. Just flip the pen over and erase! If your pen does not have an eraser tip you can add an Eraser button on the Toolbar. See ***Chapter 10 - Score Management*** for details on how to set this up in Settings.

What You Can Erase

Notes and **Rests** - any type of augmentation that you added to the note (or rest) such as dots, ties, slurs, and any text will be also removed along with it since there is no meaning to those things if the notes no longer exist.

Ties and **Slurs** - unlike erasing a note with a tie or slur attached, you can erase only the tie or slur and it will not affect the note.

Accidentals - sharps, flats, naturals, double sharps, and double flats can be removed without affecting the note.

Tuplets - you can erase the numeric value of groupings of 3, 5, 7, etc. Once you remove it, the notes will change value and may cause the bar to overfill. In the following example there are three tuplet groups of 7:

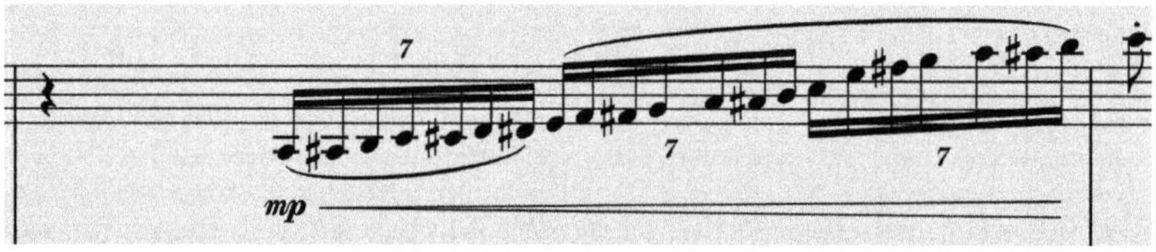

By removing the number 7 you end up with lots of 16th notes. This is too many notes to mathematically fit in the bar so the bar background color turns to **red** to indicate *overfill.*

Beams - there are several things to note about erasing beams:

1. Removing the beam(s) between two notes will convert the notes into flagged notes:

Notes with beams.

Notes after removing some of the beams.

2. When there are more than a single beam connecting notes, erasing the **outermost** beam will ungroup the notes and turn them into flagged notes. Erasing the **innermost** beam will simply remove the beam, changing the note value.

In the example below, removing the innermost beam from sixteenth notes turns them into eighth notes.

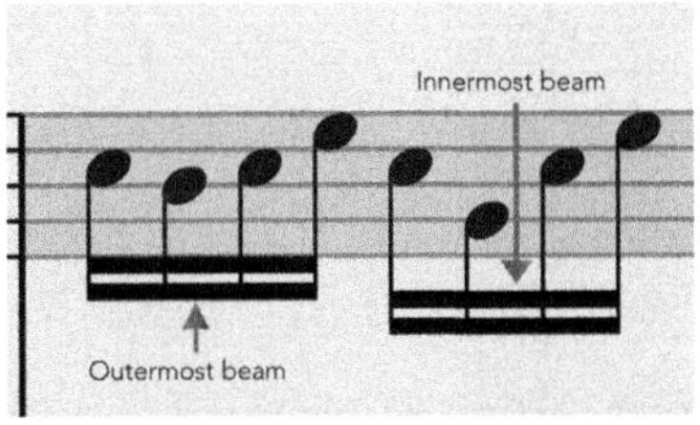

Each sixteenth note has become an eighth note.

Flags - erasing flags will change the note value. In the example below, flagged eighth notes become quarter notes. Also notice that the bar has become overfilled since the note values doubled.

Notes with flags.

Removing flags changes note values (bar is overfilled).

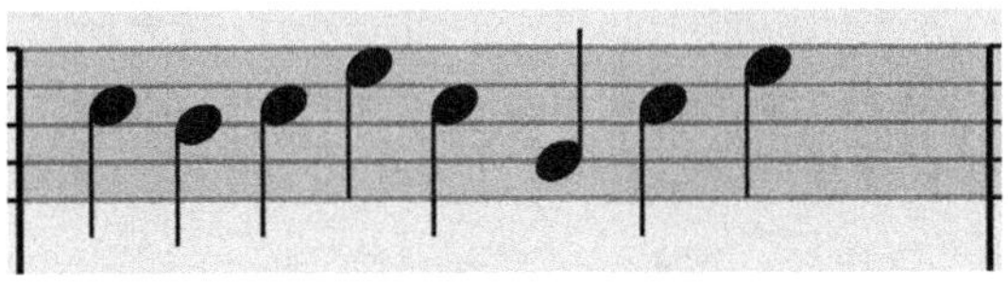

Unrecognized strokes - any pencil mark, intentional or not, whether it is in a **Pending Bar** or an **Active Bar** can be erased.

Markup - all markup drawings can be erased, but **Drawing Mode** must be enabled first.

Other items that can be erased:

- Text
- Symbols
- Pedal retakes
- Bar repeats
- Repeat endings
- D.C.
- D.S.
- Coda signs

Expression and **Automation** - erase any modified automation and reset it to the initialized values.

Accidentals

StaffPad supports the drawing of sharps, flats, double sharps, double flats, and naturals.

Sharps - requires four strokes: two vertical and two horizontal. Make sure the center of the sharp covers the pitch whether it is on a line or a space.

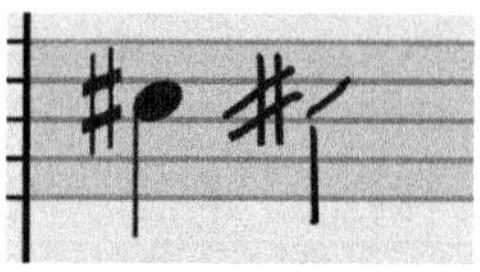

Flats - draw a lowercase b. It can be drawn in two separate strokes or one continuous stroke. Make sure the center of the flat covers the pitch whether it is on a line or a space.

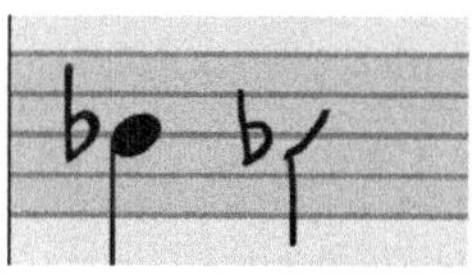

Double Sharps - draw the letter x (two strokes). Make sure the center of the double sharp covers the pitch whether it is on a line or a space.

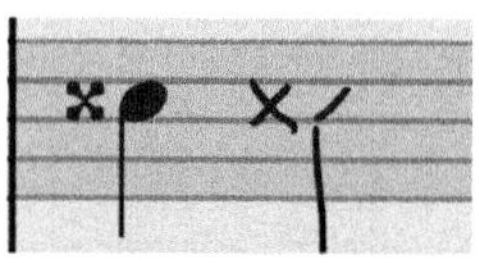

Double Flats - draw the letter b, two of them, side-by-side. Make sure the center of the flat covers the pitch whether it is on a line or a space.

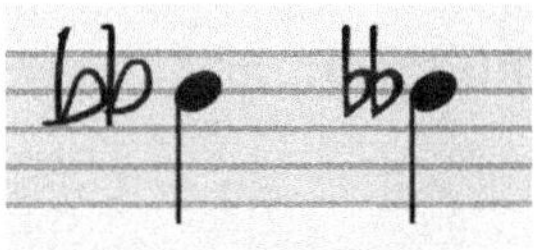

Naturals - drawn in two strokes. The first stroke resembles a capital letter L, followed by the same shape upside down (like the number 7). Make sure the center of the natural covers the pitch whether it is on a line or a space.

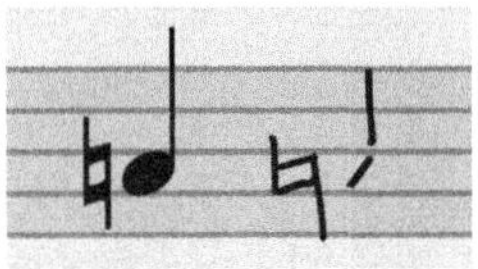

Slurs and Ties

Tied notes are created by drawing a slightly curved line connecting two notes of the same pitch. The line should be close but does not have to touch the note heads. Ties can even cross a barline.

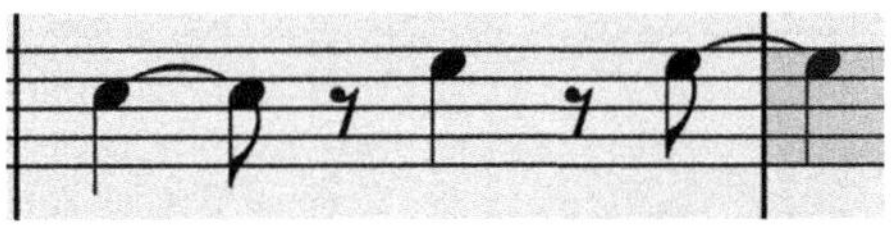

Slurs are curved lines that cover more than two notes. A slur can be drawn above or below a group of notes.

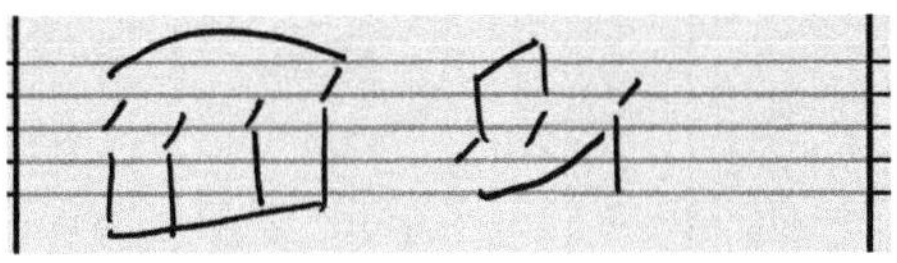

The slur can be repositioned so that it sits above or below the staff by dragging the line to its new position. You can also change the starting and ending points of the slur by dragging either end and sliding to its new position.

Articulations

Articulations include various accent marks such as staccato, tenuto, marcato, etc. The articulation must be drawn above the note head (when stems point down), and below the note head (when stems point up).

Accent - the most common articulation for accented notes. The > symbol can be drawn above or below the note, but it will always be rendered above the note.

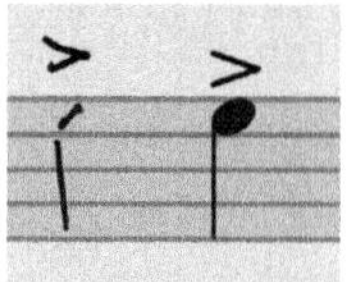

Staccato - a small dot over or under the note. You do not need to make the dot large as if you were drawing a note head. Even if it is almost too small to see, StaffPad will understand the drawing based on context. A small dot in the middle of nowhere would be ignored but sitting over a note head will be understood to indicate a staccato is being added.

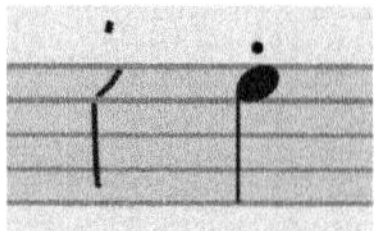

Staccatissimo - a vertical line over or under the note.

Marcato - the marcato can also be drawn above or below the note. Draw a hat (Λ) above the note or a V below the note. The marcato symbol will always be rendered above the note.

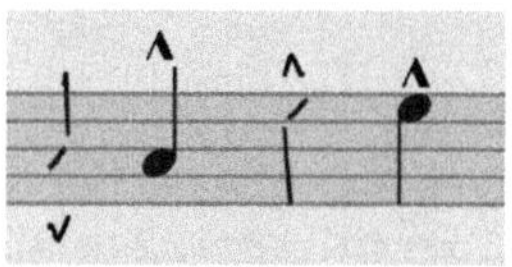

Tenuto - a tenuto mark is represented by a short horizontal line above or below the note. It will always be rendered above the note.

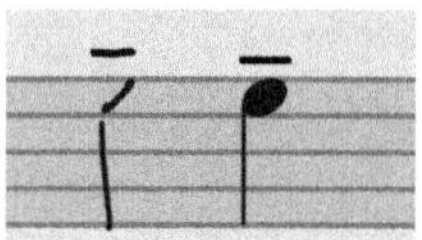

Combining Articulations - you can have multiple articulation marks on a note. It doesn't matter in what order you stack them or whether you place them above or below the note. They will always be rendered above the note. The staccato mark will always be placed just above the note. The marcato mark will always be the uppermost mark. Once caveat, staccato and staccatissimo marks are mutually exclusive. Only one can be active. The latter mark will replace the previous mark.

Multiple Voices (Voice Layer)

StaffPad allows up to four separate voices to appear on a staff. Which voice you are writing in depends on which voice is currently selected on the Toolbar:

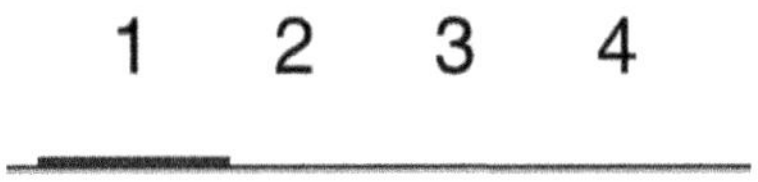

Normally, only a single voice is needed on the staff. Flutes, for example, are often in pairs (a2) and both instruments will play the same written notes. But when you want to have each flute play separate lines (divisi) you have two choices:

1. Split the staff into two staves
2. Combine both parts on a single stave differentiating by stem direction

Using a single stave is where selecting a "voice" comes in. This is common practice for French Horns; horns 1 & 2 share one stave and horns 3 & 4 share another.

Without separating the parts into multiple voices, they would be written as double-stops.

Rarely would you actually need to write more than two voices on one stave. Technically it is possible, but you end up with more than a single voice sharing a stem direction:

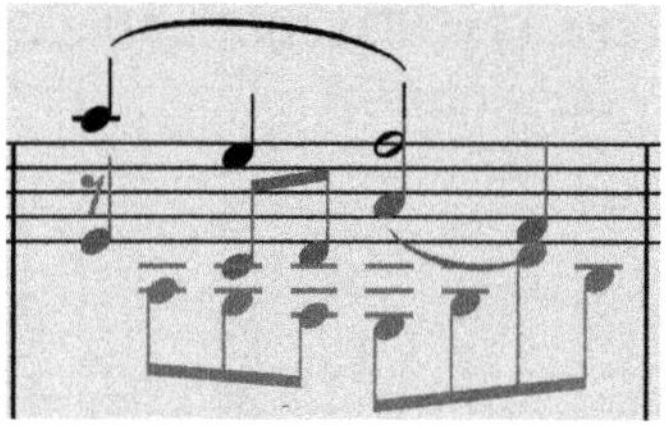

Three players trying to read their independent parts would have a very difficult time to sort through this! If you do utilize multiple voices, StaffPad will display them in the following colors:

- Voice 1 - black
- Voice 2 - green
- Voice 3 - red
- Voice 4 - orange

You can choose to turn off colors by turning off this option in Settings. See ***Chapter 10 - Score Management*** for details.

Voices can be swapped by selecting the notes and tapping the Swap Voices button: Voice 1 will become Voice 2; Voice 2 will become Voice 3; Voice 3 will become Voice 4; Voice 4 will become Voice 1. In the above example with only three voices, Voice 3 would become Voice 1.

Stem direction can also be applied by selecting the notes and tapping the Stem Direction button.

Divisi Staffs

Above we saw how you can utilize multiple voices to accommodate more than one instrument reading from the same stave. In some cases that may be adequate, but sometimes you need a more independent solution for the players: the Divisi Staff.

Having a separate staff to split up the instruments creates complete independence from one another. Each instrument can play at different dynamics as well as dissimilar types of lines (legato vs staccato, for example). It also adds clarity to each part since they are totally separate.

A divisi staff can be added by “long pressing”, that is, pressing your finger on the screen with added pressure, on a measure. A context menu will appear.

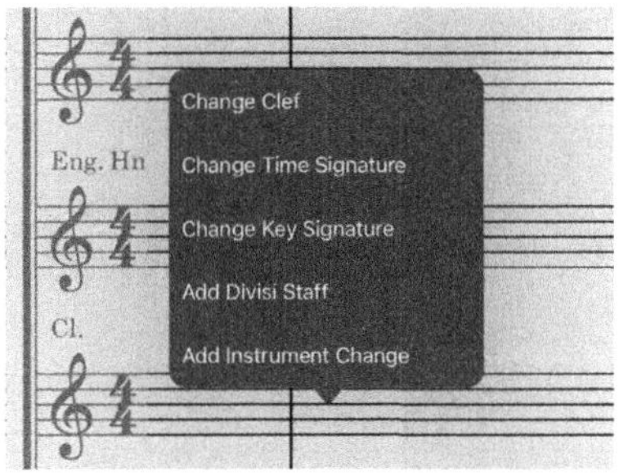

After selecting **Add Divisi Staff** you will see an additional staff for the instrument.

If you change your mind and wish to remove the divisi staff, long press either staff of the divisi parts and you will be presented with this context menu. Select **Remove Divisi Staff** and the newly added divisi staff will be removed, not the original staff. Everything you entered on the divisi staff will be lost!

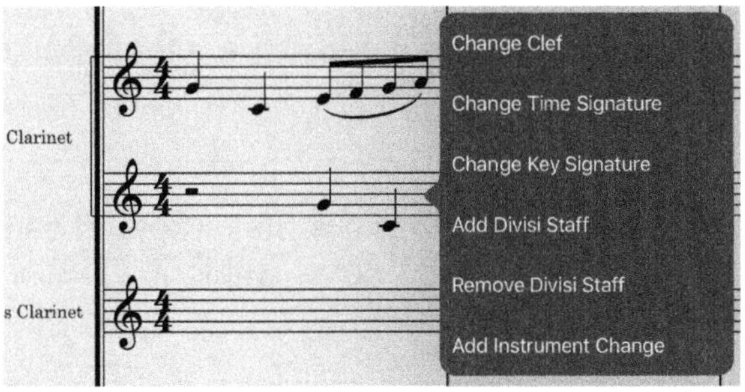

Pickup Bars

A pickup bar is a measure of music at the beginning of a piece that contains less than the full number of beats. StaffPad has a special designation to mark a bar as a pickup bar. If you didn’t mark the bar as a pickup bar, StaffPad would consider this an error and flag the measure as *underfilled*.

Only the first bar can become a pickup bar.

Long-press the first measure of the piece to select **Create Pickup Bar**. This menu option will not appear in any measure except the first. Notice that the current first measure has a gray background. This indicates that

StaffPad considers the bar in its current state to be underfilled.

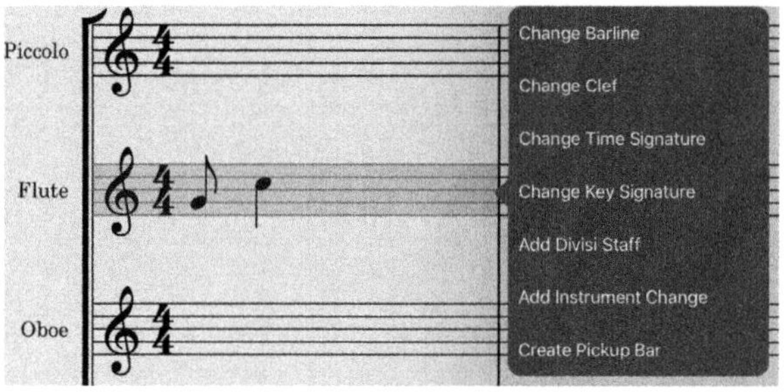

After making the bar a pickup bar the background color of the bar is back to normal and considered neither under- or over-filled. A pickup bar does not have to contain a beat and a half as in the example above. Any number of beats less than the expected time signature can be written.

NOTE: Whatever you initially write as a pickup bar, that will be considered the time signature for that measure. The example above would make the first measure a 3/8 bar. Any other instrument written in the pickup bar must now adhere to this time signature.

Adding an Oboe note in the pickup measure must equate to the 3/8 time signature. In the example above the bar is considered to be underfilled.

To return this measure to a non-pickup bar, long-press the measure and select **Remove Pickup Bar**. Removing a pickup bar does not delete the bar or any of the notes within it. Once you remove the pickup bar any notes in it will then be considered underfilled.

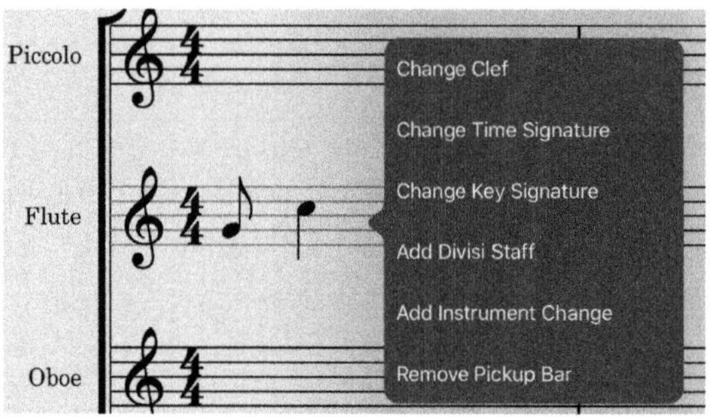

StaffPad will resize the pickup bar to fit the number of notes just as it would reformat the score to fit the notes. The pickup bar will not have a measure number and is considered measure 0. The first full bar of music will be bar 1.

Time Signatures

When you create a new project the default time signature will be 4/4. You can change not only the initial time signature but the time signature of any measure in the score. Long-press anywhere in the measure to popup the context menu and select **Change Time Signature**.

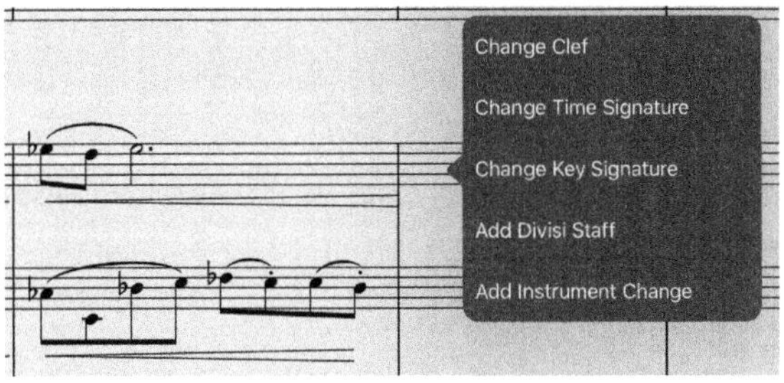

A second popup will display a list of typical time signatures to choose from.

If none of the options offer a time signature you wish to use, scroll all the way to the right and tap the **more** (...) button.

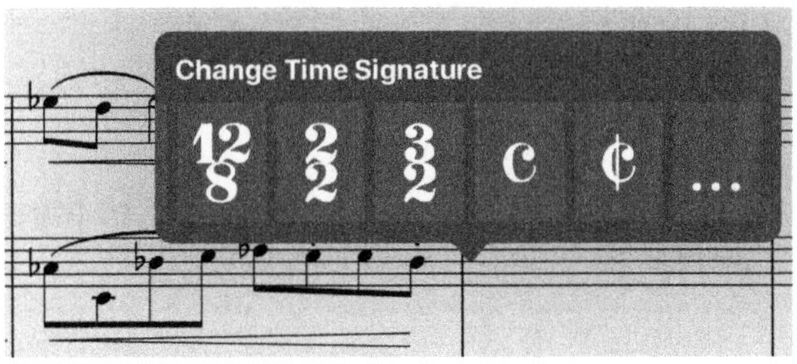

You can define your own custom time signature by typing in the beat number (numerator) and the note base (denominator).

Numerator:

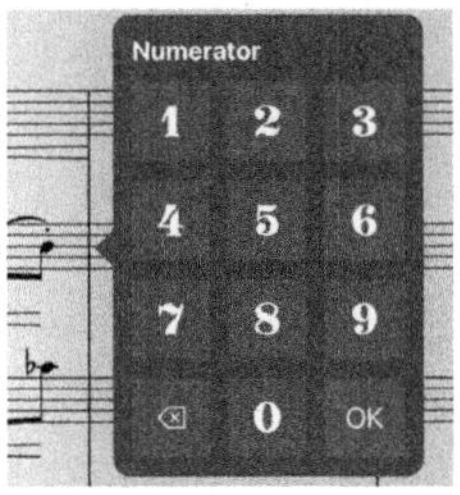

Denominator:

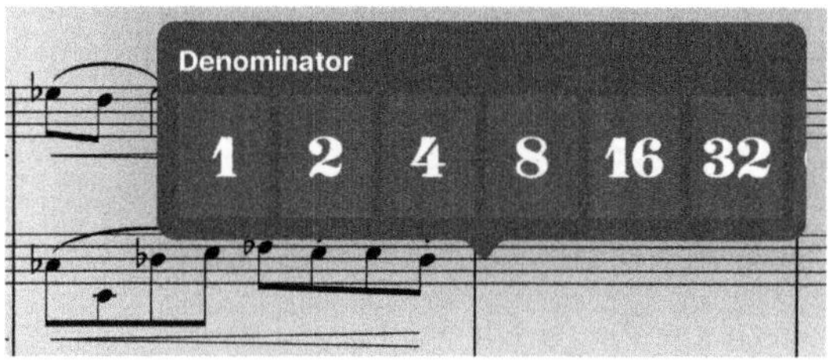

Changing the time signature when there is already music in the bar will not affect those notes. The result will likely be an under- or over-filled bar.

Key Signatures

The key signature can be changed not only at the beginning of the score, but at the beginning of any bar in the piece. Changing key signature makes sense when there is a strong direction in the music to do so. Otherwise, without a new key signature there will be lots of accidentals (sharps and flats).

Long-press on a measure to reveal the context menu. Select **Change Key Signature**.

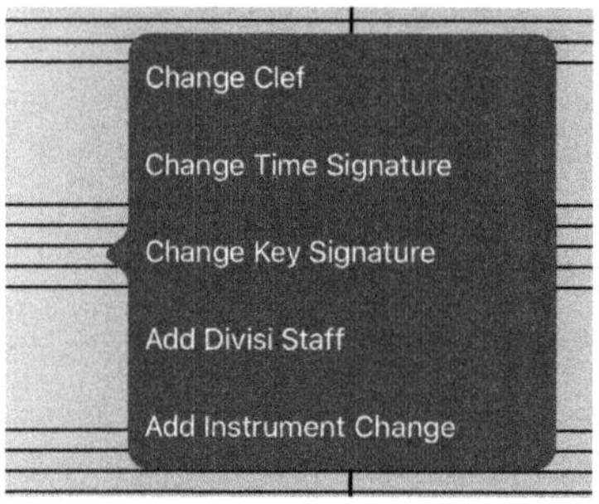

Beginning with the key of C Major, a list of keys in order of the cycle of fifths will be presented. Select **Minor** to change the names to the relative minor keys of the shown keys.

To remove a key signature, long-press the measure and select **Change Key Signature** again. This time select the same key signature as the previous measure, and it will be removed.

Transposed Score vs C Score

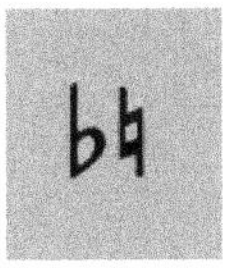

Select the **transpose** button from the Toolbar to toggle between C Score and Transposed score.

StaffPad allows you to work in C Score or Transposed Score. A “C” score, often referred to as *Score in C*, or *Concert Score*, is when every note sounds exactly as written. This is often easier for sight reading the score and eliminates having to transpose the notes in your head to understand the harmony.

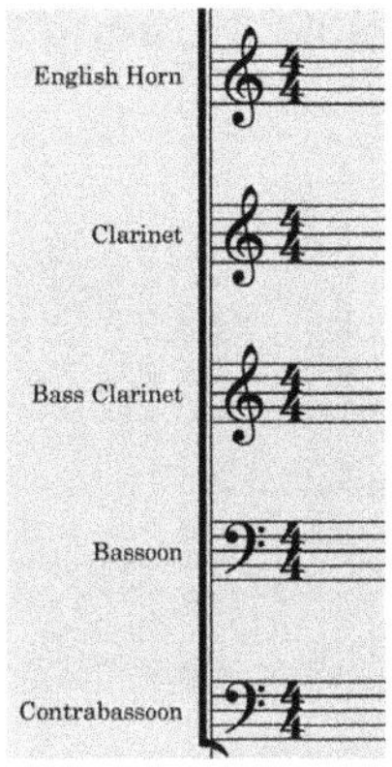

A transposed score is written exactly as the player will read it. For example, if the score is in the key of C, a Bb Clarinet will transpose its part up a whole step to the key of D. The English Horn (Cor Anglais) sounds a fifth lower than it is written. So a score written in the key of C will be written in the key of G for the English Horn.

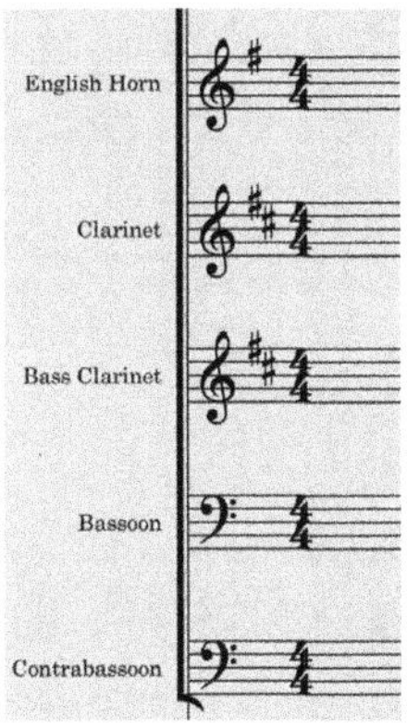

Why have these options? Obviously, the transposed notes that the players will see makes it easier for the conductor to communicate with the player when discussing the notes. The C Score makes it easier from the composer’s point of view so that the focus is on the creative process and notating the music as it is being created versus having to switch the brain and figure out if the transposed version is correct.

It really comes down to personal preference. Some people can do this with ease. I prefer C Score. The only drawback with C Score is that you must know what the instrument's range is (lowest to highest notes). Fortunately, StaffPad will only play valid notes for any instrument. You can place an out-of-range note anywhere on the score (StaffPad will still let you do that), but you should always check the note to make sure it actually sounds if you're in doubt.

Clefs

You are free to assign any clef for an instrument. StaffPad will initially assign the clef most used for that instrument, but you can change it whether it makes sense or not.

To change clefs, long-press on a measure and select **Change Clef**.

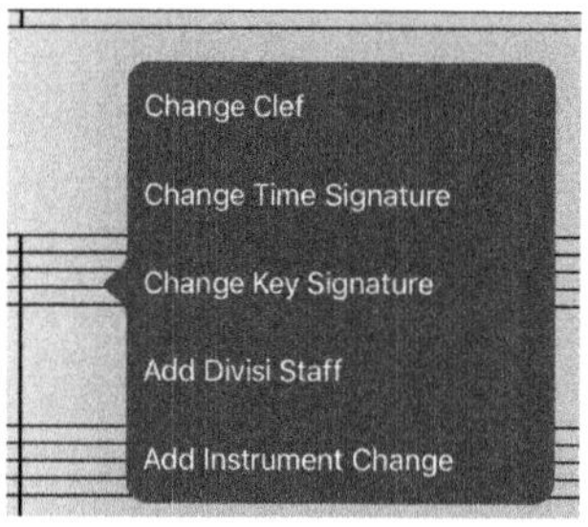

A popup menu will appear with a list of several types of clefs.

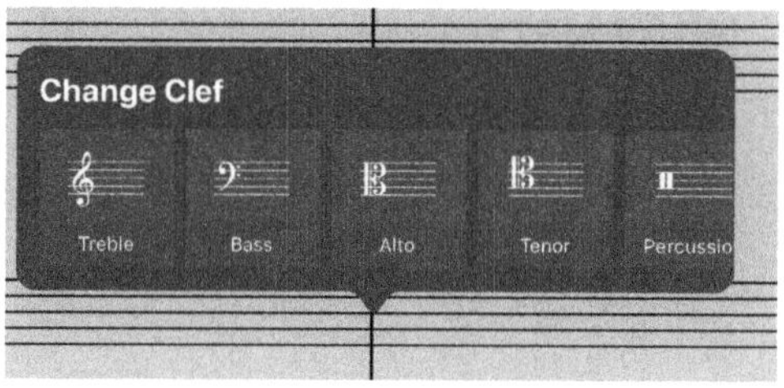

Scroll the list horizontally to see all clef choices.

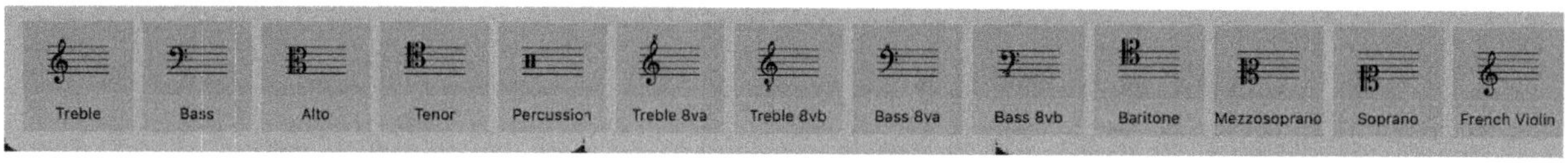

StaffPad will currently only allow you to change the clef at the beginning of a bar. Mid-bar and redundant clefs are not supported.

Barlines

All barlines in StaffPad are single line to begin with. You may change the barline type by long-pressing on a barline. A context menu will appear with the option to **Change Barline**.

If you press too far to the left or right of the barline you won't see the Change Barline option.

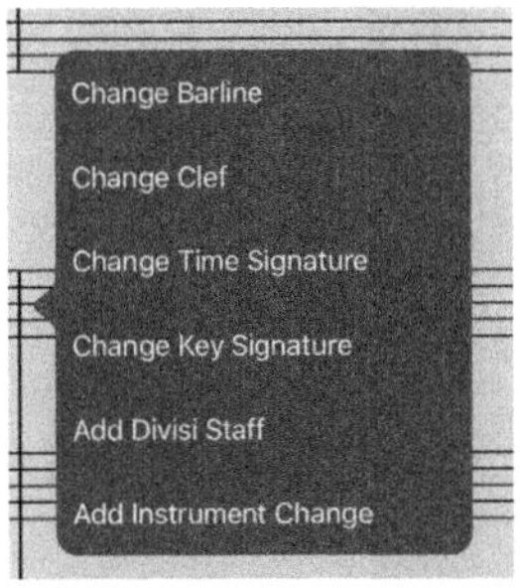

The barline choices will be shown in a scrollable list. The popup menu will be pointing to the bar that will be modified and the current barline will be colored blue.

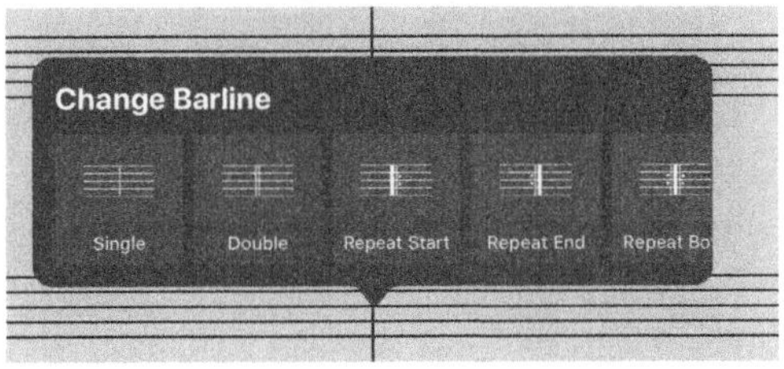

Here is the complete list of barline options.

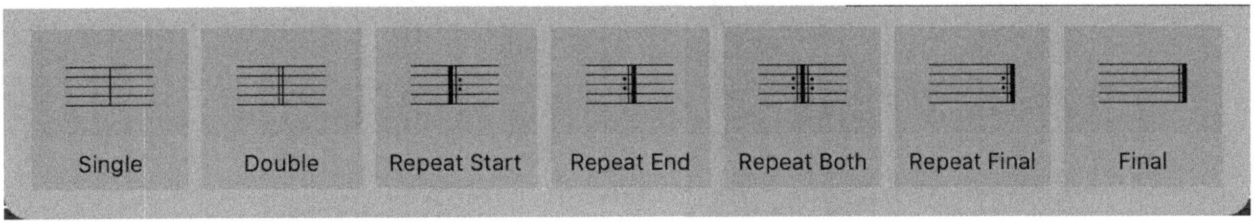

Single - the default barline style.

Double - used to indicate a new section of music. Will be automatically applied when changing the Key Signature.

Repeat Start - the beginning of a section that will be repeated. StaffPad playback will return to this bar when reaching a Repeat End barline.

Repeat End - once the music reaches this barline it will return to the previous Repeat Start bar (or beginning of the score if no Repeat Start exists).

Repeat Both - functions as both a Repeat End and a new Repeat Start.

Repeat Final - functions the same as a Repeat End but also acts as a Final bar.

Final - the end of the piece.

There can only be one **Final** (or **Repeat Final**) barline. That will be at the end of the piece. Any music in measures following where you place the final barline will be deleted!

Repeat Endings

Adding repeat barlines as described above is limited. For complete flexibility you can add **Repeat Endings**. Long-press on the bar to the left of the Repeat End barline and the context menu will give you the option to **Add First Ending**.

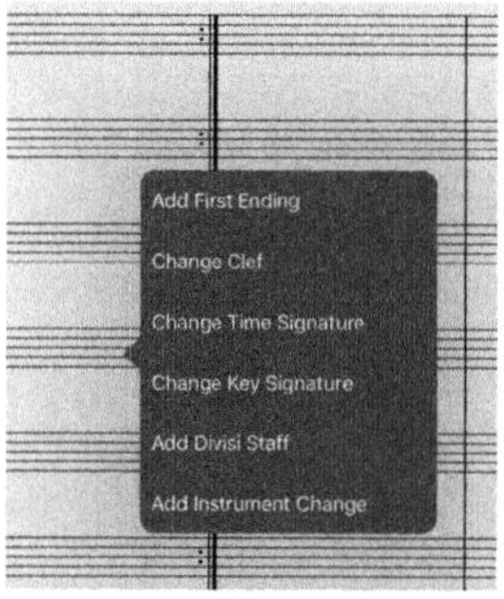

Alternatively, long-press the bar *after* the Repeat End barline and you will be given the option to **Add Second Ending**.

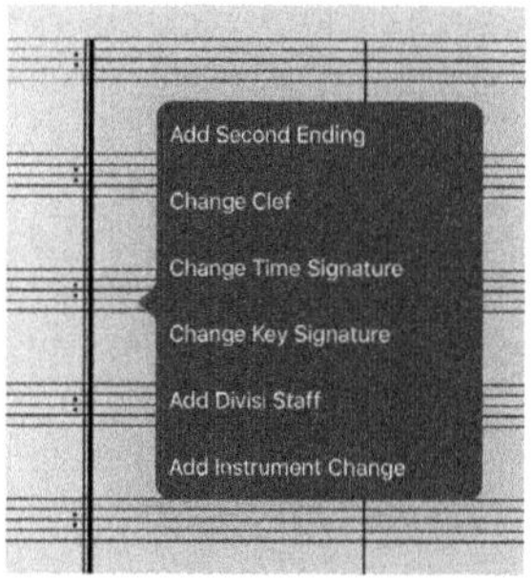

In either case, the end result will be the same.

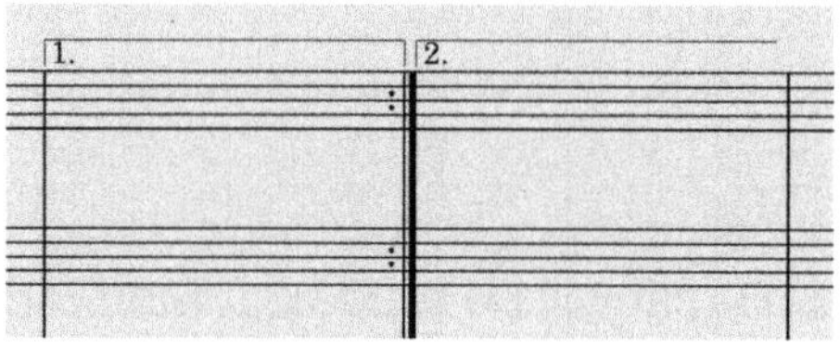

StaffPad will create both a **first** and **second** ending. You are not limited to only a first and second ending. You can add additional endings. Long-press the first ending (1.) and you will be presented with a context menu to **Add Additional Ending**.

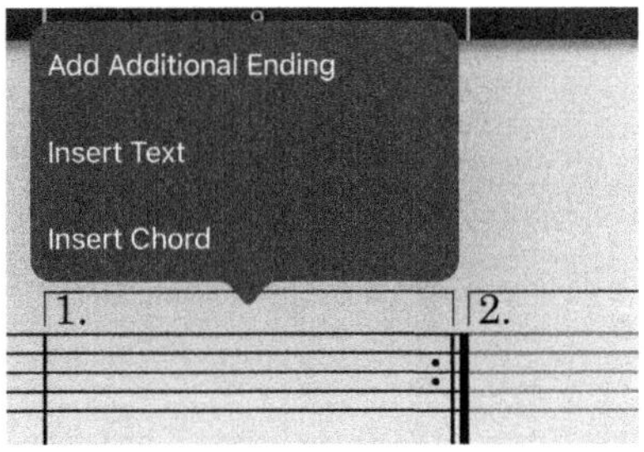

The first ending will now become a first *and* second ending, and the second ending will become a third ending.

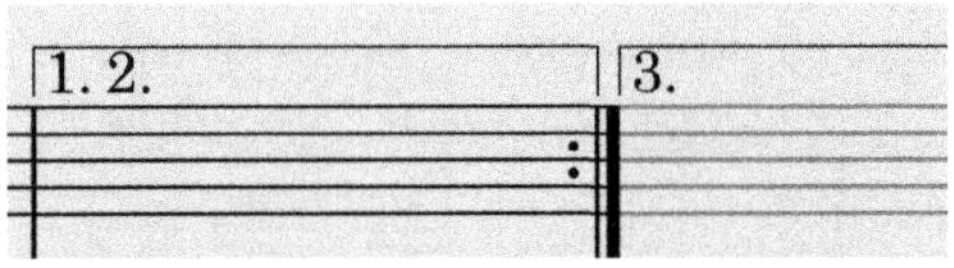

Long-press the first ending again to **Add Additional Ending** or to **Remove** (the last) **Additional Ending**.

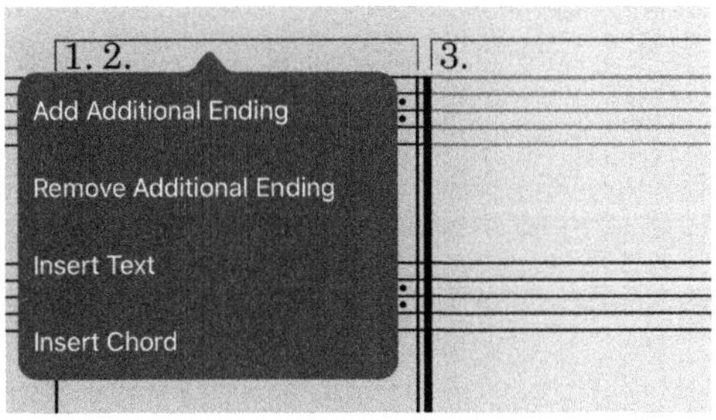

There is not a limit to the number of endings you can add.

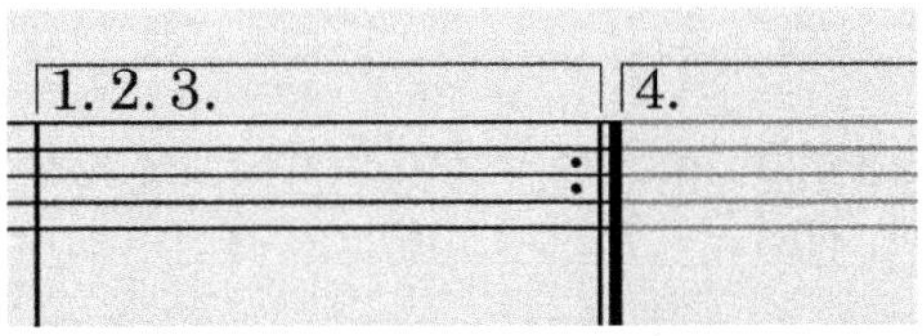

If your repeat endings turn **red,** it means it is not clear where the repeat should go. Make sure you've properly set up and **Repeat Start** barline. Without a Repeat Start barline, StaffPad will follow music theory rules and repeat to the beginning of the piece.

Drum Kit Notation

StaffPad supports standard drum notation. This will only apply to the **Drum Kit** instrument. In the example below, hi-hat and snare drum are written in **Voice 1**. The kick drum is written in **Voice 2**. Stems will be rendered accordingly.

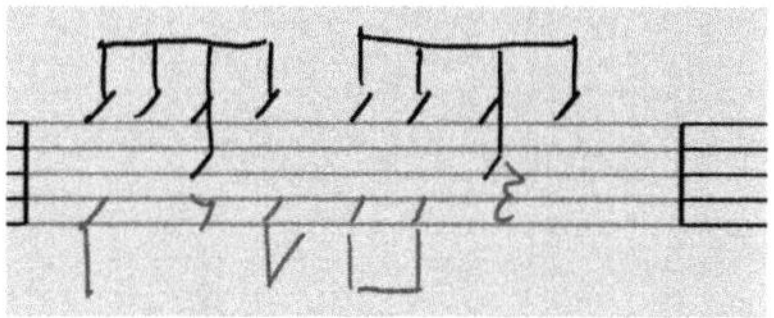

The hi-hat and all other cymbals will be rendered with X note heads. Each line and space on the staff is assigned General MIDI drum instruments. For example, the notes between the top space and the second line (counting up from the bottom) and excluding the third space (the snare) are assigned to the tom-toms.

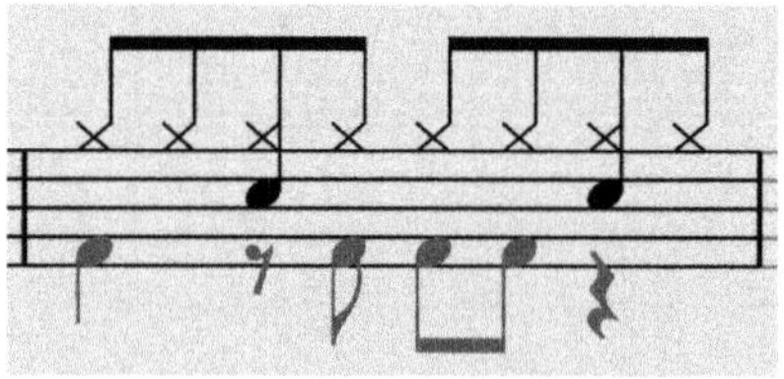

When exporting the score as a MIDI file or MusicXML file, the drum notation will export as a General MIDI drum track, common to all DAWs.

Percussion Notation

Other percussion instruments such as snare drum, gran casa, piatti, and triangle will be given the non-pitched percussion clef.

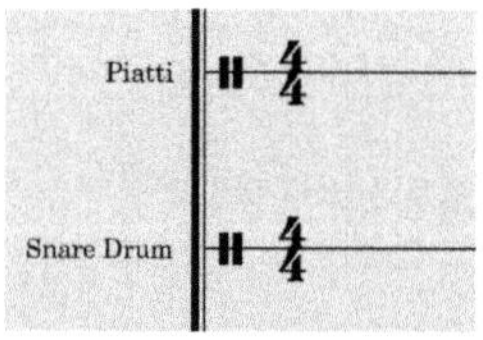

At least for the included stock StaffPad instruments, non-pitched instruments can generally be written in three places: on the line, just above the line, and just below the line. You can draw either a slash or an X.

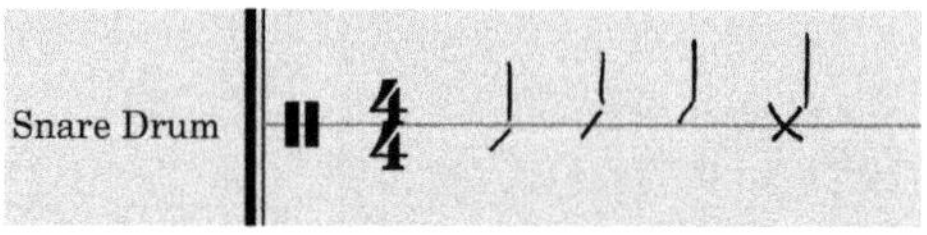

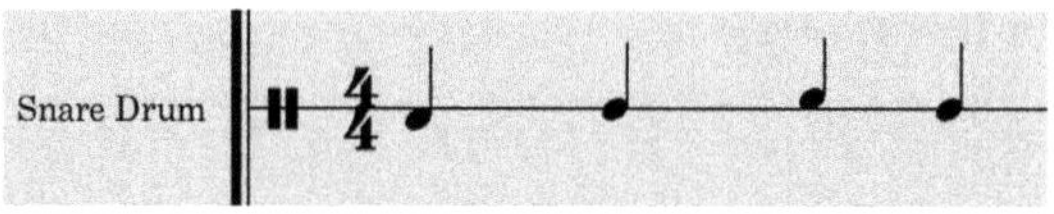

The three locations for note selection will provide slightly different timbres with the instruments. Third party add-on libraries may offer additional notes to give you even more sound alternatives. See ***Appendix A: Add-on Sample Libraries*** for more details as well as ***Writing Tips: #22 – Experiment with Pitches.***

Markup

StaffPad gives you the ability to make annotations on the score with a custom drawing tool called **Markup**. These annotations will be ignored recognized by the notation engine. They will, however, be broadcast over to the individual parts and can be seen by the StaffPad Reader app, with some exceptions.

Tap the Markup button on the Toolbar. The Command Bar will drop down and present you with three different types of pens to draw with.

The three pens are: red pen, blue pen, and a yellow highlighter.

Red pen - this is a **private** pen. Only you can see these annotations. They will not be visible in the StaffPad Reader.

Blue pen - this is the **public** pen and is the default pen. Annotations made with this pen are the only ones that will be visible in the StaffPad Reader.

Yellow highlighter - this is also a **private** pen. Like a real-world highlighter, it is useful for drawing attention to things, not for textual notations.

This annotation is blue (public) and will be seen in the StaffPad Reader:

The upper right side of the Command Bar will now give you some markup options.

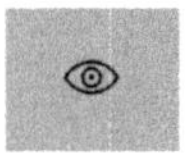

The eyeball icon indicates that markup visibility is on and you will see all annotations.

The eyeball icon with a slash through it indicates that markup visibility is off, and you will not see any annotations.

Erasing Markup

The same technique for erasing notes works with markup. Apply pressure to the pencil to trigger eraser mode. As with erasing notes once you lift the pencil off the screen eraser mode is terminated.

The trash can icon will remove **ALL** markup! Be careful with this action because you will not be given a chance to abort. You can, however, use the **UNDO** button to restore your markup.

Chapter 5
Text

Text is used throughout StaffPad to fill in the areas where drawing with a pencil doesn't succeed or is just plain simpler. This reduces the responsibilities of the notation recognition engine and lets it focus on understanding music notation.

Most text features begin with a long-press on the screen to activate a context menu. Each of these menus only offer options related to where your finger is pressing. This reduces clutter in menus by limiting the scope to what you are doing.

We saw in ***Chapter 4 - Music Input*** that long-pressing on a bar offered options that make sense to a measure of music. The following text options relate to how the musician will interpret the intentions of the composer.

Dynamics

Dynamics can be entered in two different ways: write the dynamic such as ***mf***, or ***ppp*** with the pencil or long-press on the screen directly under the staff where the dynamic will be.

Draw a dynamic marking under the note in the measure where you want it to appear.

Alternatively, long-press in that same location and tap **Insert Text**.

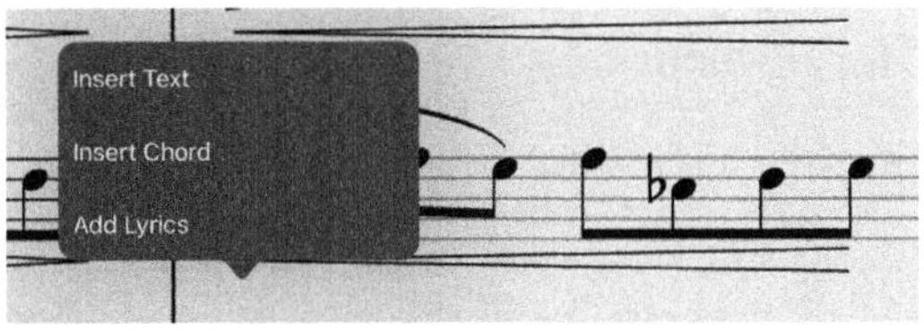

As you type a letter a list of suggestions will display above the keyboard. Tap on any available dynamic.

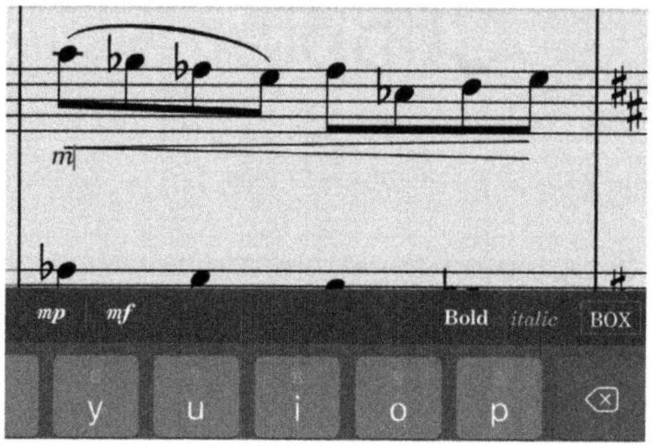

To change the dynamic at any time after it has completed, tap the dynamic. The keyboard will appear, and you may tap the delete (backspace) key on the keyboard to modify the text. If it is a valid dynamic marking it will display properly in the correct font, otherwise it will display as you typed it. The playback engine only understands valid dynamic markings.

Which dynamic markings does StaffPad understand? Here is the official list:

- All terraced dynamics from ***pppp*** to ***ffff***
- Sforzando dynamics such as ***sfz*** and ***sffz***
- Rinforzando dynamics such as ***rf*** and ***rfz***
- Subito dynamics such as ***sp***, ***sf***, ***sfp***, and ***sfpp***

Technique text

Unlike dynamics, technique text sits *above* the staff. Technique text might include articulations such as "arco", "con sord", "pizz" (pizzicato), "stacc" (staccato), "spic" (spiccato), and "marc" (marcato). Many of these apply to woodwinds, brass, and strings, and some, like arco and pizz are only for strings. For additional information, refer to books on orchestration for specifics on any instrument's technique capabilities.

As with dynamics and most text input in StaffPad, long-press on the screen where the text will sit and select **Insert Text**. In the case of technique text, it will be placed above the staff where you wish the technique - or articulation - to begin.

Enter "pizz" for pizzicato and "arco" for bowing.

When the part is performed by a live musician the articulation will be played as you have directed them to. But in the case of StaffPad, it will depend on which sample library you are using and if that articulation is support-ed.

Preset Change

While not exactly a text item, a preset change sits where you would normally find text. Some sample library instruments come with alternate sounds, *presets*, that you can access at a moment's notice. Think of Preset Changes like key switches in your DAW.

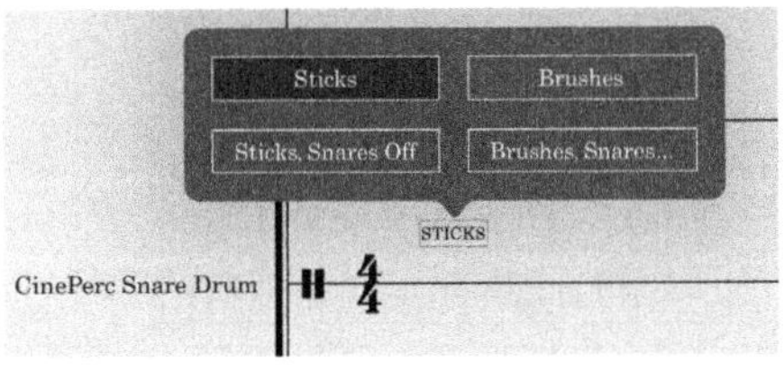

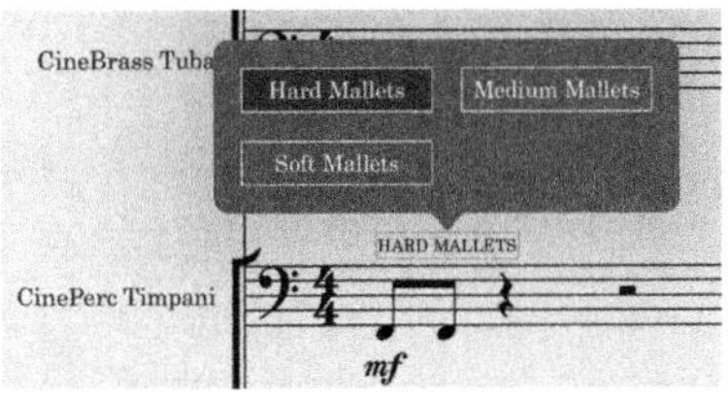

Any instrument that uses presets will display the default preset in the first bar. By tapping on the boxed preset name, you will be given a selection of included presets to choose from.

At any point in the score you can change to a different preset. Long-press on the staff where the preset change will occur, select **Change Preset** from the context menu and you will be given a selection of alternate presets that you can substitute. StaffPad will switch to that sound during playback.

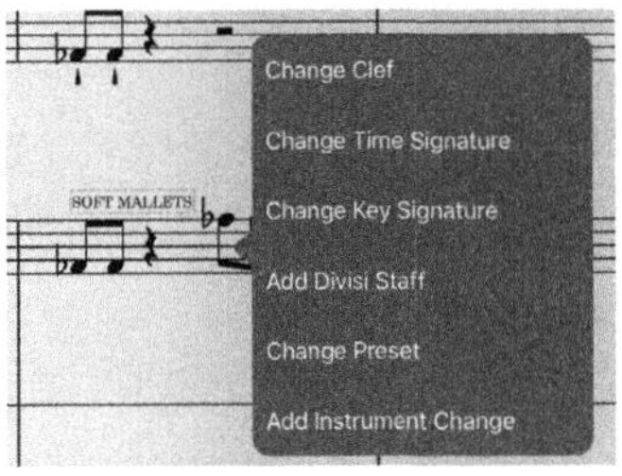

Swing Playback

You can add a "swing" instruction so that notes such as eighth and sixteenth notes will be played as if they were triplets. Long-press above the staff and enter **swing** or **swung**.

It doesn't matter which staff you add this directive, it will always be added to the very top of the score. Every individual instrument will see this on their part. During playback in StaffPad, any instrument playing during a swung section will play in a swing style.

When you wish to end the swing style, insert new text with the directive, "**Straight**".

You cannot direct only some instruments to play swing and others to play straight. This is a limitation in StaffPad.

Tempo

Tempo can be specified anywhere in the score in two ways: as a classical style tempo description or by specifying the exact beats-per-minute.

Long-press above the staff and type in one of many standard tempo descriptions. As you type each letter a list of suggested tempos will be given.

Alternatively, type in a number - by itself - that represents a bpm (beats-per-minute) value. A list of suggestions will be given for that number equaling different note values.

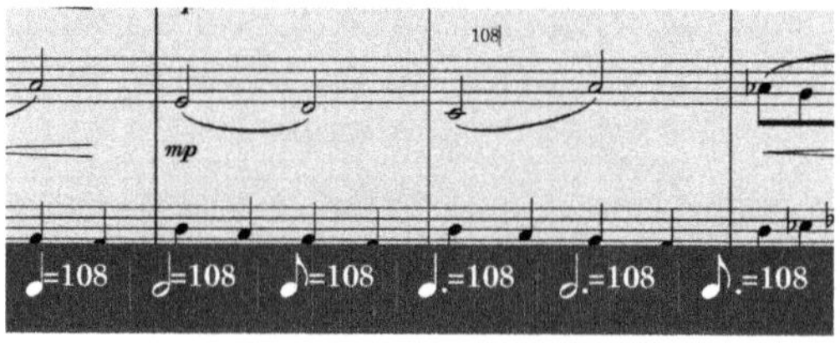

You can even ask Fenby to change the tempo by saying something like, "Tempo is one-oh-eight at bar 20".

Tempo Staff and Importing Tempo Maps

Beside setting the tempo via text you can also create a **Tempo Staff** where you can control tempo at a granular level from within the Automation Layer.

In addition to the Tempo Staff, you can import a tempo map from a MIDI file. See ***Chapter 9 - Playback*** for details.

Expressive text

Expressive text is a descriptive word or phrase intended to invoke an emotion in the music. Words like "espressivo" (abbreviated as *espr*) conjure up images of a Gypsy violinist playing in an overly animated fashion at your table while enjoying a romantic evening with a loved one.

Expressive directions like this won't have any impact on playback from within StaffPad, but it can be an important description for the musician performing the part. Create expressive text by long-pressing under the staff and select **Insert Text**, just as you would when entering dynamics.

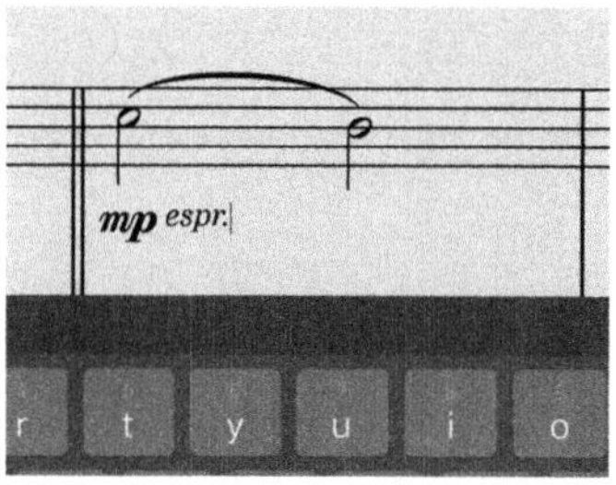

In fact, if you already have a dynamic marking notated, you can append the expressive text right after it and StaffPad will render it accordingly. You can combine both, the dynamic and the expressive text at once by entering "*mp espr.*". Again, StaffPad will know what to do.

Text Options

Here is a complete list of text options (excluding dynamics). As you type a letter of the alphabet the list of options will be refined. Many items reflect tempo. As we saw earlier, rhythmic changes such as *swing* are included. *Rit*, or *Ritando* will create a gradual slowdown in tempo.

💡 You can control the tempo changes of the Ritando using the Tempo Staff. Resume the previous tempo with *A Tempo*.

A Tempo	Lento	Poco stringendo
A tempo	Marcia moderato	Prestissimo
Accel.	Moderato	Presto
Accelerando	Molto accel.	Rall.
Adagietto	Molto accelerando	Rallentando
Adagio	Molto rall.	Rit.
Allegretto	Molto rallentando	Ritardando
Allegrissimo	Molto rit.	Shuffle
Allegro	Molto ritardando	Straight
Andante	Molto stringendo	Stringendo
Andante moderato	Poco accel.	Swing
Andantino	Poco accelerando	Swung
Grave	Poco rall.	Vivace
Larghetto	Poco rallentando	Vivacissimo
Larghissimo	Poco rit.	
Largo	Poco ritardando	

Lyrics

What good would a notation program be if it couldn't handle adding lyrics? StaffPad handles lyrics like a champ! Similar to all other text you've been adding, long-press below the staff, but instead of selecting Insert Text, select **Add Lyrics**.

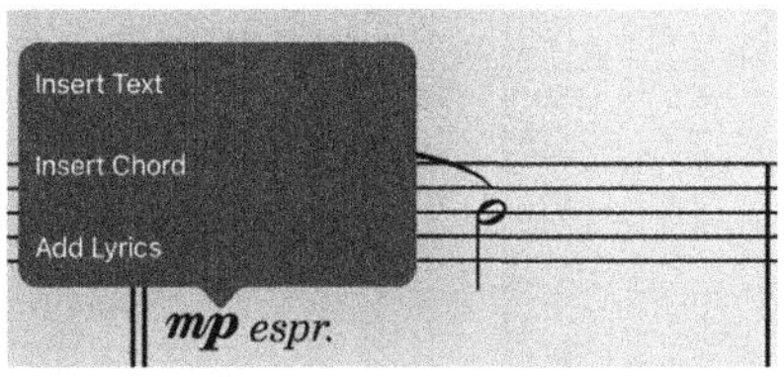

Start typing your lyrics. Separate syllables by typing a hyphen (-) between them. For example, the lyric "StaffPad" is two syllables so you would enter it as "Staff-Pad". No spaces, just the hyphen. StaffPad is smart enough to associate the hyphenated syllables with the musical notes. After typing a word, enter a space character to move on to the next note. If you need to include any punctuation such as a comma or period, enter it following the word, but before typing the space character.

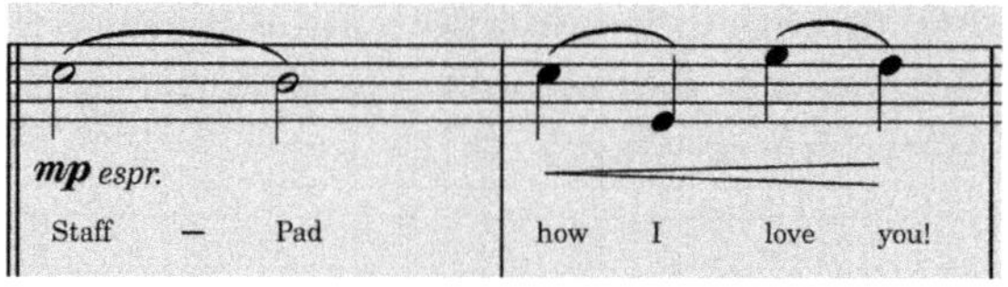

When a word must extend over several musical notes, use an underscore character (_) to represent each note it's matching. Again, just like the hyphen, enter it without any spaces.

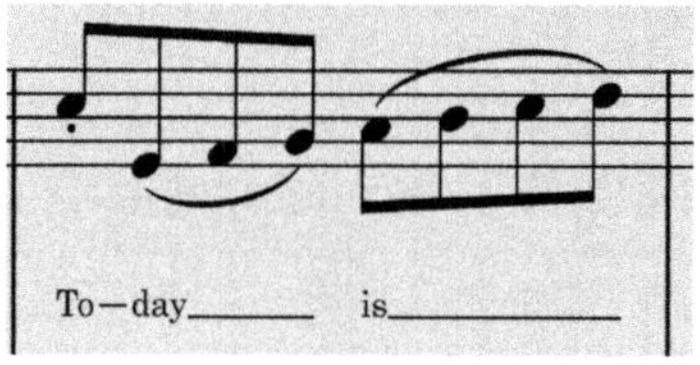

When you are done entering the lyric, tap **Enter** to exit Lyric Mode.

Additional verses can be added before or after a verse that already exists. Long-press an existing lyric at the word where you want the other verse to appear.

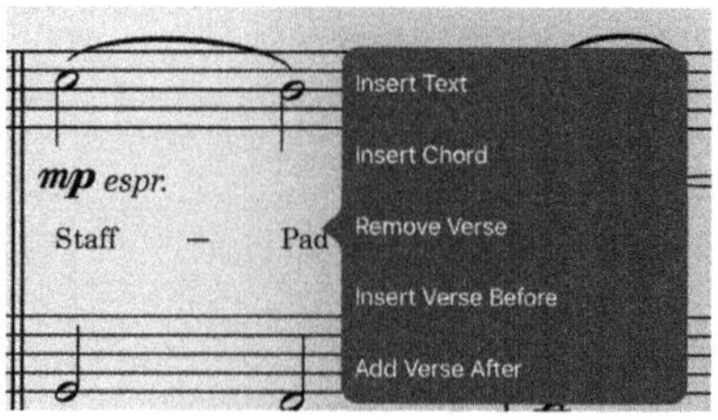

Your options now are **Add Verse After**, **Insert Verse Before**, and **Remove Verse**. Removing a verse will be whichever verse you tap when opening this menu.

Chapter 6
Symbols

About Symbols

The pencil usage in StaffPad was designed to replicate the process of writing music on paper. While much music writing in StaffPad does rely on the pencil for drawing notes, rests, and various accent marks, not every marking will be drawn the “old fashioned” way.

StaffPad provides a palette of common symbols accessible by tapping the Symbols button on the Toolbar. The symbols palette is a scrollable list of actions to be drawn onto your music.

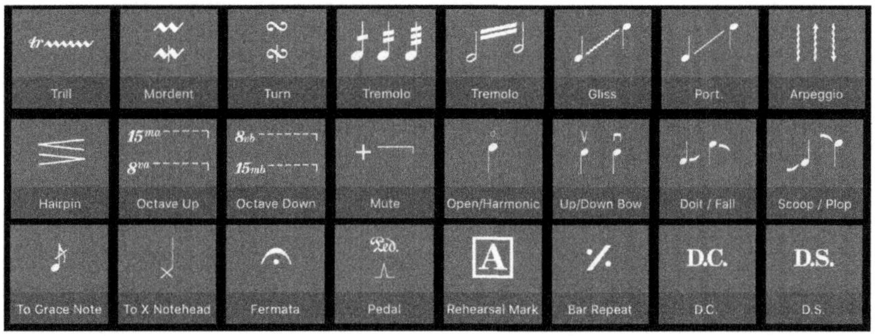

Twenty-four symbol buttons are available initially. As you will see, additional buttons will become visible based on other actions that you take. In all cases with symbols, once you select a symbol you will continue to use your pencil to “draw” the markings onto your score.

Trills

The trill is a technique that goes back to the days of Baroque music. A trill is a rapid movement between the written note and a note above it, usually a half- or whole-step interval. StaffPad supports half and whole step trills. To achieve a trill effect with a wider interval, choose the **Tremolo** (see below).

Select the **Trill** button and touch the pencil anywhere near the note to be trilled. This could be above, below, or anywhere on the note or stem. Initially, the trill will be drawn as a **whole step** interval. A smaller note head in parenthesis will be shown notating the interval to trill to.

While holding down the pencil, drag it up or down to change the interval. Dragging it up will change to a whole step while dragging it down will change to a half step interval.

A squiggly line will be drawn from the ***tr*** abbreviation to the duration of the note. Its length cannot be modified.

If you wish to change the interval, tap and hold the pencil on the small note head in parenthesis and drag it either up or down to change it. Once you release it, the new interval will be shown.

During playback, StaffPad will perform the trill if the sample library being used supports it.

Mordents & Turns

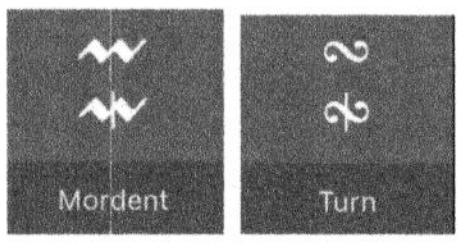

Both mordents and turns are referred to as embellishments, ornaments, and decorations in musical literature, used extensively in the Baroque period. In StaffPad, a note can either have a mordent or a turn, but not both at the same time.

As defined in Wikipedia, "A **mordent** is a rapid alternation between an indicated note, the note above (called the upper mordent, inverted mordent, or pralltriller) or below (called the lower mordent or mordent), and the indicated note again. The upper mordent is indicated by a short thick tilde (which may also indicate a trill); the lower mordent is the same with a short vertical line through it.", and "*A **turn** is a short figure consisting of the note above the one indicated, the note itself, the note below the one indicated, and the note itself again. It is marked by a backwards S-shape lying on its side above the staff. The details of its execution depend partly on the exact placement of the turn mark.*".

Select either the **Mordent** or **Turn** button and draw or tap in the area of the note. Move the pencil up or down in either case to switch the type of the mordent/turn. To modify the direction of the mordent or turn, select the appropriate mordent/turn button again and drag the pencil up or down to change it.

Mordent with up-stroke.

Mordent with down-stroke.

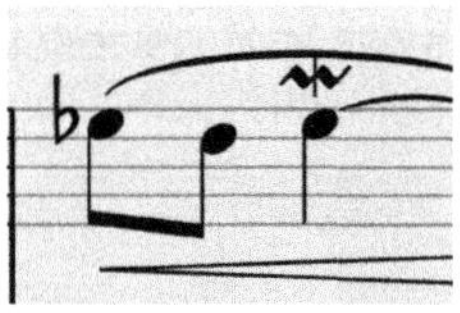

Turn with up-stroke.

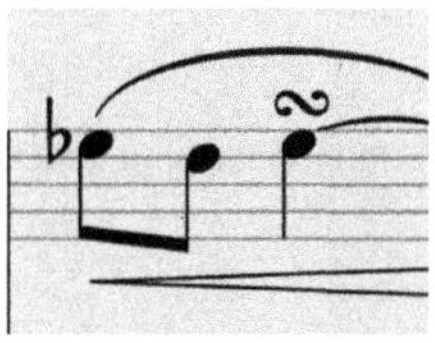

Turn with down-stroke.

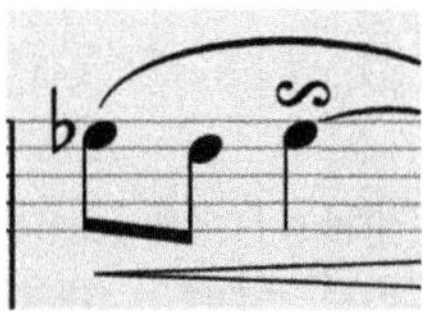

Tremolos

StaffPad offers two types of tremolos: single-note tremolos and two-note tremolos.

Single-Note Tremolo

The single-note tremolo is the rapid repeated playing of a single note. Select the **single-note tremolo** button and draw the pencil over a note. When the tremolo slash symbol appears, drag the pencil up or down to increase or decrease the number of slashes. You can draw from one to three slashes.

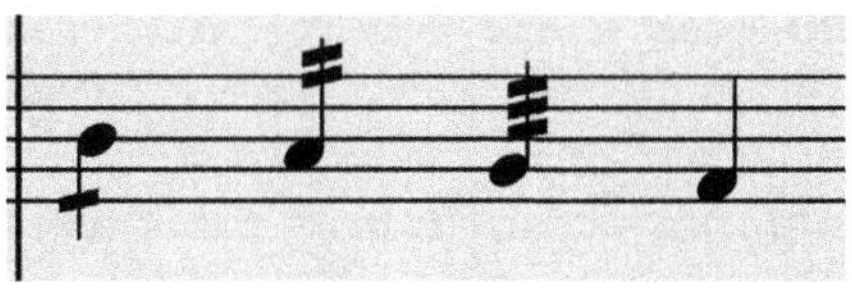

A single slash on a quarter note would be played as if you wrote repeated eighth notes. Think of the single slash as an additional beam between two notes. Adding a single slash to an eighth note would treat it the same as a sixteenth note.

A double slash on a quarter note would be played as if you wrote repeated sixteenth notes. Think of the double slash as adding two beams to the existing note. A quarter would be performed like a sixteenth note, an eighth note would be performed like a thirty-second note.

A triple slash will be played as rapidly as possible - not necessarily the same as treating it as thirty-second notes. This is referred to as an *"unmeasured"* tremolo.

Two-Note Tremolo

The two-note tremolo offers the same abilities as the single-note tremolo with the exception that you can specify intervals larger than a whole step.

Tap the **two-note tremolo** button and draw slashes between two notes of the same value. The example above has a tremolo between the notes D and F, E and A, and F and A. The first and second groups would span the duration of a quarter note each while the third group would span the duration of a half note.

Just as with the single-note tremolo, you can specify from one to three slashes by dragging the pencil up or down. The single slash would perform the tremolo equivalent to that of playing eighth notes; the double slash would perform the tremolo equivalent to that of playing sixteenth notes; and the triple slash would perform the tremolo as fast as possible as an *unmeasured* tremolo.

Glissando & Portamento

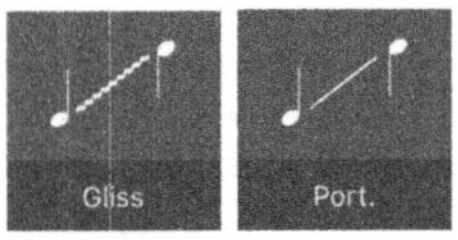

Gliss (glissando) and Port (portamento) are methods of playing from one note to the next in quick succession. Select either symbol and draw from one note to another. You can have either a gliss or portamento between two notes, but not both at the same time.

A glissando will essentially perform a fast moving scale from the lowest note to the highest. It may follow the diatonic scale of the key it is in or add accidentals depending on how many notes it needs to reach the highest note in the amount of time allotted.

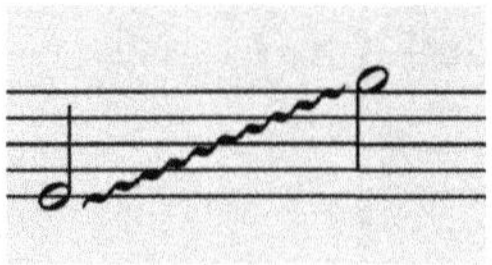

Most any instrument can perform a glissando since it's really just playing a fast scale. A portamento, on the other hand, is a smooth glide from the lowest note to the highest. A portamento is commonly found in string parts. You usually need to consider which string the highest note is on so the player can begin sliding from the lowest note on the same string, uninterrupted.

While it's possible to notate a portamento of a great distance, it could require a string player to cross strings to get from point A to point B. The player would most likely only be able to play the lowest note on the target note's string, giving you an effect similar to what you're requesting.

If you change the pitch of either note the angle of the gliss or portamento will adjust itself so it's still following the direction of the notes.

Arpeggios

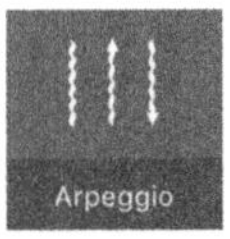

An arpeggio is the playing of a chord (multiple notes) in rapid succession. Even though the chord may be written as if every note is to be played at the same time, an arpeggio will stagger each note. Arpeggios are common in harp playing and are referred to as a "roll".

Arpeggios can be found in keyboard-like instruments where more than one note can be played at the same time: piano, marimba, celesta, etc., even guitar.

Tap the **Arpeggio** button and draw the arpeggio symbol over the notes. Drag the pencil up or down to see one of three types of arpeggios: up, down, neutral.

An up-arrow arpeggio will play the notes from the lowest to the highest. The down-arrow arpeggio will play the notes from the highest to the lowest. The neutral arpeggio (no arrow) will leave the direction at the player's discretion, but for the sake of StaffPad it will be played the same as the up-arrow arpeggio.

Hairpins (Crescendo & Decrescendo)

The hairpin is the symbol for crescendos and decrescendos. A crescendo tells the music to get louder and the decrescendo does the opposite: get quieter.

You can choose to draw the hairpins by hand, but it's more fun to use the hairpin symbol tool.

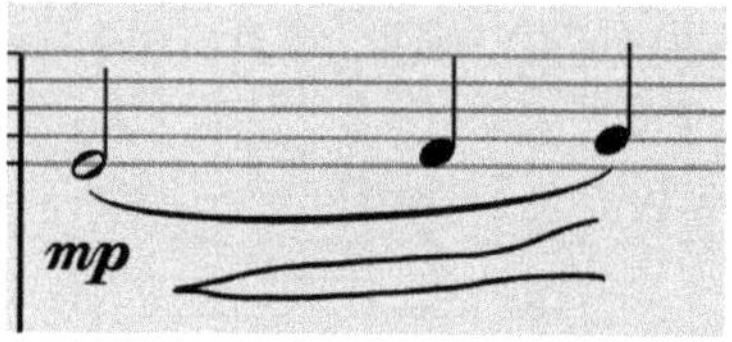

Tap the **Hairpin** symbol button and start drawing from the note where you want the hairpin to begin to where you want the hairpin to end. Here's the fun part: As you are moving the pencil, drag the pencil ***up*** to turn it into a crescendo (<) or drag the pencil ***down*** to turn it into a decrescendo (>).

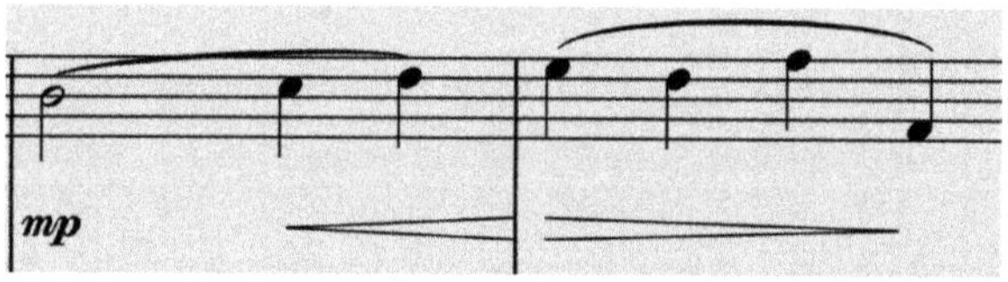

You can shorten or lengthen the hairpin by grabbing either end and moving it left or right. Drawing hairpins in this manner is super fast!

Octave Lines

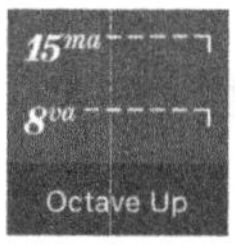

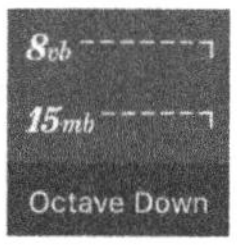

To avoid writing too many ledger lines above or below the staff it is common practice to direct the player to play the notes up or down one (or two) octaves. Most players should be able to work this out without any problems.

StaffPad provides symbols for both **up** and **down** an octave (or two). Select either octave button (Up or Down) and drag the pencil across the range of notes you wish to affect. A series of dashes will encompass the notes affected and will be terminated by a vertical slash.

For **Octave Up**, drag the pencil up to change the octave to 15ma (two octaves) or down for 8va (one octave) above the written pitches. The octave marking will appear above the staff.

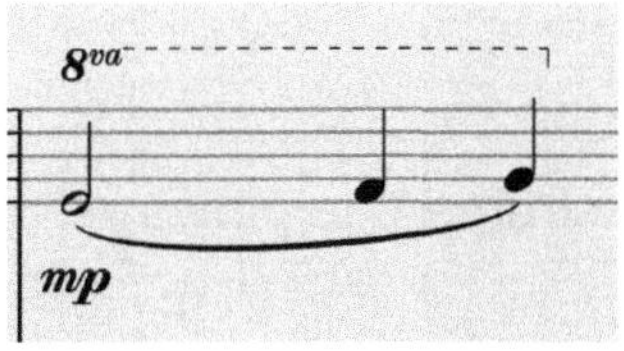

For **Octave Down**, drag the pencil up to change the octave to 8vb (one octave) or down for 15mb (two octaves) below the written pitches. Moving the pencil up or down to change the octave is very intuitive. The octave marking will appear below the staff.

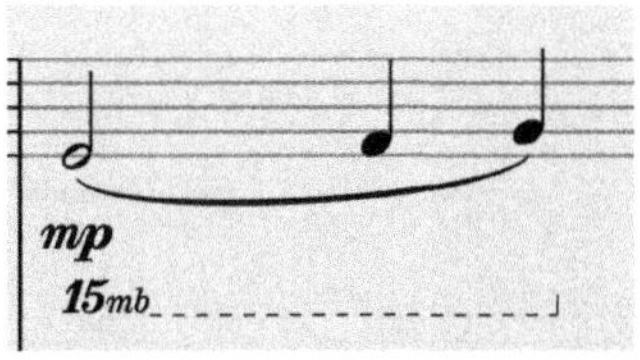

Mute

Muting is handled in different ways by each instrument group. Strings, for example, will attach a device to the bridge of the instrument to reduce the amount of vibration resonating from it. Brass players will stuff a mute into the bell of their instrument to muffle the sound. Brass mutes range from a straight mute, Harmon mute, stuffing a hand into the bell (stopped), or covering it with a plunger.

Tap the **Mute** symbol button and drag the pencil across a range of notes that will be performed in a muted way. Dragging from the left side will change where the mute begins. Dragging from the right side extends or shortens the length of the muted notes.

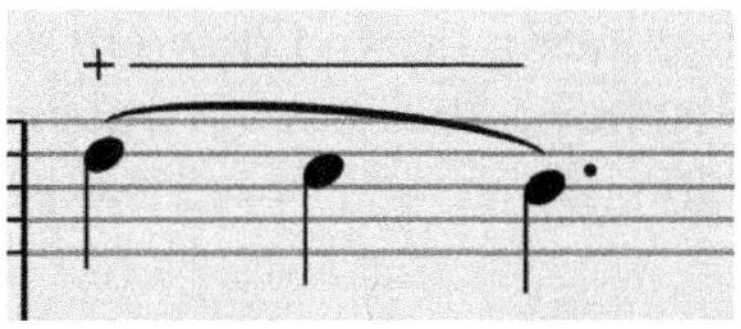

A note about muting in StaffPad. The mute symbol (+) will only apply to brass instruments. To mute strings you will enter *technique text* (see ***Chapter 5 - Text*** for details) “con sord” to indicate to the players to mute their instruments (if the sample library supports this). The plus (+) symbol for strings technically means to pluck the string with their left hand but will have no effect in StaffPad. The same symbol on French Horn means to stop the sound by stuffing the player’s hand into the bell. On instruments like the trumpet, it will depend on the sample library and what muting sounds they provide. Some will default to the straight mute. Others might require a *Preset Change* to trigger the Harmon mute, for example.

Open / Harmonic

The Open/Harmonic symbol instructs the instrument to play the note as a harmonic (strings),

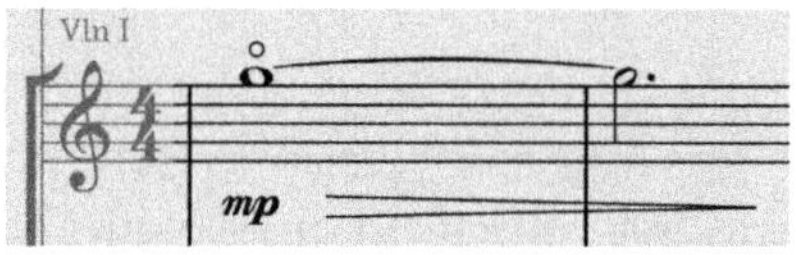

or open, specifically the hi-hat cymbal.

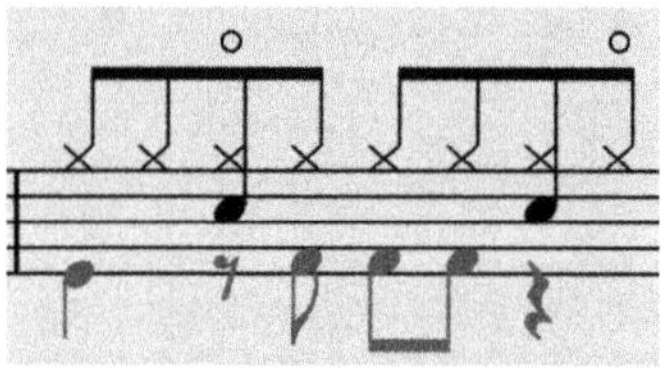

It can also imply an open string, such as on a guitar or string instrument such as the violin or viola, but that would only be a written instruction for a live musician and would have no effect with how StaffPad performs the note.

Up / Down Bow

Up and down bowing is critical in performance by a string instrument (violin, viola, cello, contrabass). When you need the musician to specifically bow one direction or the other, you notate either an up or down bow.

After selecting the **Up/Down Bow** button, drawing up and down bows are as easy as drawing up-strokes for the Up bow and down-strokes for the Down bow. This is a very quick way to notate what is often considered an extremely tedious part of music notation.

The Down bow symbol (⊓) directs the player to draw the bow in a downward motion while the Up bow symbol (V) directs the player to draw the bow in an upward motion.

Doits, Falls, Plops and Scoops

The terms Doit, Fall, Plop, and Scoop are derived from the jazz world. Each of these are performance directives instructing the player to attack the note starting from other pitches, either in an upward or downward trajectory.

With the **Doit/Fall** button, drag the pencil in an upward or downward motion to point the articulation in that direction. Dragging up is a Doit, dragging down is a Fall.

With the **Scoop/Plop** button, drag the pencil in an upward or downward motion to point the articulation in that direction. Dragging up is a Scoop, dragging down is a Plop.

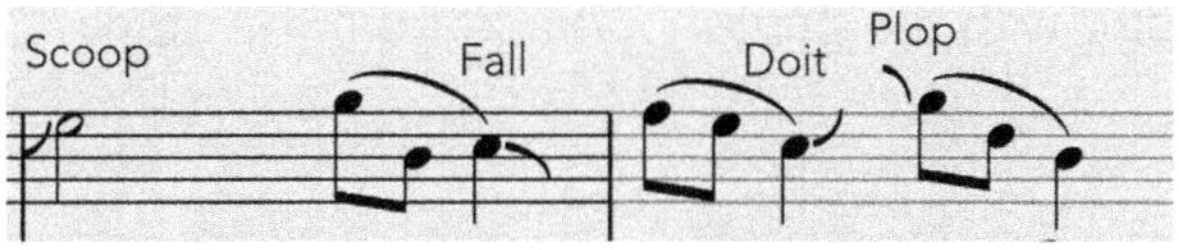

While this musical example is not exactly phrased in a true jazz vein, it illustrates the usage of these jazz articulations.

Scoop - the note is played by sliding up from a note a half step or even a quarter tone below. This is *bending* the note. Can be also used on French Horns to "*rip*" into the note.

Fall - the note falls off with no exact note specified. It is left to the player to interpret how much time and space is available to travel.

Doit - the opposite of the fall. The note falls in an upward direction. It is left to the player to interpret how much time and space is available to travel.

Plop - the opposite of the scoop. The player bends the note from above.

Grace Notes

Grace notes are ornaments added to a phrase that give it an exciting flourish. Grace notes are represented by small note heads. These notes are meant to be played without a strict rhythm, but rather a quick run ending on the target note.

Grace notes can be added to an existing phrase or created with that intention from the start. Here is the example phrase without grace notes.

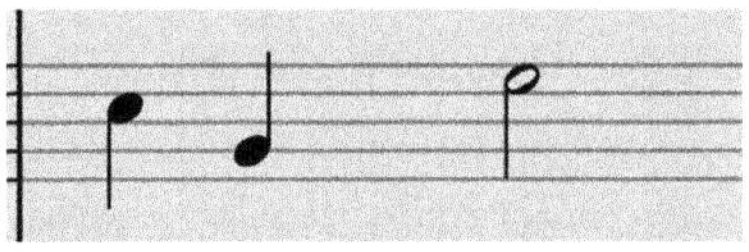

The intended grace notes can be added as an afterthought.

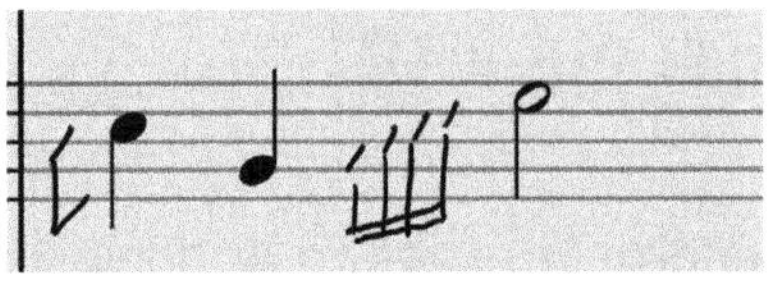

Or grace notes can be drawn along with the primary phrase from the start.

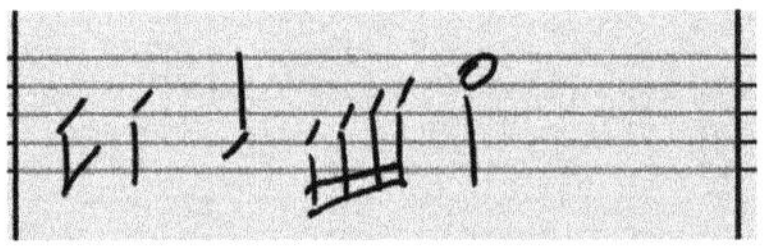

Any notes you add intended to be grace notes may result in an *overfilled* bar.

Select the **Grace Note** button and draw on each note that you want to become grace notes.

Finally, add any slurs or other articulations.

X Noteheads

Non-pitched percussion instruments are often represented by a note head bearing the letter X rather than a black oval sitting on the staff. Instruments such as the snare drum are written on the percussion staff featuring only a single staff line to represent the rhythmic value rather than pitch. In this case, the note heads are often shown as X.

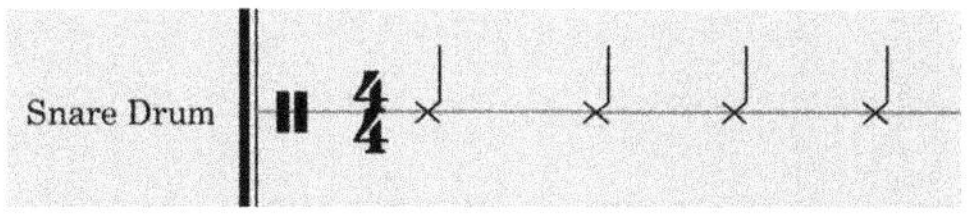

In the case of drum kit notation, you will find a regular 5-line staff with regular note heads representing the kick drum, snare, and tom-toms, but an X note head for the hi-hat and other cymbals.

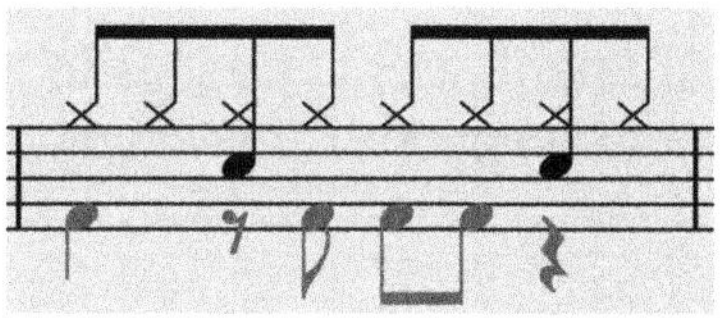

Tap the **To X Notehead** button and draw on any note head. The note head will toggle back and forth from regular note head to the X note head.

Use of the X Notehead on strings will be interpreted by StaffPad to represent the Bartok snap pizz effect (depending on the support of the sample library).

Fermata

A fermata is a “pause” in the music. The duration of this pause is controlled by the conductor, however, in the case of playback in StaffPad, the tempo will be halved for the length of the written note. Tap the **Fermata** button and draw the fermata on a note. It will appear above the note.

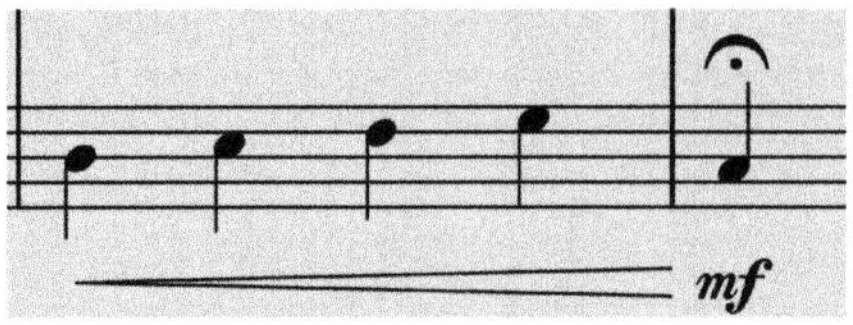

In this example, at a tempo of 90 bpm, the tempo will become 45 bpm for the duration of one quarter note.

The duration of the pause can be customized by adding a Tempo Staff and editing tempo changes.

Pedals and Retakes

Although you can draw Pedals on any instrument, it only applies to keyboard notation such as piano and celesta. Tap the **Pedal** button to draw at note positions. Just tapping a note will insert a Pedal mark with its shortest default duration.

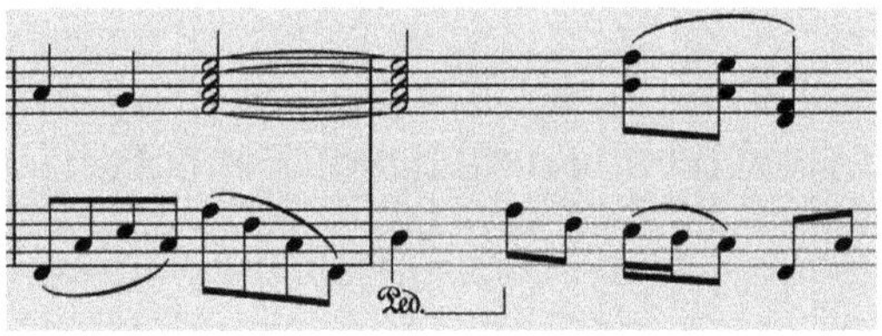

Drag the left end of the Pedal mark to reposition where the pedal begins and drag the right end to extend the pedal's duration.

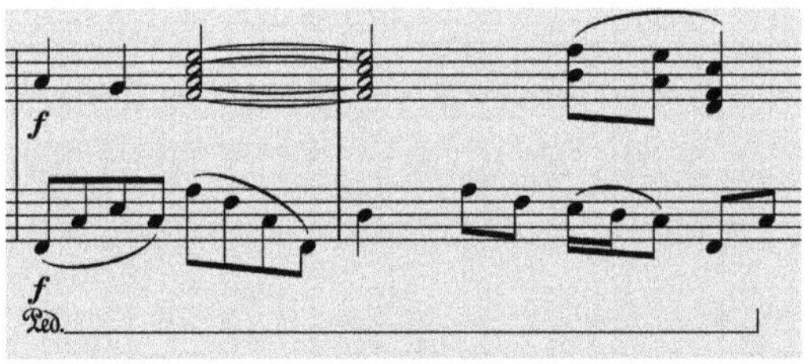

A "retake" is when your foot lifts off the pedal and presses down again. This is notated by drawing upward at any note position.

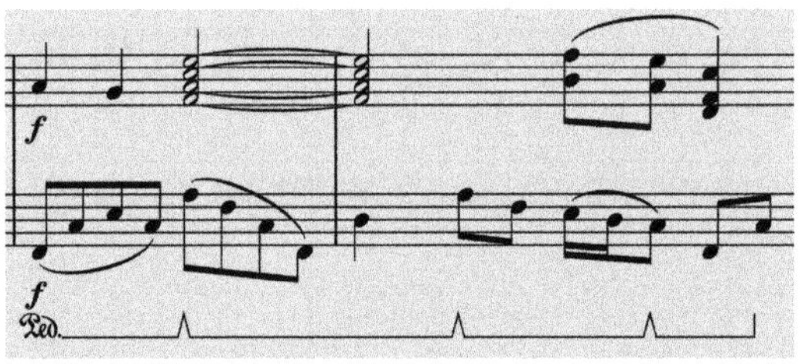

The previous examples are using the modern, default notation style in StaffPad. You can toggle the style to the traditional notation by long-pressing on a pedal mark and selecting **Switch Pedal Style**.

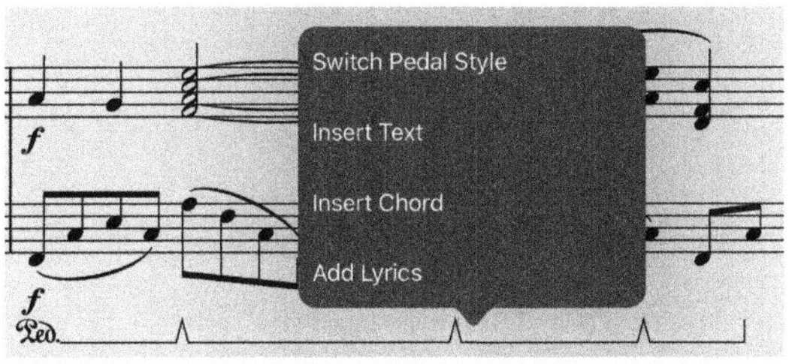

The style switch will affect any pedal marks throughout the entire score.

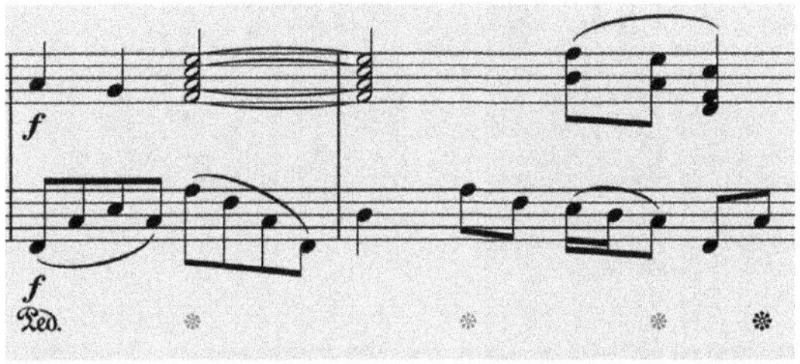

Rehearsal Marks

Rehearsal marks are designed to be used, as the name implies, for rehearsal. A boxed letter or number will appear at the top of the score. The default style is an alphabetic sequence starting with the letter A. Tap the **Rehearsal Mark** button and draw a new rehearsal mark anywhere in a bar to add a new rehearsal mark.

Imagine a dividing line in the middle of the bar. Tapping anywhere in the left half of the bar will place the rehearsal mark at the beginning of that bar. Tapping anywhere in the right half will place the rehearsal mark at the beginning of the *next* bar.

It doesn't matter on which staff (instrument) you add a rehearsal mark, it will be displayed above the topmost staff and also included in the bar numbers at the top.

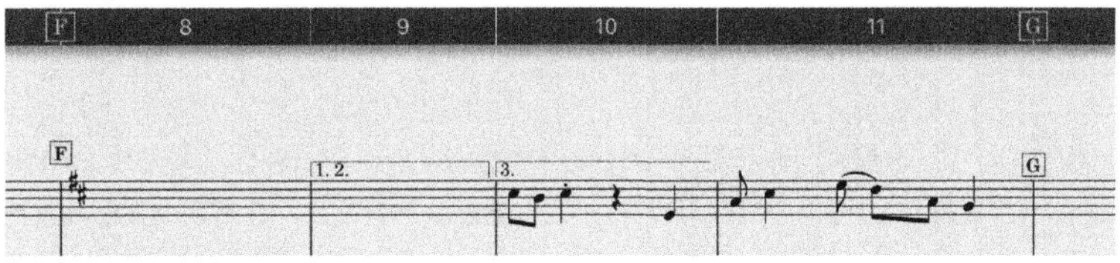

In the above example you see rehearsal marks F and G. Adding a new rehearsal mark anywhere between the two marks will automatically update the sequence. The new mark is now G and the previous G mark becomes H.

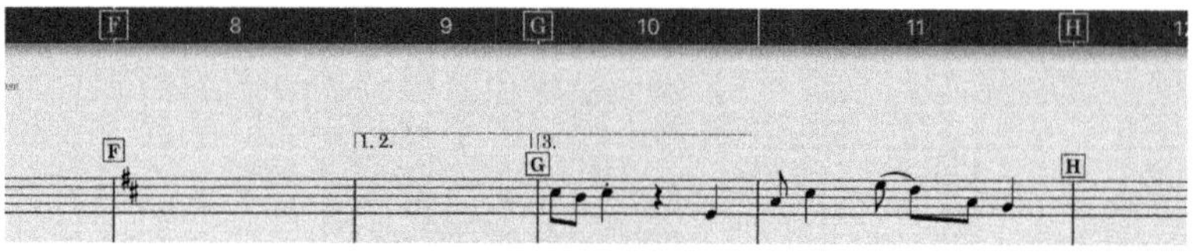

Long-press on a rehearsal mark and select **Switch Rehearsal Mark Style** in the context menu.

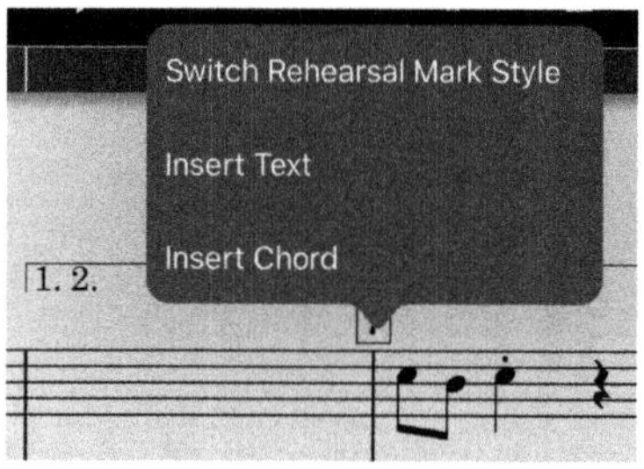

Each time you switch the rehearsal mark style it will cycle between Alphabetic - Numeric - Bar Number. The example below converts alphabetic marks to numeric. There is no relationship to bar numbers.

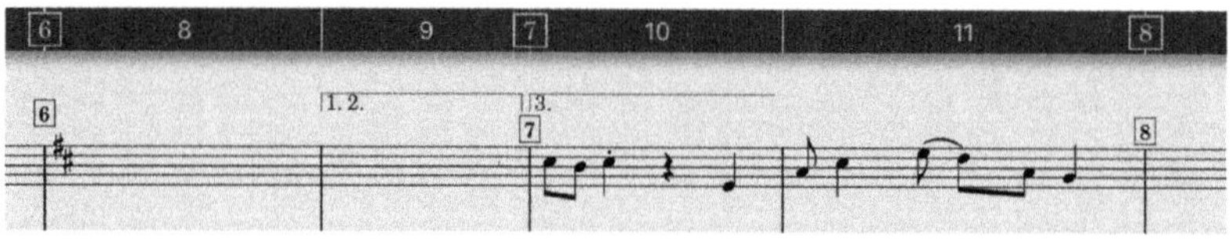

Switch the rehearsal mark type again and the numeric type will become **bar numbers**. Notice the marks match the bar numbers listed in the bar number row at the top.

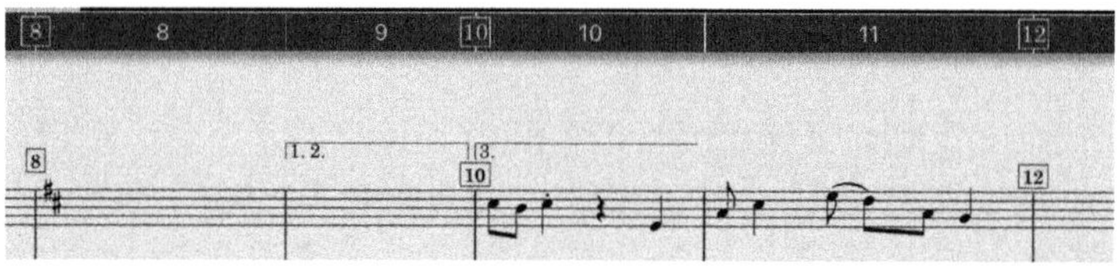

Bar repeats

The bar repeat symbol is commonly used in jazz and commercial music. Used primarily in writing "charts", the repeat symbol tells the player to play the same thing that was written in the previous bar(s).

Tap on the **Bar Repeat** button and draw on any bar. A single bar repeat symbol will appear. If there are any notes in the measure they will be lost and replaced with the repeat mark.

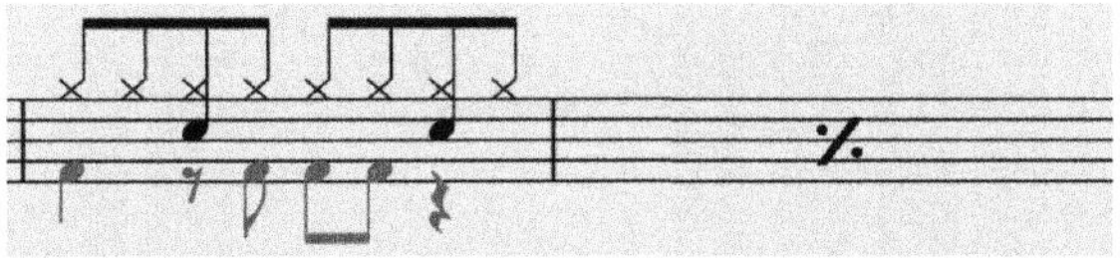

Drag the pencil down to convert the repeat mark to a **two-bar** repeat. The previous two bars of music will be repeated.

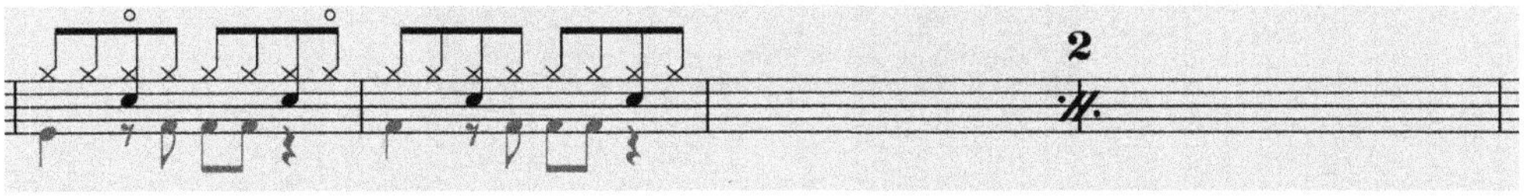

Drag the pencil up to convert it to a **four-bar** repeat. The previous four bars of music will be repeated.

The span of bars covered by the repeat mark is restricted to the repeats. If you draw any notes (or rests) in the repeated bars the repeat mark will be removed and replaced with the notes you've written.

DC, DS, Coda Repeats

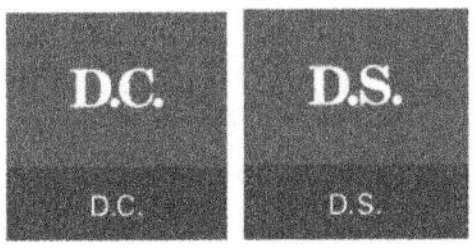

D.C. is the Italian abbreviation for *Da Capo*, meaning, "from the head" (go back to the beginning). D.S. is the abbreviation for *Dal Segno*, meaning "from the sign". Along with repeat bars, first and second endings, D.C. and D.S. define a roadmap on how to navigate the score.

StaffPad offers a very clever and unique method for adding these navigation symbols.

D.C.

Tap the **D.C.** button and draw the D.C. mark on any bar. Press the pencil on a bar where you want the D.C. mark to appear.

DO NOT LIFT THE PENCIL!

By default, you will see a D.C. mark.

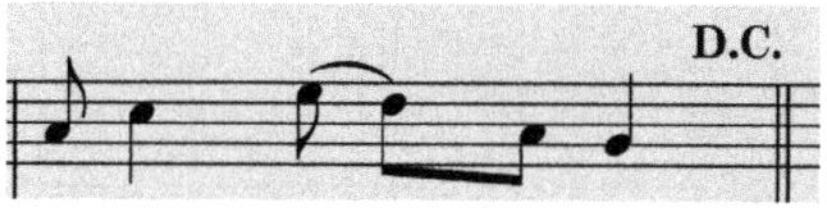

D.C. al Coda

Drag the pencil up and it will change to D.C. al Coda:

The **D.C.** button in the Symbols palette becomes a **to Coda** button. The very next touch of the pencil will place the **to Coda** symbol on that bar:

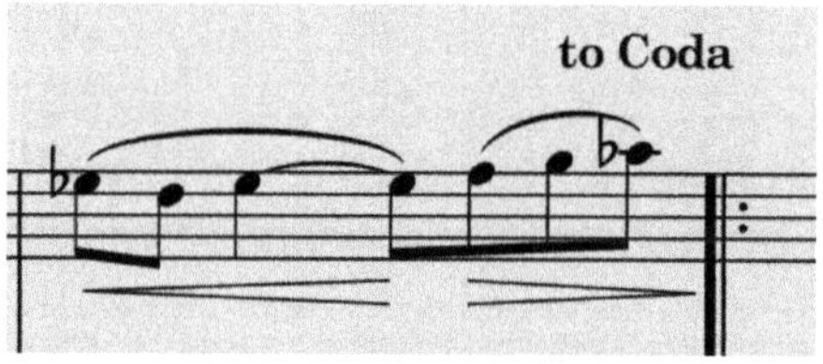

The actual Coda symbol was automatically placed in the bar immediately after the **D.C. al Coda** symbol, defined by a double-barline. This is the bar that the **to Coda** instruction will jump to.

D.C. al Fine

Or...drag the pencil down and it will change to D.C. al Fine:

The **D.C.** button in the Symbols palette becomes a **Fine** button. The very next touch of the pencil will place the Fine symbol on that bar:

NOTE: Any music in bars located *after* where you place **Fine** will be lost.

An **End** barline will be added at that point. You can always drag the **Fine** symbol to a different bar if you tapped the wrong location. The **End** barline will always follow the **Fine** symbol.

D.S.

Tap the **D.S.** button and draw the D.S. mark on any bar. Press the pencil on a bar where you want the D.S. mark to appear.

DO NOT LIFT THE PENCIL!

By default, you will see a D.S. mark.

The **D.S.** button in the Symbols palette becomes a **Segno** button. The very next touch of the pencil will place the 𝄋 symbol on that bar:

D.S. al Coda

Drag the pencil up and it will change to:

The **D.S.** button in the Symbols palette becomes a **Segno** button. The very next touch of the pencil will place the 𝄋 symbol on that bar:

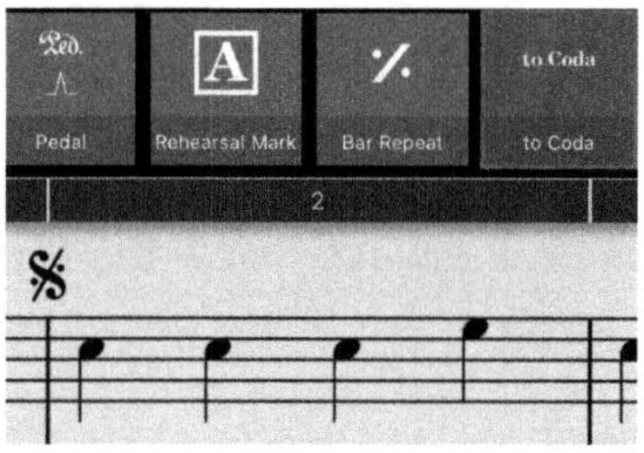

The **Segno** button in the Symbols palette will be changed once again! This time it becomes a **to Coda** button. The very next touch of the pencil will place the **to Coda** mark on that bar:

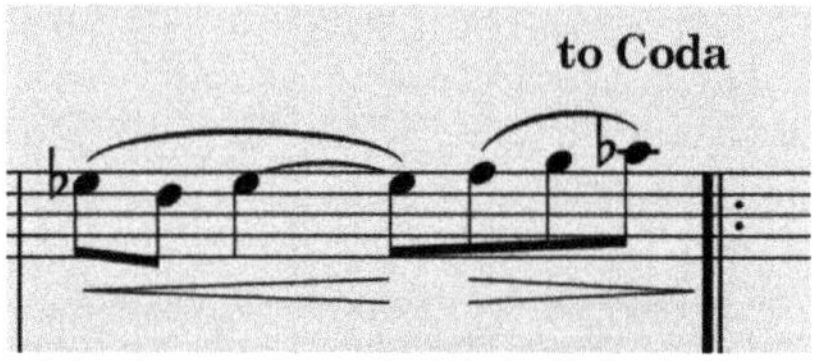

The actual Coda 𝄌 symbol was automatically placed in the bar immediately after the **D.S. al Coda** symbol, defined by a double-barline. This is the bar that the **to Coda** instruction will jump to.

D.S. al Fine

Or...drag the pencil down and it will change to:

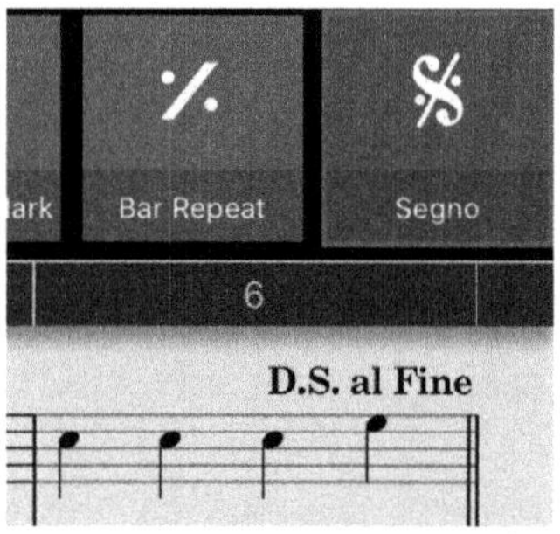

The **D.S.** button in the Symbols palette becomes a **Segno** button. The very next touch of the pencil will place the 𝄋 symbol on that bar:

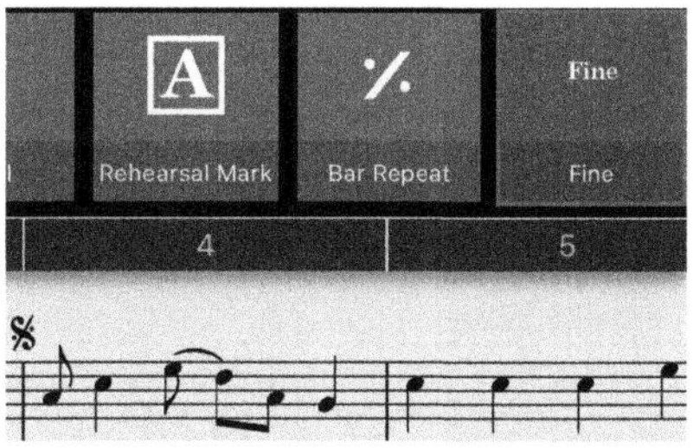

NOTE: Any music in bars located *after* where you place **Fine** will be lost!

The **Segno** button in the Symbols palette becomes a **Fine** button. The very next touch of the pencil will place the **Fine** symbol on that bar:

An **End** barline will be added at that point. You can always drag the **Fine** symbol to a different bar if you tapped the wrong location. The **End** barline will always follow the **Fine** symbol.

Chapter 7
Chords

Chord symbols in StaffPad can be used in a variety of ways. You can type the chords in manually like you would when creating a lead sheet, or you can let StaffPad analyze your music and display the results.

Manual Entry

Chords can be entered manually the same way you would enter lyrics. Long-press below the staff and select **Insert Chord** from the context menu.

Type a chord name. StaffPad understands the common chord naming conventions such as C, C major, Cmaj7, Cmaj7(#11), etc. Each chord you type will be placed above an existing musical note or rest. If the bar is empty the chord symbol will be displayed above the first beat.

Type a space to advance the cursor to the next note or rest. Keep typing a space to skip any notes where a new chord will not be included. If the bar is empty, any additional chord after a space will be replaced over the first beat in that bar.

StaffPad will render chords you enter in modern chord syntax. For example, entering Cmaj7 will convert the chord spelling using the triangle symbol.

Tap on the chord name to edit the chord. The modern syntax will revert to the common spelling for you to modify but will be converted back when completed.

Show Chords

StaffPad will analyze an instrument's part and display a chord symbol above the staff. Even with simple melodies it will make its best guess while displaying a chord.

To turn on this feature, tap the name of the instrument on the left side of the screen. The instrument's details page will appear. Turn on **Show Chords** to make the chord symbols visible. If you don't want these chords to be part of the automatic analysis feature (see below), turn on **Exclude from Chords**.

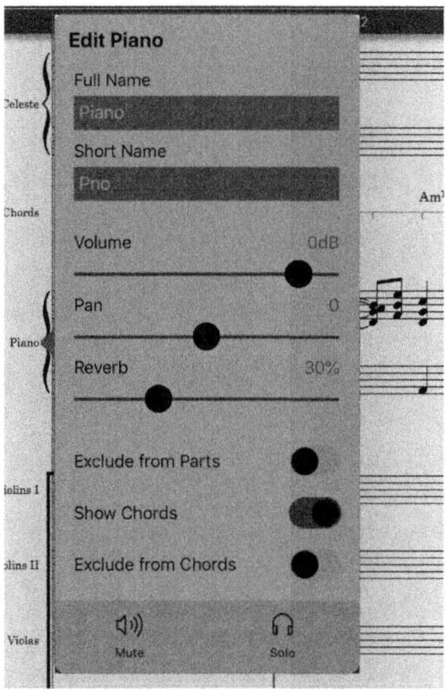

Chords Staff

The Chords staff is an independent music staff that will analyze your entire score and display chord names. It will consider the notes of every instrument in the score unless an instrument has selected **Exclude from Chords** (see above).

Another reason you may wish to exclude an instrument's notes from chord analysis is when a part contains many chromatic notes and would skew the harmonic analysis.

From the **Instruments** page, locate the **Utility** category and select **Chords** from the Staff column. The Chords staff can be placed in any position within the score.

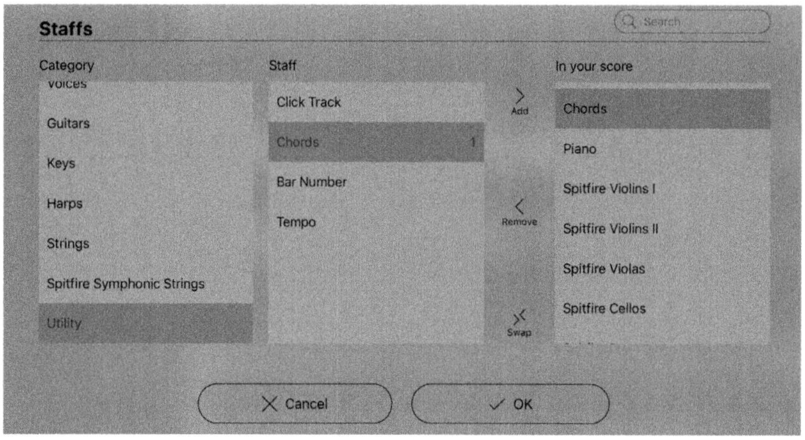

Tap the name of the instrument (Chords) from the left side of the screen to open the details page. Here, you can adjust the complexity of how chords are displayed. They range from Easy Play, Simple, Moderate, and Complex.

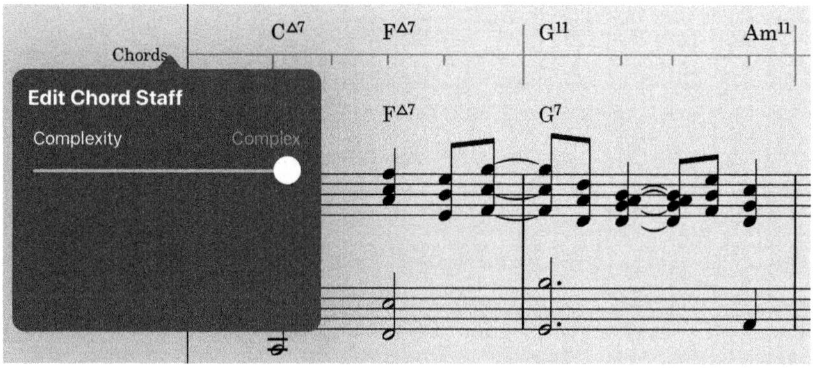

You can customize the Chords staff by adding your own chords by tapping a beat marker and typing in a chord, the same as you would with manual chord entry. The chord name you type in doesn't even have to make sense, but you are given this flexibility.

The chord staff is an extremely useful tool to help you analyze the harmony of your score!

Chapter 8
Selections

Like a word-processor, StaffPad gives you ways to select things - or groups of things - and modify them in many ways: cut, copy, paste. But the editing choices include things like transposing notes, cloning dynamics, and many more tasks specific to music notation.

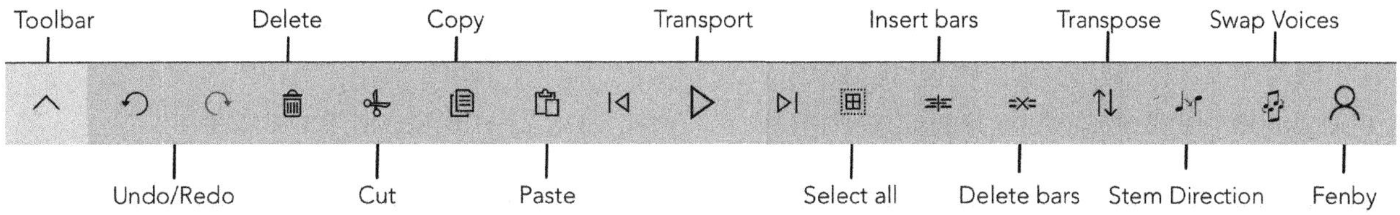

As we saw in ***Chapter 3 - Where to Begin,*** the Selection Bar is where you'll find the Delete, Cut, Copy, and Paste buttons. The Selection Bar (replacing the Command Bar) will only appear when something has been selected.

How to Select

There are two types of selection: **Bar selection** and **Note selection**.

To select an entire bar, double-tap a bar with your finger, not the pencil. To de-select the bar - or a range of bars - double-tap again. It can be the same bar or a different bar.

To extend the range of bars selected, tap on another bar and the selection will be extended.

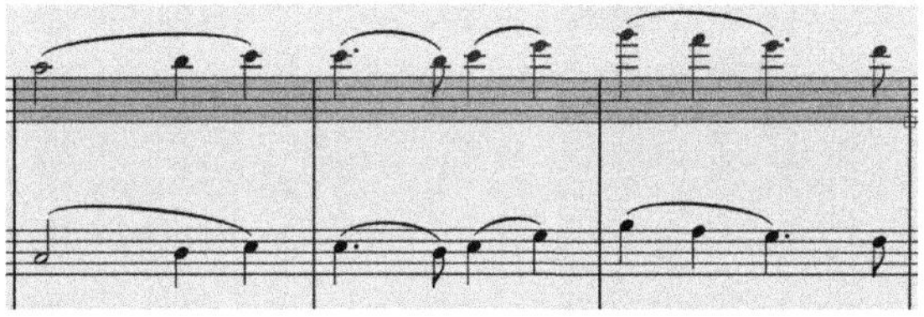

The range can be extended vertically as well.

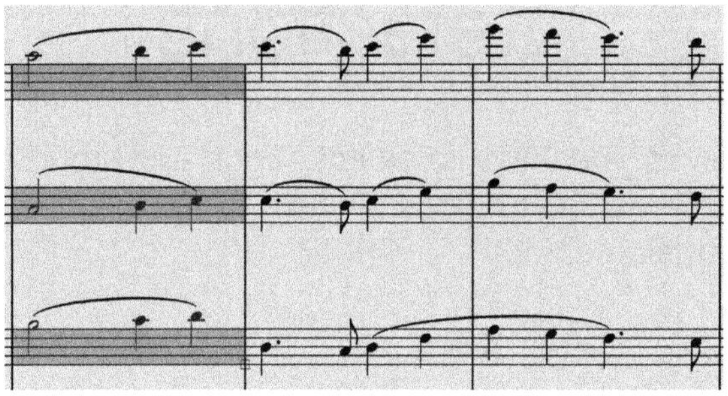

A block of bars can be selected by tapping a bar to the right (or left) and below (or above).

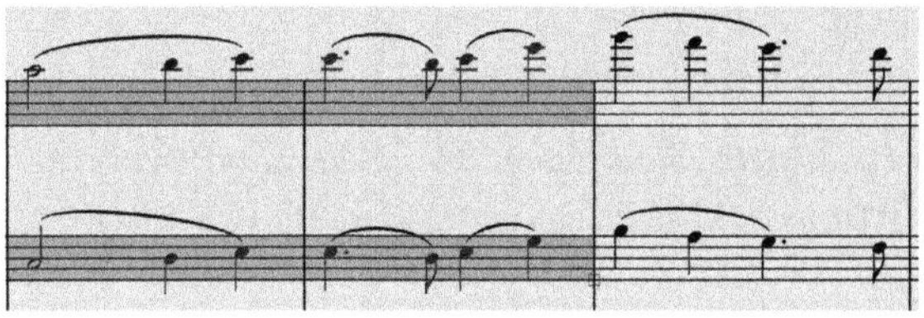

Using the pencil, a selected bar can be dragged and moved to a new location.

Before:

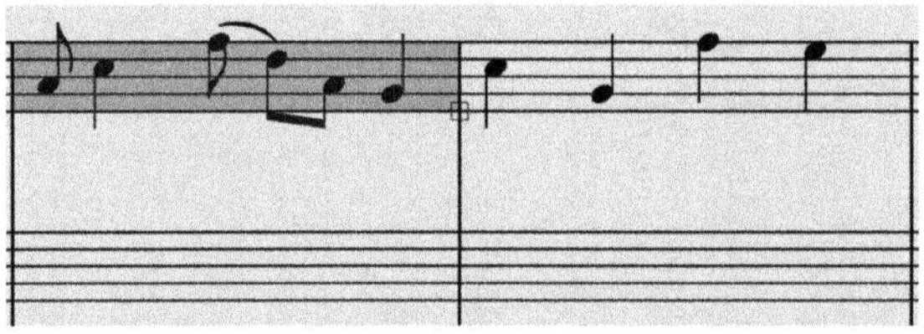

After:

Duplicating a Bar

Once you select a bar, you'll notice a small square handle in the lower right corner.

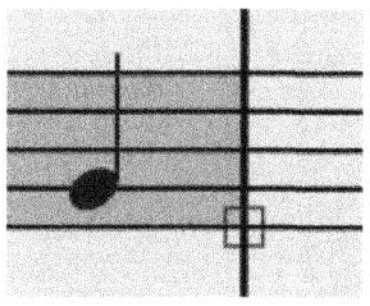

With the pencil, tap the handle and drag it to the right.

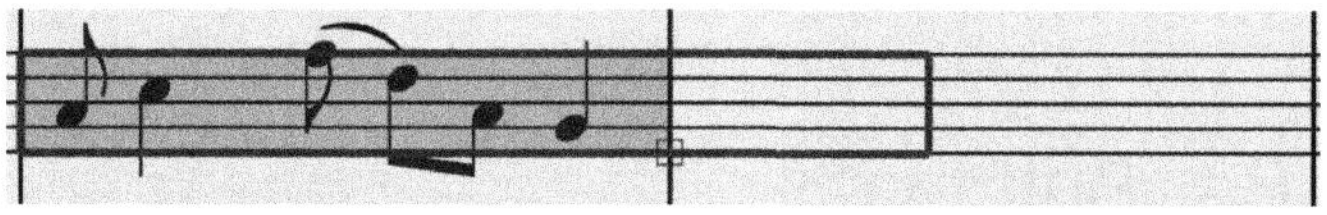

You will see a thick blue border surrounding the bar and will move along with the pencil. Once the pencil reaches past mid-bar and you release the pencil your notes in the selected bar will be duplicated in the next bar.

As long as the pencil remains touching the screen you can extend the duplication of the bar numerous times.

Copy and Share

One very cool feature with selecting bars in StaffPad is that you can copy the selection and paste the music in other applications such as email.

After you've made your selection of bars, tap the Copy  button. The selection will now be in the clip-board and can be pasted into any application that accepts graphic images.

The great thing about this feature is that it will take the selected bars and include the instrument name, clef, and time signature.

Review of Selection Bar Buttons

Although this was stated in ***Chapter 3 - Where to Begin***, let's reiterate what these edit buttons are for.

Delete. Selected items will be deleted and *not* placed on the clipboard.

Cut. Selected items will be deleted (cut) and placed on the clipboard to be pasted elsewhere.

Copy. Selected items will be copied and placed on the clipboard.

Paste. The contents of the clipboard will be pasted into the currently selected measure.

Select All. The entire score will be selected.  In order to use this function, you must first select at least one measure.

Insert Bars. You determine how many bars you will be inserting by selecting *that* number of bars. The existing bars will move to the right by that many measures.

Select how many bars to insert.

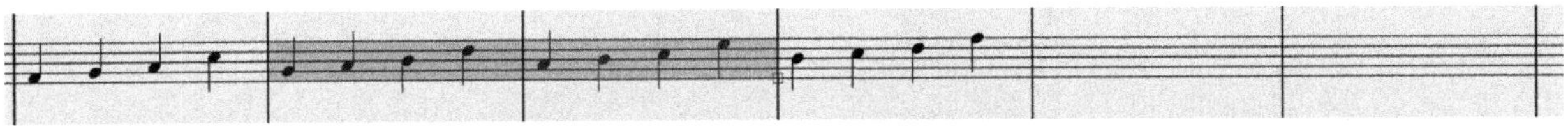

After inserting bars.

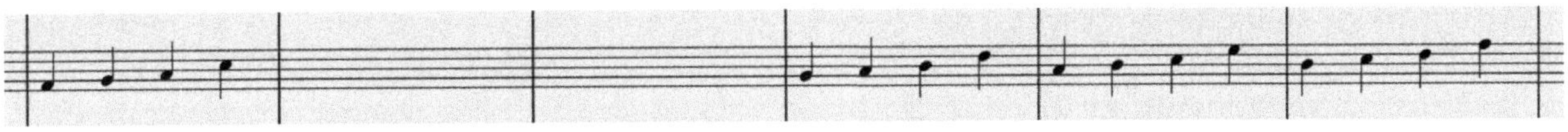

Delete Bars. Similarly, select the number of bars you wish to remove. All measures to the right of the selection will be moved to the left by that number of bars.

Select bars to delete.

After deleting bars.

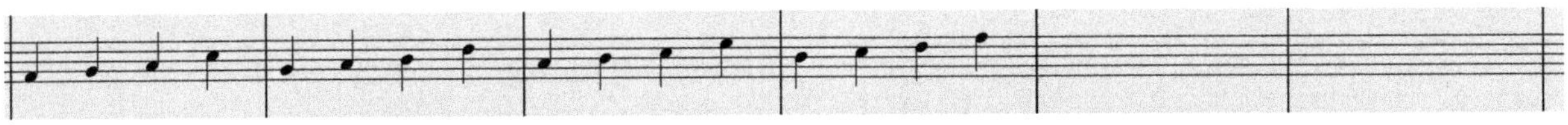

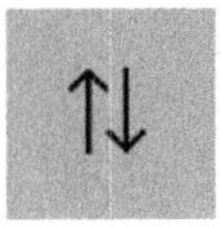

Transpose. Transpose the selected notes up or down from any interval up to a 15th (two octaves). Intervals may be designated as diminished, minor, perfect, major, and augmented. You can also have StaffPad change the key signature. This may make sense to do so depending on the interval selected.

💡 Initially, only the selected measure(s) are transposed. If you don't close the dialog and tap OK again, the *entire staff* will be transposed using the current value selected.

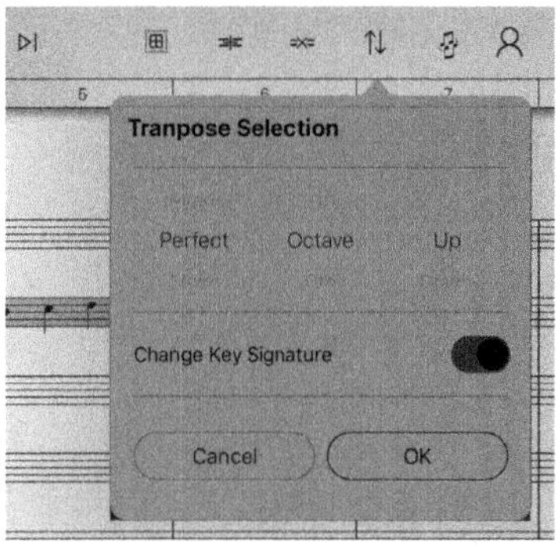

Stem Direction. Reverses the direction of whatever stems are selected. Especially useful when beaming notes that are currently flagged. Use the **lasso** tool to select a single note. See ***Chapter 8 - Selections*** for more info on using the lasso tool and ***Chapter 13 - Writing Tips*** (Tip #3 Beaming Trouble).

Before changing stem direction.

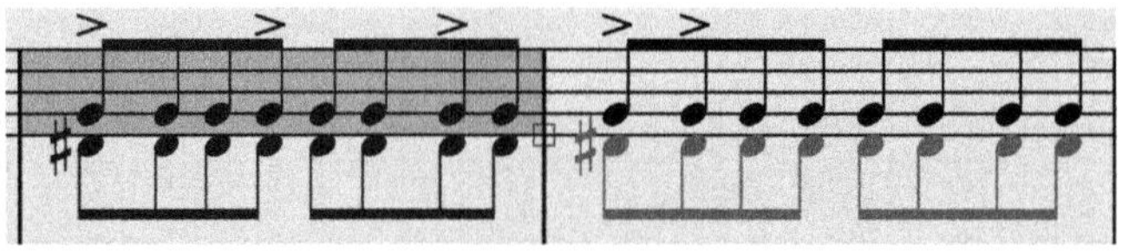

After changing stem direction.

Swap Voices. As the name implies, whatever notes are associated with one voice will be swapped with those of another voice. In the example below, the note G (stems up) are in voice layer one and the note D# (stems down) are in voice layer two. See ***Chapter 4 - Music Input*** for details on using multiple voices.

Before swapping voices.

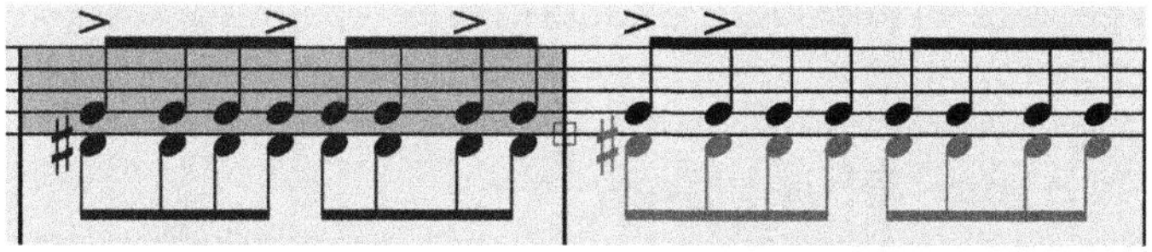

After swapping voices. Voice stem directions remain the same.

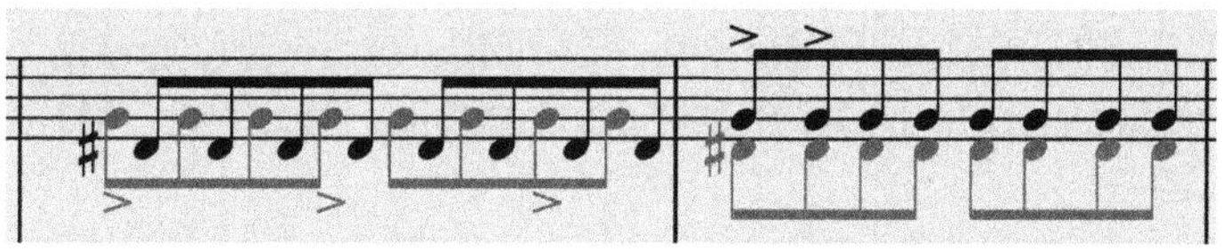

Copy-Paste Tips

StaffPad gives you two ways to copy and store the selection onto the clipboard for later pasting. Once a selection has been made, tap the **Copy** button on the Selection Bar.

A second method - and a lot more fun - is to use the 3-finger *pinch* maneuver (this is only for **iPad** users).

Using your thumb and two other fingers, touch the screen and slide your fingers together, as if you are grabbing those notes in your hand! Your data will now be on the clipboard.

To paste you can either tap the **Paste** button on the Selection Bar or...

Use the 3-finger *reverse pinch* maneuver. This is the exact opposite of grabbing the data. First, select a bar where you will be pasting data (double-tap a bar with your finger), touch the screen with three fingers again and *flick* your fingers apart as if you are tossing the data back onto the page. Very intuitive!

Copy Between Projects

Copying data (notes, dynamics, text, etc.) between projects is as easy as selecting a range of bars and placing it onto the clipboard using one of the methods described above. You can then open a different project, select a destination bar, and paste it into the new project by tapping the Paste button on the Selection Bar.

Use the 3-finger pinch gesture, or type Cmd-V (if you have a Bluetooth keyboard attached).

Use Ctrl-V (if you have a Bluetooth keyboard attached).

Selecting Individual Notes: The Lasso

The lasso is a freeform selection tool for grabbing individual notes rather than entire bars at a time.

Tap the **Lasso** button on the Toolbar. Simply draw the pencil around any group of notes you wish to modify. Notes can even extend into nearby bars. Draw a complete circle. The two ends of the lasso must meet in order to complete your selection.

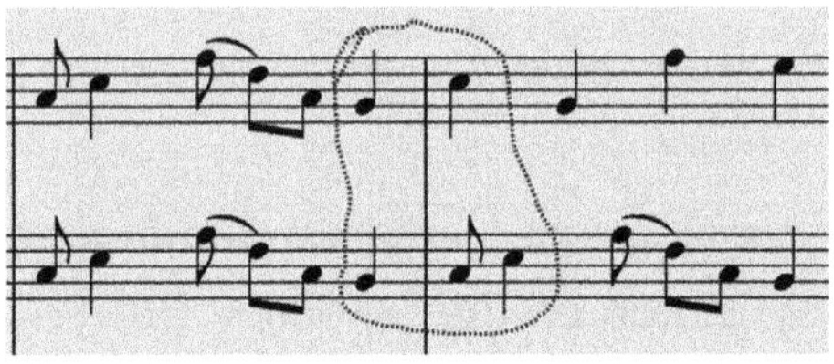

Lift the pencil when your selection is complete. The notes you selected will now turn **blue**.

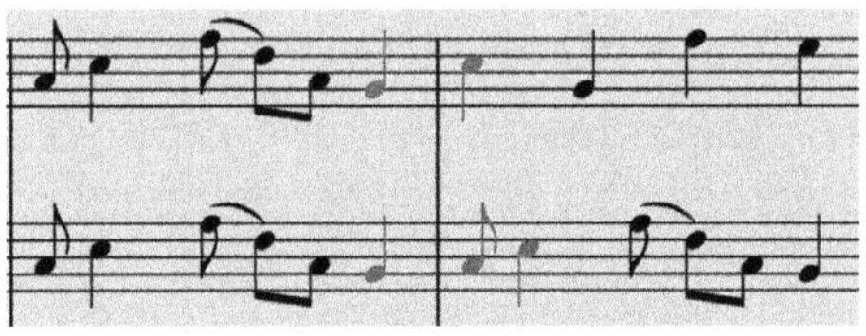

The **Selection Bar** will now show buttons related to lassoed items.

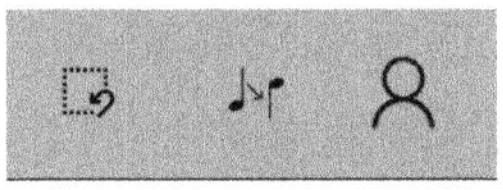

Tap the **Deselection** button to deselect your lassoed notes.

Tap the **Stem Direction** button to reverse the direction of stems.

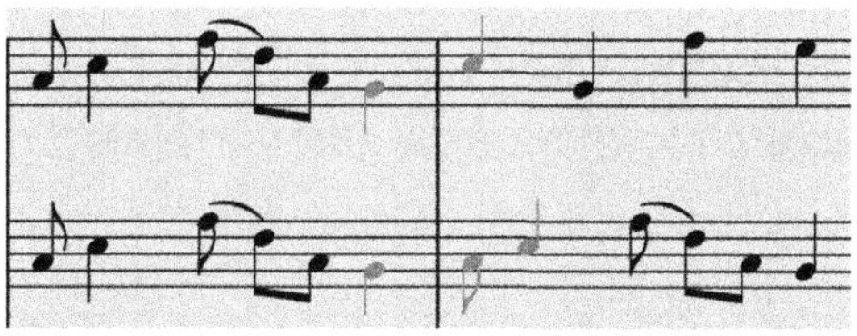

Automatic Copy

Once notes are lassoed, they are automatically copied onto the clipboard. Now you can paste the copied notes over and over by tapping the pencil in their new location(s).

In the following example, the first three notes of the phrase have been lassoed and copied to the clipboard. The notes will appear **blue**.

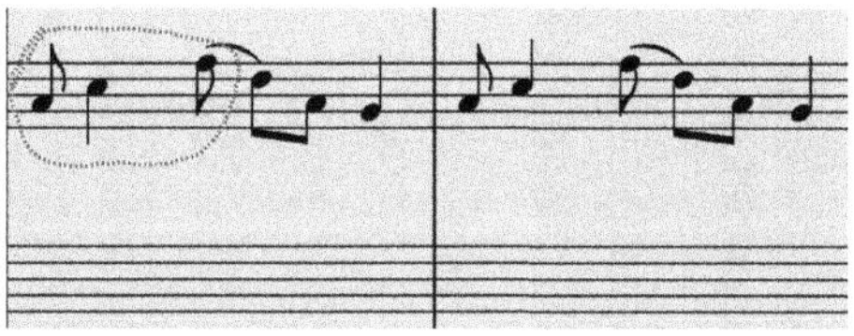

The phrase is now being pasted in the bar below. Each time the pencil taps the screen it will be pasted.

 Lasso pasting is also **Voice** sensitive. Select a different voice from the Toolbar and paste. Notice the original Voice 1 notes (selected blue) with upward pointing stems and the newly pasted Voice 2 notes (green) with stems down.

Dynamics

Draw a lasso around a dynamic marking and the dynamic will also be automatically copied to the clipboard.

Now you can simply draw the selected dynamic into new locations, and it will be pasted into place. This is a very quick and useful feature for duplicating dynamics among related groups of instruments, e.g., strings.

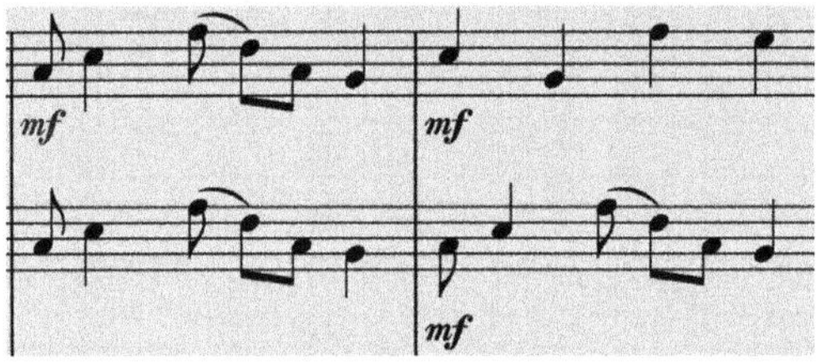

Exit Lasso Mode

Once you complete editing in lasso mode, double tap on any measure or tap the **Deselect All** button on the Selection Bar to exist lasso mode.

Selecting Items

Individual notes can be moved up and down to change pitch. Tap the note with the pencil and drag it up or down. If two notes are tied together, both notes will move together.

Two notes tied together.

Moving one tied note up moves it's tied companion. The note D moved up to a G.

Both notes and rests can be moved horizontally in order to make room for adding additional notes or rests.

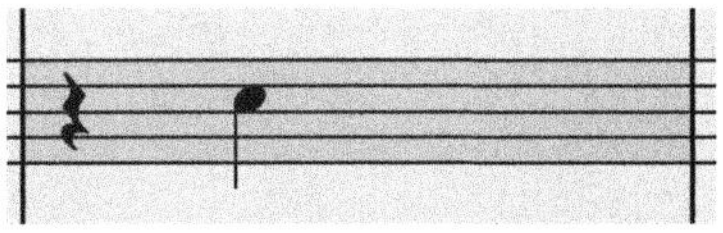

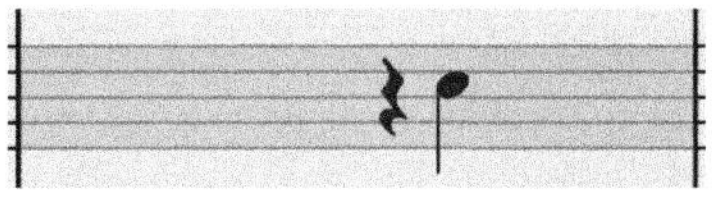

Selecting Other Items

Pretty much anything on the score can be selected and moved by tapping the item with the pencil and dragging it to a new location. Here is a complete list of items that can be addressed.

The following items can be moved left or right:

- Text
- Rehearsal Marks
- D.C.
- D.C. al Coda
- D.C. al Fine
- D.S.
- D.S. al Coda
- D.S. al Fine
- Fine mark
- Segno mark
- The Coda symbol cannot be moved on its own. It will always be placed in the bar after a D.C. al Coda or D.S. al Coda

The following items can be extended or contracted by moving their endpoints left or right:

- Trills
- Glissandos
- Portamentos
- Hairpins
- Octave Lines
- Pedal & Retake Lines

The following items can be moved from one note to a different note:

- Mordent
- Turn
- Fermata

The following items can change their state by dragging up and down:

- Arpeggio
- Octave line
- Up/Down bow
- Doits
- Falls
- Scoops
- Plops
- Bar repeats

The **trill-to** note (D*b* in this example) can be changed from a half-note interval to a whole-step interval by selecting the note and dragging up or down.

Dragging a barline to the right will expand its size to allow additional notes, rests, or accidentals to be added. There is no limit to how wide the bar can be expanded to.

Dragging a barline to the left will contract its size, but StaffPad will limit its width based on how many notes are in the bar to maintain readability.

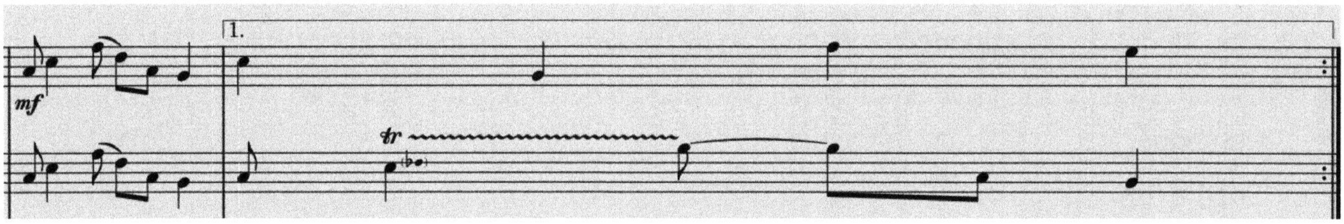

Chapter 9
Playback

Playing Back Your Score

Playback in StaffPad is your reward for all your hard work entering music notation. Playback can be accessed at any time during your score writing: audition each bar of music as you complete them or after every single note you write! You have immediate feedback on what you're composing and orchestrating.

Playback transport controls are always visible at the top of the screen.

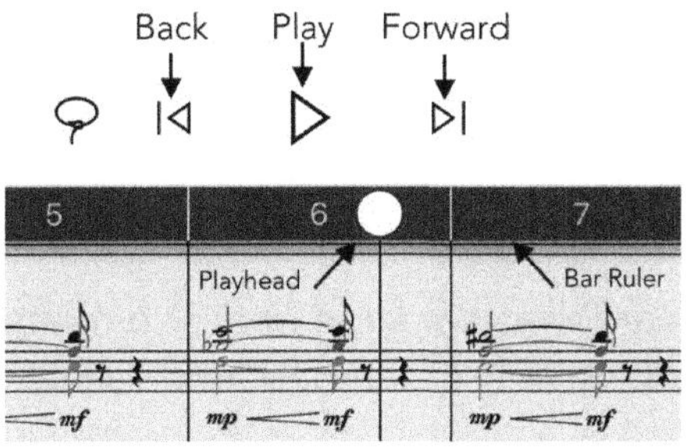

In the center of the transport is the Play button. Tap once to begin playing music.

While music is playing the button will become a Pause button. Tap once to pause (stop) playback.

To the left of the Play button is the Back button. Tapping once will move the playhead back one bar. Double-tap will send the playback head to the first bar.

To the right of the Play button is the Forward button. Tapping once will move the playhead forward one bar. Double-tap will send the playback head to the last bar.

Moving the Playhead

Drag the playhead left or right to set the current play position. Tapping anywhere on the Bar Ruler will move the playhead to that spot. Double-tapping the bar ruler will move the playhead to that spot and begin play!

Soloing a Part

Occasionally you will have a need to solo a certain part to hear details of what you've written. You can, of course, select any combination of Solo and Mute from the Details panel of multiple instruments, but a quick method is to select any number of bars.

When you hit play you will now only hear those selected bars. No matter where the playhead is, it will jump to the beginning of the selected bars and play only those bars and will stop when the selected bars end.

This works not only on a single instrument but across multiple instruments. This is a very convenient way to hear, for example, the entire string section for a specific passage.

Automation Layer

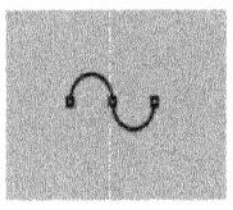

Tap the Automation Layer button to engage the automation layer. The automation layer is a graphic representation of three types of automation in StaffPad: expression, volume, and pan. If you've ever worked with a DAW before, this type editing should not be new to you.

Expression (blue) - Controls the loudness, but not the same as volume. In MIDI terms, this is CC 11. How expression affects an instrument's sound varies greatly and depends on how many dynamic layers are provided by the instrument's maker.

Volume (green) - The overall volume. In MIDI terms, this is CC 7. If you modify any data here it will disable the Volume setting in the staff's **Edit Staff** control.

Pan (orange) - The panning position. In MIDI terms, this is CC 10. If you modify any data here it will disable the Pan setting in the staff's **Edit Staff** control.

Tempo - tempo automation is technically part of the automation layer, but it is not part of the automation cycle: expression, volume, and pan. Tempo automation is viewed independently on the **Tempo Staff** (see below for details). The staff is always visible as long as you have included a Tempo Staff in your score, but the automation data will only be visible - like all other automation - when engaging the Automation Layer.

While the automation layer is active, you cannot edit notes and rests. You must disengage the automation layer to go back to regular editing. You can, however, add text, lyrics, and chords.

When you first engage the automation layer you will be viewing Expression data. It will be represented by a light purple color (let's not argue whether it's really violet, magenta, or otherwise! StaffPad insists it's blue, but I'm not so sure...).

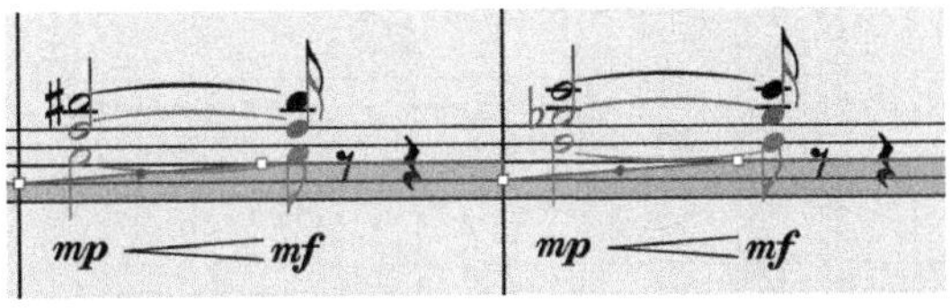

All dynamics will be converted into expression data. In the example above, the notes begin at ***mp*** followed by a crescendo into ***mf***. The expression data rises, and each dynamic has a small data handle - a small square box - at the point where the expression value changes. There is also a small blue dot that sits between two data handles. This controls where changes to the next data handle begins. More on this in a moment.

Using the pencil, you can make changes to the data by:

- Grabbing a data handle and moving it up, down, left, or right. Once you do this you are overriding the written dynamics. You will know this has happened because the dynamics and hairpins will change color from black to orange.
- Drawing new data from anywhere to anywhere

By moving the data handle, you are changing the data value. In the example below, the dynamic marking indicated a crescendo to ***mf***, but now the expression value will really be more like ***f***, or possibly even ***fff***. The dynamic marking and the hairpin have changed color from black to orange to indicate you've overridden those values. The orange dynamics color will only appear this way while the automation layer is active.

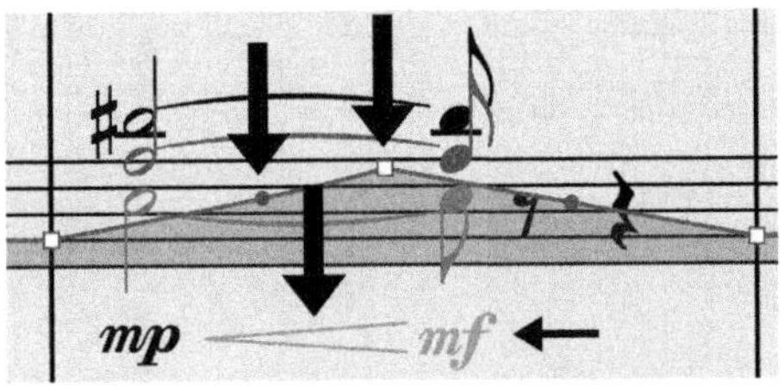

If you change just the blue dot you are only affecting the crescendo so only the hairpin changes color from black to orange. This means you are telling the playback engine to start the crescendo a few milliseconds later (or earlier). The blue dot defines the shape of the curve and influences when the automation begins to change from one data point to the next.

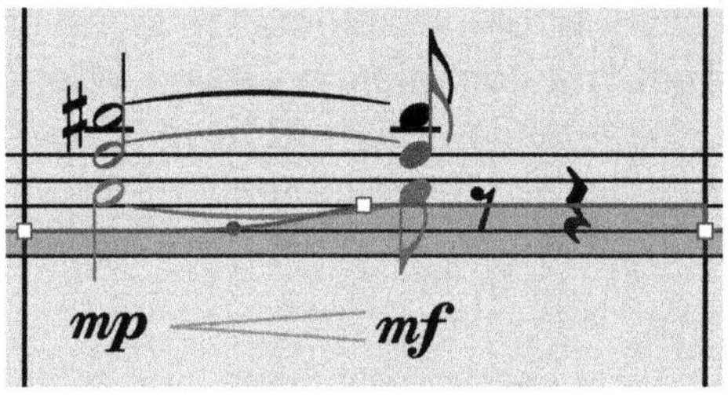

You can draw in a freeform fashion with the pencil for custom changes. If you don't see a blue dot it means the change in data from one point (handle) to another moves in a linear fashion.

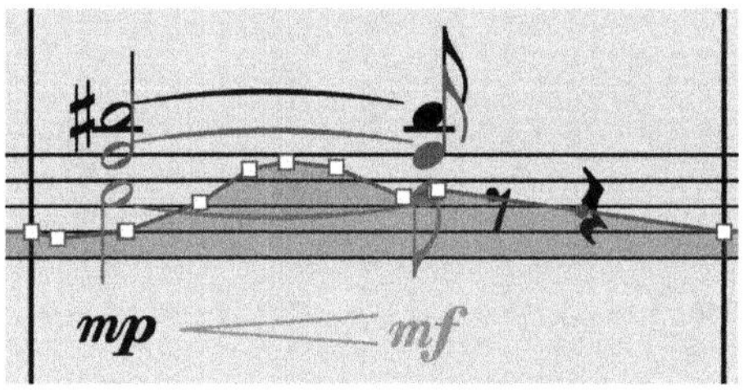

Volume (green) automation data will also display dB values at each data point.

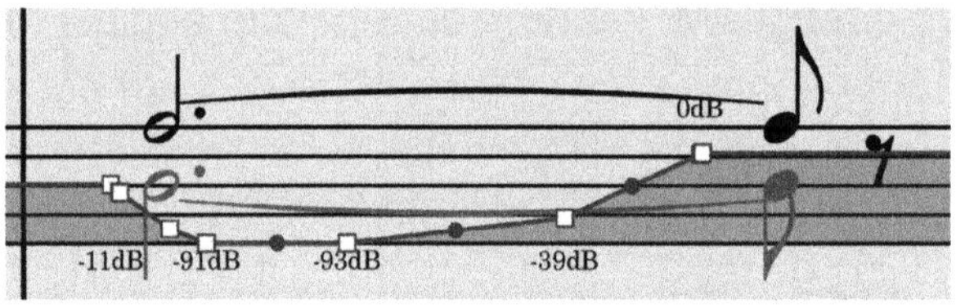

Erasing Automation

Data points (handles) can be deleted by using the **eraser** tool. This works the same as deleting notes and rests. Once you delete a data handle a blue dot will appear in its place so you can adjust where the change - ramping up or down - begins.

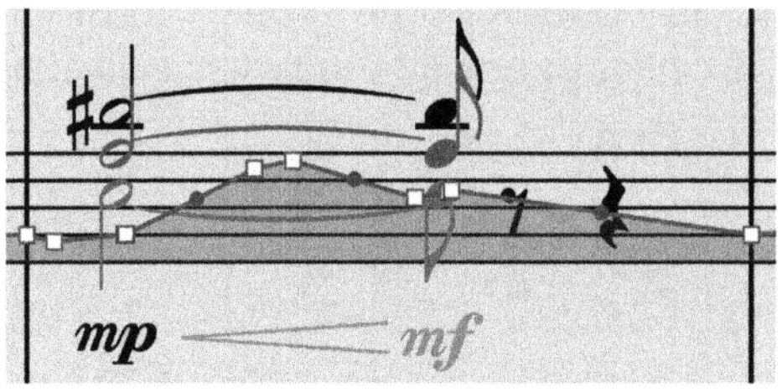

You can only delete data points, not the blue dots.

Viewing Other Automation Types

Long-press on the staff to cycle between all automation types. While Expression automation is visible you can next view Pan automation. Pan automation will appear in an orange color.

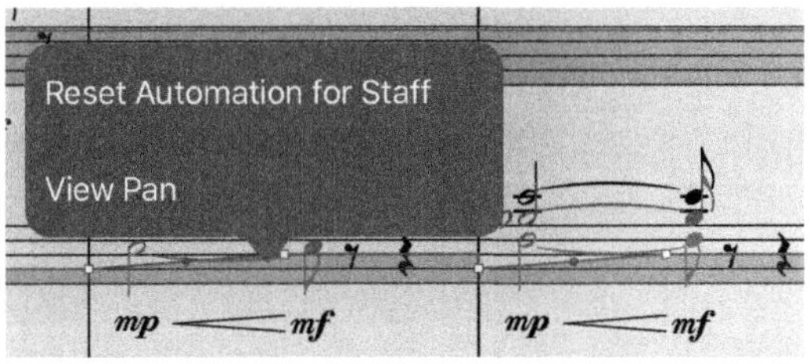

Long-press on the staff for the next automation type, Volume. Volume automation will appear in a green color.

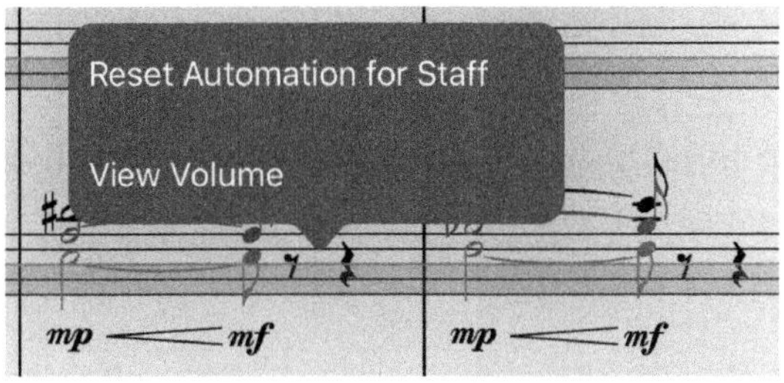

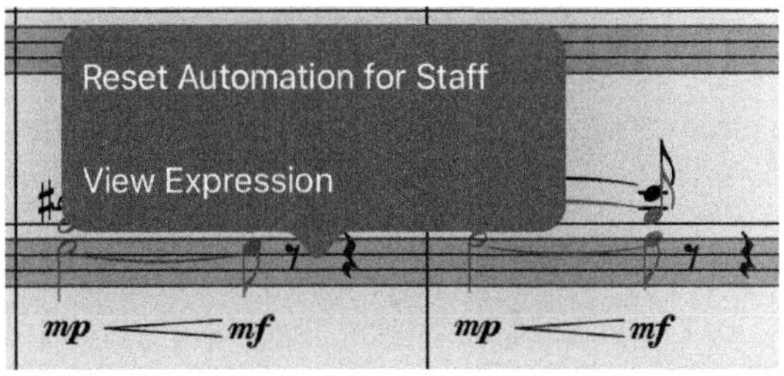

All data editing rules apply to each automation type.

Resetting Automation

If you need to undo all of your automation changes in one go, long-press on the staff and select **Reset Automation for Staff**. As you saw before, this item appeared along with selecting a different automation type (expression, volume, pan).

Resetting automation will return all automation values to their original settings based on current dynamic markings. This will only affect the current automation type you are working with. To reset those types, cycle through the different types and reset them individually.

To reset **all** automation globally (not just the current staff) for a particular automation type, long-press on an empty space between bars and select **Reset Current Automation**.

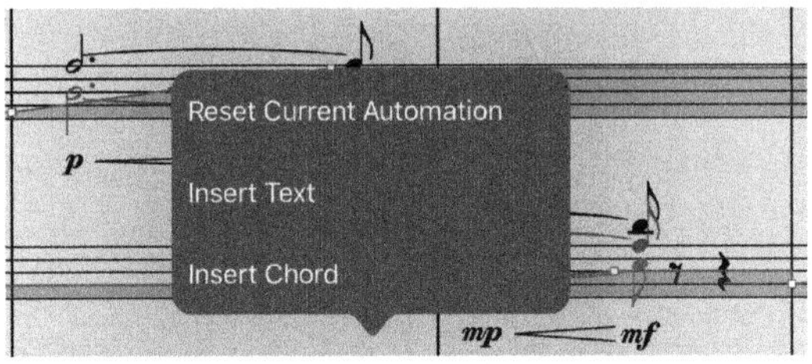

Changing Bar Numbers

The bar ruler at the top of the screen can be customized. Bar 1 does *not* need to begin with "1". Why would you want to do this? You might be working on an excerpt from another score and need to preserve the bar numbers you are referencing in the original score.

Long-press on any bar number and the **Change Bar Number** palette will appear.

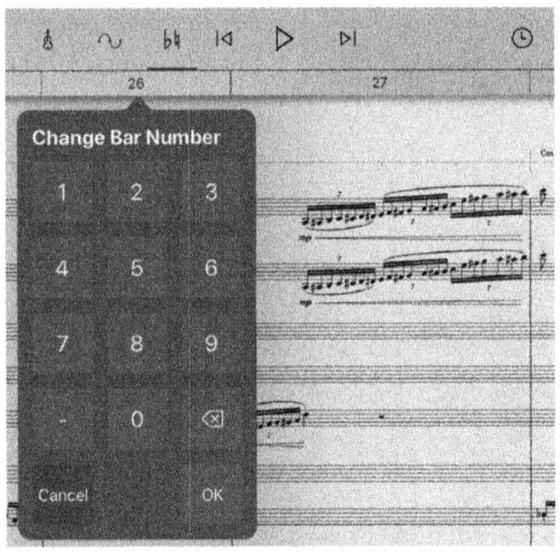

Type in any numeric value. All other bar numbers will now change relative to the bar number you entered. It's possible that changing a bar number will result in a bar number with negative numbers!

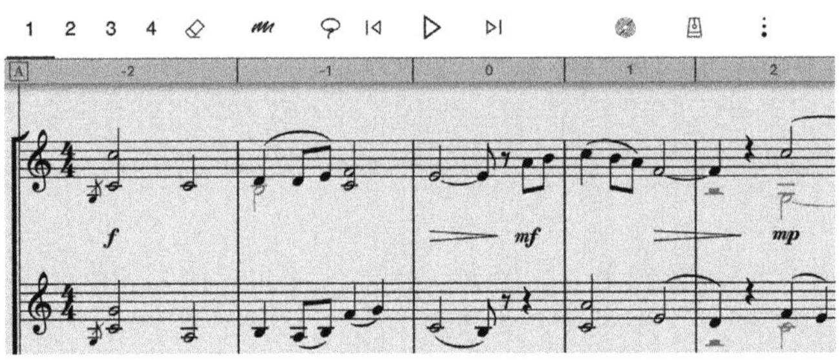

Controlling the Tempo

Music lives and breathes when the tempo of a piece of music is flexible. Speeding up, slowing down, these are generally controlled by the conductor of the orchestra. But in the digital world we don't have the luxury of being directed by a conductor. In the digital world we have to rely on the **Tempo Map**.

Tempo Staff

For even finer control over the tempo you can create a **Tempo Staff** from the **Utility** category in the **Instruments** page. The tempo staff can be positioned anywhere on the score page.

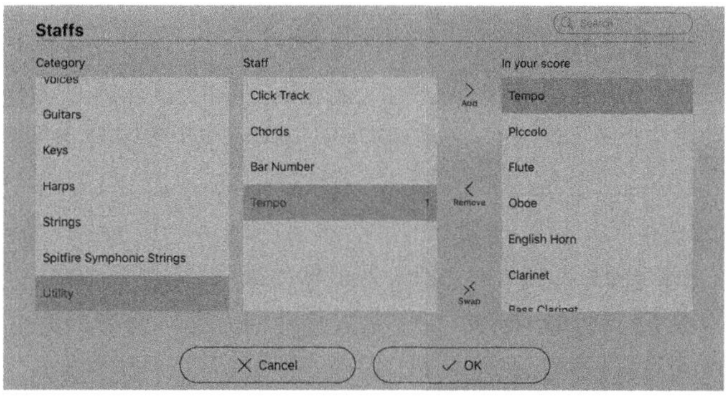

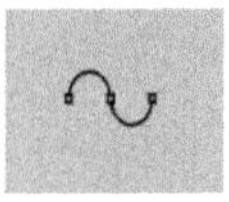

The tempo staff's tempo map can be viewed by turning on the **Automation Layer**. A graph is presented representing where any tempo change occurs. Nodes can be added indicating a new tempo at various points. Drag the node up or down to change the tempo.

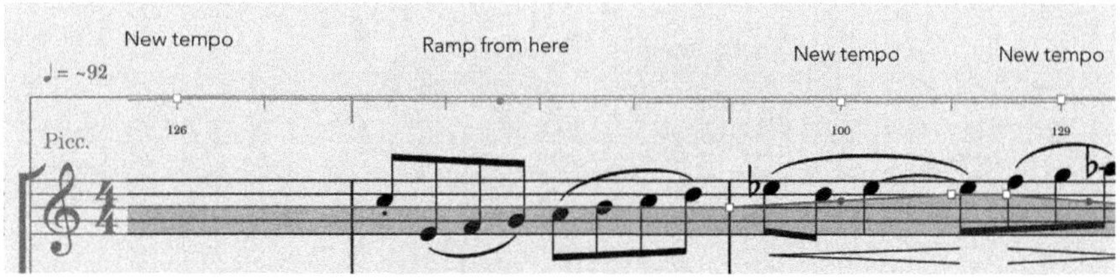

A closer look reveals that the square nodes represent where a new tempo has been added.

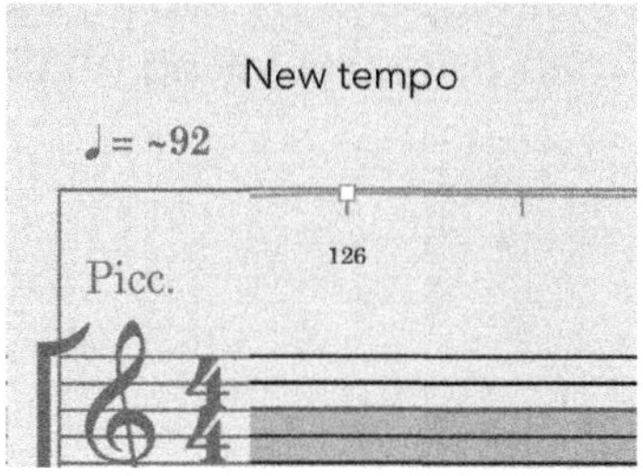

By sliding the blue dot between two tempo nodes you specify where a gradual ramp up or down to the next tempo will begin.

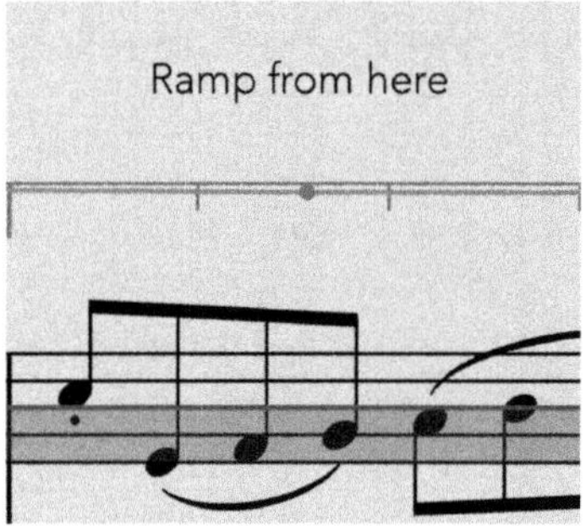

Without adding this ramping node, a new tempo will increase or decrease in linear fashion at a constant speed. Ramping the tempo would give you precise control over ritardando and accelerando.

After entering all of the tempo changes with ramping, the tempo staff will convert these instructions to text such as **Accel.** and **Rit**.

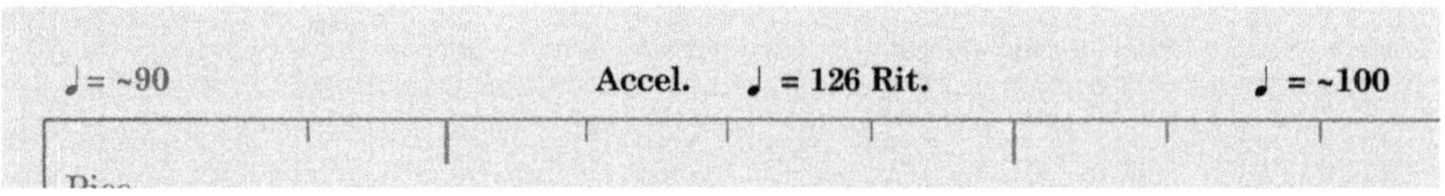

You may not wish to have this much detail displayed on the individual player's parts. Tap the name of the staff, **Tempo**, and bring up the Tempo Staff Edit Details dialog.

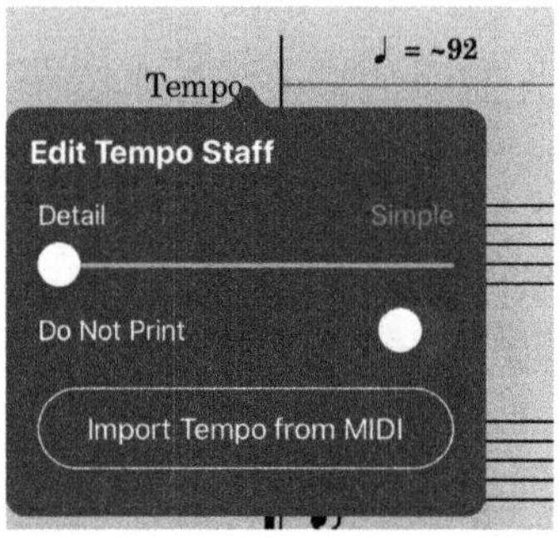

Here you can control the amount of detail that displays by sliding the **Detail** horizontal slider from **Simple** to **Precise**. You can also prevent the tempo map from displaying on the extracted parts by turning on the **Do Not Print** option.

Import Tempo Map from MIDI File

The **Edit Tempo Staff** details dialog also contains an option to **Import Tempo from MIDI**. Tapping this button will allow you to select a MIDI file (.mid or .midi). A tempo map will be applied to the score. The bars from the imported file must match the bars in your score exactly.

This import feature is especially useful if you are using StaffPad to "score to picture". Film scoring typically requires many tempo changes in order to match the film. You can create a tempo map in your DAW that is timed to a video, export a MIDI file, and import it into StaffPad.

Mixing Your Score

Currently, StaffPad does not contain a dedicated mixer pager like you might find in a DAW. Instead, each instrument's volume, pan, and reverb setting will be accessed by tapping on the name of the instrument on the left side of the staff. The **Edit Staff** dialog box will appear.

The following properties are available:

- **Instrument Name** - The name of the current instrument. If you've replaced the instrument with a third-party sample library (In-App Purchase) you will also see the manufacturer's logo.
- **Full Name** - The name of the instrument that will display on the leftmost end of the working score. It will also display on the printed instrument part. This is editable.
- **Short Name** - The abbreviated name that remains fixed on the left side of the screen as the score scrolls. Along with the short name, the staff's clef and time signature remain visible. This is editable.
- **Volume** - The volume slider adjusts the instrument's overall volume. If you override the volume through the automation layer this control will become disabled.
- **Pan** - The pan slider adjusts the instrument's overall panning position. If you override the pan through the automation layer this control will become disabled.
- **Reverb** - The reverb slider adjusts the amount of the instrument's reverb return.
- **Exclude from Parts** - Checking this box will exclude the instrument from the printed parts. The instrument will continue to sound during playback unless muted (see **Mute** below).
- **Show Chords** - This will display a chord above the staff based on the notes contained in each bar as it is analyzed by StaffPad.
- **Exclude from Chords** - Analysis of notes on every staff will be included in the Chord Staff unless this button is selected. Parts with many chromatic notes might skew the harmonic analysis so this allows you to avoid that.

- **Mute** - Sounds from this instrument will not be heard. Muted staves will become gray.

- **Solo** - Only this instrument (along with any other soloed instruments) will be heard.

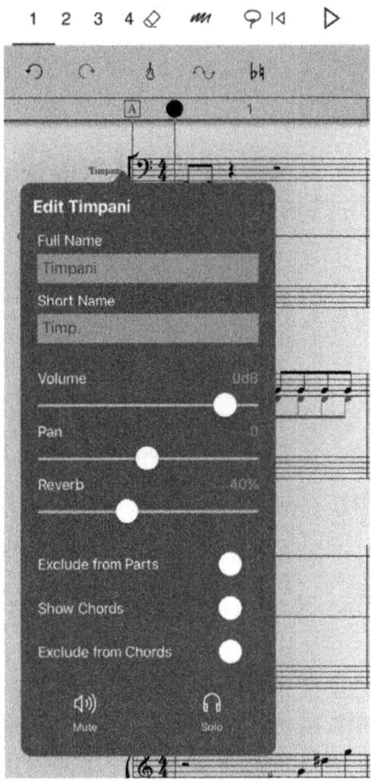

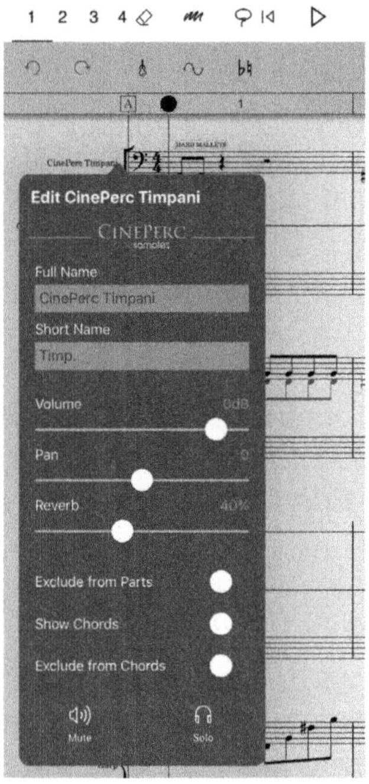

ScoreSync and StaffPad Reader

ScoreSync is an amazing concept and the future of orchestral performance and recording. The concept is simple: synchronize multiple mobile devices with the StaffPad score with each device displaying the player's individual instrument part.

Changes to anything in the score will be instantly reflected onto the player's part without any intervention by the player. It's completely automatic!

By enabling the ScoreSync button on the Toolbar, any mobile device running the free StaffPad Reader app and connected to the same Wi-Fi network will be given the ability to select an instrument part (hopefully theirs!). Once they choose an instrument it will be remembered for all future ScoreSync sessions.

Players can annotate their parts with various pens that can be either private or public. Public pens can be seen by other musicians and is the perfect choice for a section leader to convey important information.

Deselecting the ScoreSync button will disconnect *all* readers. The score will immediately disappear from their screens, however, any annotations made will be saved and can be viewed again once the score is reenabled by StaffPad. The removal of parts from a player's Reader is a valuable tool for protecting copyrighted music.

For complete details about using the StaffPad Reader, see ***Chapter 14 - StaffPad Reader.***

Chapter 10
Score Management

From the Welcome Page, you can manage details by tapping the three dots below the score thumbnail image which will reveal options for Edit Details, Duplicate, Add to Collection, Share, and Delete. Keep in mind that only the six most recent scores you've worked on are presented here on the Welcome Page.

Details about these score management options will be described below as the same options can be accessed from the **Library** and **Collections** pages.

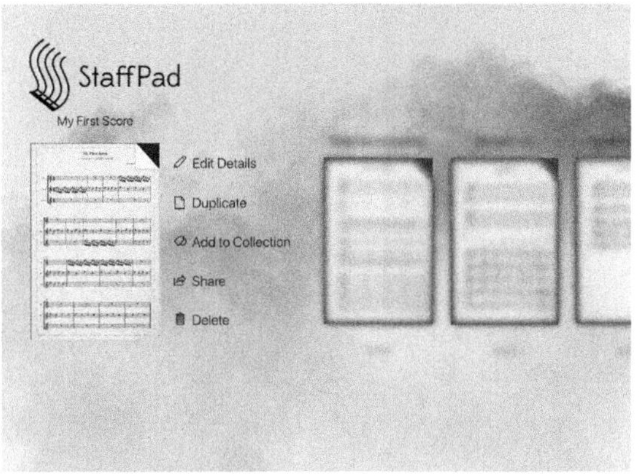

StaffPad keeps track of all your scores in two locations, **Library** and **Collections**.

Library

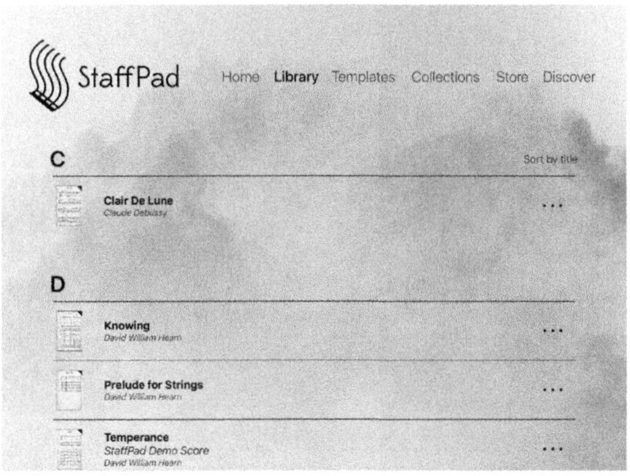

All your scores are contained in the library. By default, they are sorted alphabetically by the title of the score. Alternatively, you can sort the list by the composer's name by toggling the button:

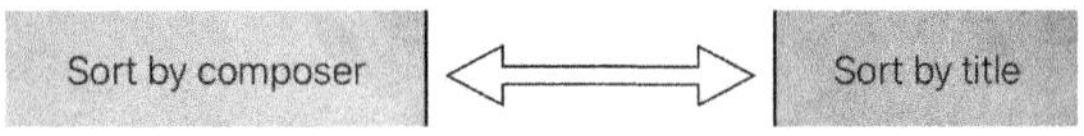

Pulling down the list from the top reveals a search field:

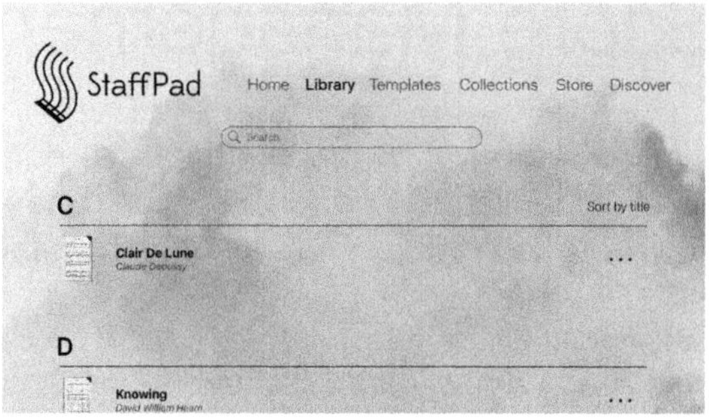

As you type letters, the search results are refined:

Further score management can be accessed by tapping on the three dots on the far right of the score name. Note that the same options are also available from the Welcome Page by tapping the three dots below the score thumbnail image.

A list of icons will be presented:

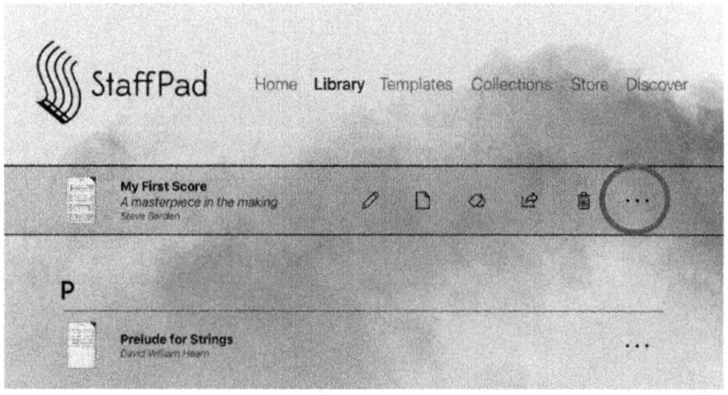

Edit Details

From here you can change the title, subtitle, composer, arranger or lyricist, and copyright fields. You could also do this on the score itself, but this shortcut is quicker. You don't have to open the score and wait for it to load. You can edit all the fields in one convenient place.

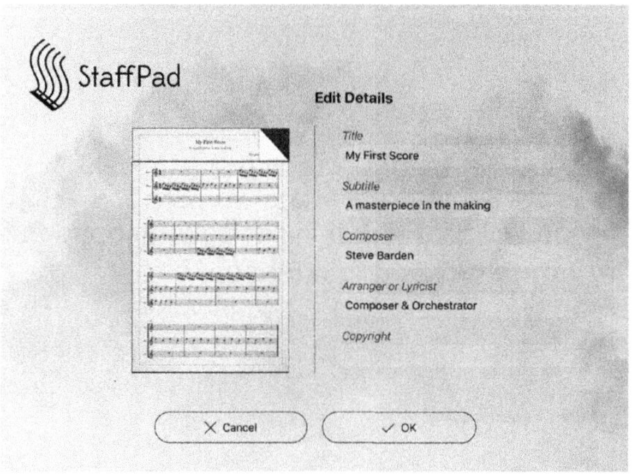

Duplicate Score

An exact duplicate copy of your score can be created. It will be given the same title with a number 2 after it, indicating it is not the original version. If you duplicate it additional times, the number after the title will increment to 3, 4, etc.

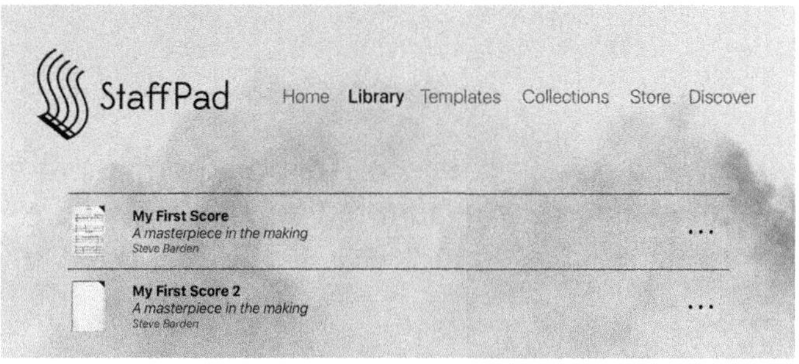

Tag Score - Add to Collection

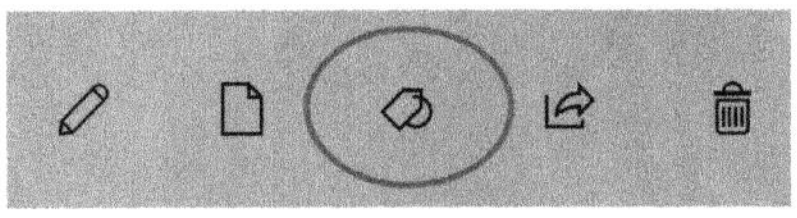

Tapping the button with the Tag icon will give you the option to add this score to one or more collections. Please refer to the section on **Collections** later in this chapter.

Share/Export/Print Score

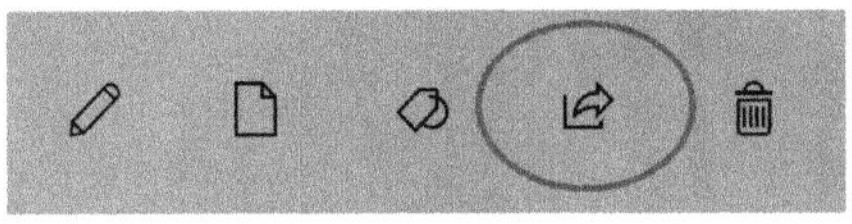

Tapping the button with the Share icon will give you a list of several options for sharing, exporting, or printing your score. See ***Chapter 11 - Sharing*** for detailed information.

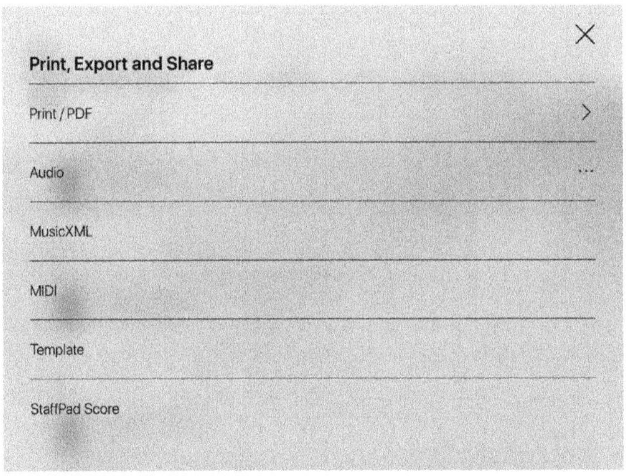

Delete Score

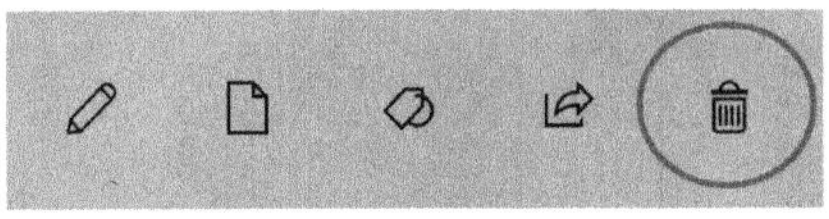

You may delete your score by tapping the trash can icon. This is a permanent action which cannot be undone. The background color of the entire row will turn red to highlight this irreversible action. You will be asked “Are you sure?”. Tap the checkmark button to delete, the X button to cancel.

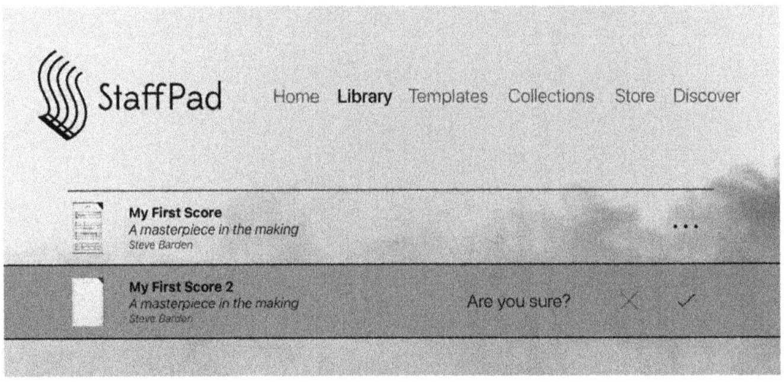

Collections

A collection is an organizational tool, like storing an item in a folder. Unlike a folder, a score can be added to multiple collections.

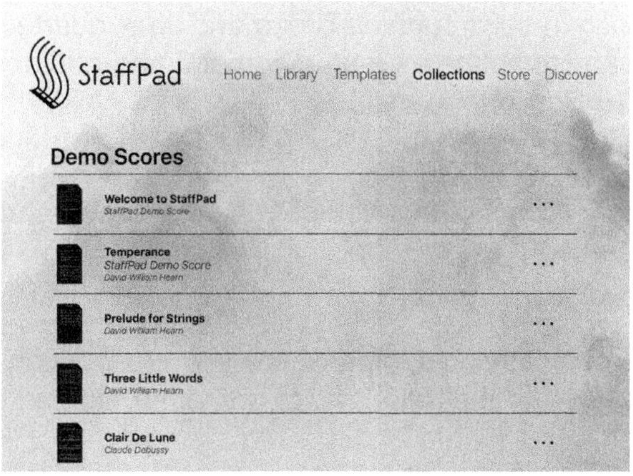

A collection may represent a group of scores in any way you like. For example, you might create a collection related to a film score you are writing, or to a concert piece. This is a convenient way to organize all the music for this particular project.

Since you can store a score in multiple collections, you can just as easily *remove* a score from a collection. This does not delete the score from StaffPad. It simply removes it from a collection. It also does not remove the score from any other collection it resides in.

Select from a list of existing collection names. You may select more than one collection to add it to. Tap the name of a collection to add it. If there is already a check mark on a collection name, tapping on the name of the collection will remove it.

Tap the **+New** button to create a new collection. Tap OK to add to the collection or Cancel to exit this page.

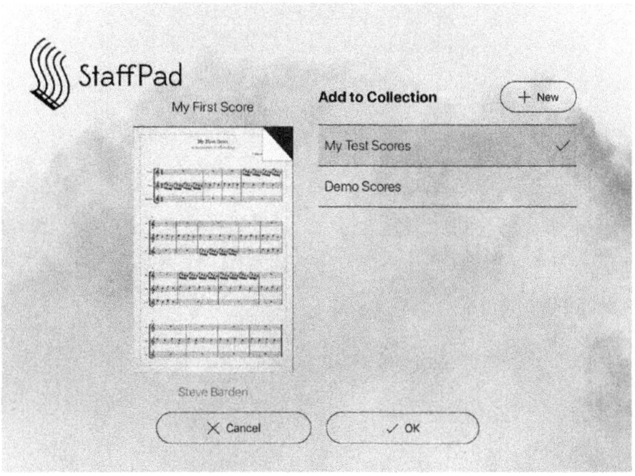

Templates

Templates are scores with pre-configured instruments, representing common orchestral configurations. These are a handy way to get started writing music.

StaffPad has created popular configurations such as String and Jazz quartets, Woodwind and Brass quintets, as well as a Full Orchestra. Pick any template as a starting point and add and remove instruments to fit your needs. See ***Chapter 3 – Where to Begin*** for details.

Templates do not have to be empty scores. Once you set up your custom orchestra you can save it as a StaffPad template to be used repeatedly.

Templates are useful for projects such as film scores where you are working with a specific musical palette. You could include tempo maps as part of the template, or any other element of the score.

Just as with the **Library** and **Collections**, scrolling the list of templates down from the top of the page will reveal a search field. As you type letters your list of search results will be refined:

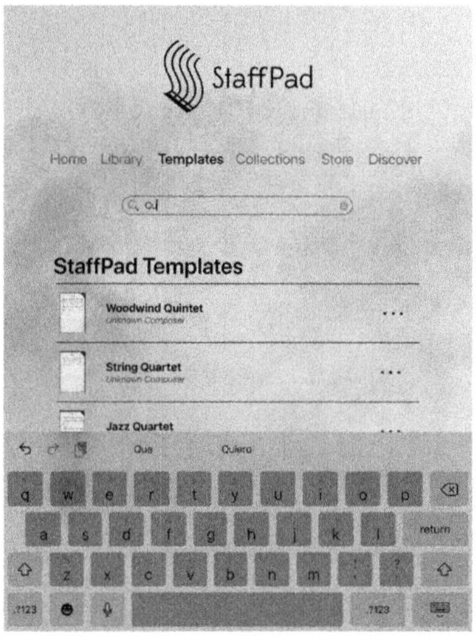

Settings

From any page, **Home**, **Library**, **Templates**, **Collections**, **Store**, or **Discover**, tapping the StaffPad logo will display the setting page. Under the StaffPad logo shows the current version number of the app followed by several options:

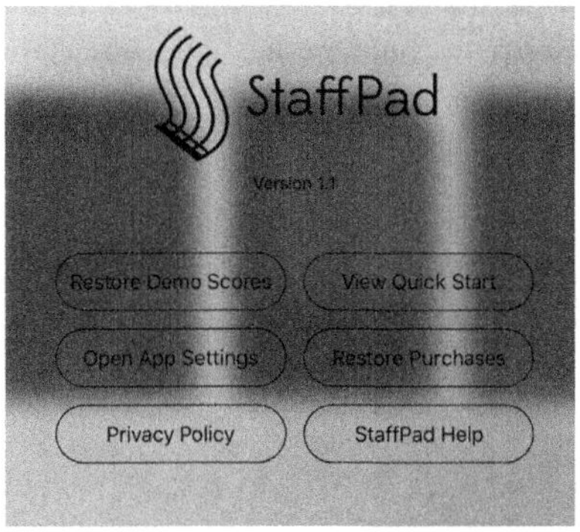

Restore Demo Scores

If you've removed any of the demo scores that were loaded when you first installed StaffPad, this option will rebuild the scores and install them once again under **Demo Scores** in the **Collections** group.

Open App Settings

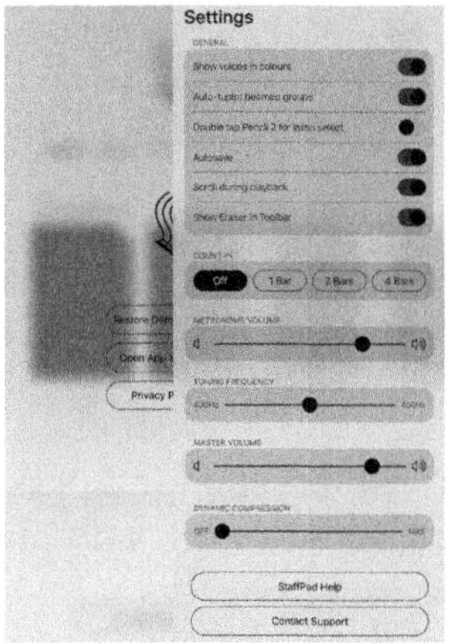

Here you can set options that are global and shared by all scores.

Show voices in colors - By default, voice colors are black (voice 1), green (voice 2), red (voice 3), and orange (voice 4). If you want to turn off this feature, deselect this option. Keep in mind that this will also affect how the printed score looks.

Eraser icon - For pens without an eraser you can make a virtual one appears when this option is set.

Auto-tuplet beamed groups - StaffPad will do its best to determine if your beamed notes constitute a tuplet of any type (groupings of 3, 5, 7, etc.). By deselecting this option, you will be responsible for writing tuplet numbers under beamed note groupings.

Double tap Pencil 2 for lasso select or eraser mode - Apple's second-generation pencil provides for a tapping gesture. Setting this option will allow double tapping to enable the lasso. When this option is turned off – *and the eraser is selected to be visible in the Toolbar* - Eraser Mode will be enabled instead of the lasso.

Autosave - Highly recommended! Your work will be saved every minute and whenever the app is put in the background when this option is enabled.

Saved Score Location - You must select your file save location. Tap **Choose...** and choose a local folder or any cloud location.

Scroll during playback - During playback StaffPad will automatically scroll the music. The playhead will remain in the center of the screen while the score scrolls. By disabling this feature, the playhead will begin moving and eventually move off-screen while the score remains stationary. You must manually navigate the score around. The playhead will appear when you have reached a point in the music where the playhead is.

Count-in - Set the metronome click to count-in 1-, 2-, or 4-bars before the music starts or leave the count-in off altogether. This is an app-wide setting and will synchronize any StaffPad Readers connected to your score.

Metronome Volume - Adjust the loudness of the metronome to your taste.

Tuning Frequency - The default tuning is 440Hz (A=440). You can change it anywhere from 430Hz to 450Hz. This will also affect the playback tuning of any connected StaffPad Readers.

Master Volume - This volume control is pre-compressor and pre-master limiter. Best to lower this volume if your music is very loud so you'll have headroom to work with. If the music is very quiet you can use the dynamic compression (below) to level it out.

Dynamic Compression - This is a master compression setting that affects the audio output of playback. The higher the setting the louder the overall perceived volume will be. However, be aware that excessive compression will defeat the use of dynamics which is a huge part of orchestral writing.

StaffPad Help - Tapping this button will take you to a website for the official StaffPad Help Desk.

Contact Support - Navigates to a web page where you can email StaffPad customer support.

Privacy Policy

Navigates to a web page displaying the company's Privacy Policy.

View Quick Start

A series of quick video tutorials describing the essence of using StaffPad.

Restore Purchases

You can download and reinstall any third-party sample libraries you may have purchased through the app's respective App Stores.

StaffPad Help

You will be taken to a website for the official StaffPad Help Desk. This is the same as selecting this option from the above App Settings panel.

Support Diagnostics

By tapping the StaffPad logo a second time will reveal a diagnostics page that is useful only for StaffPad tech support. The UUID is a unique identifier specific to your device. If you are asked to provide this info you can retrieve it by tapping on **Copy to Clipboard**. You can paste that long text string into an email if necessary.

A second diagnostic option is **Share Logs**, which is helpful for developers to determine the cause of an app crash. Tapping this item will allow you to copy the log data to a location of your choosing.

When you are finished here, tap **Done**.

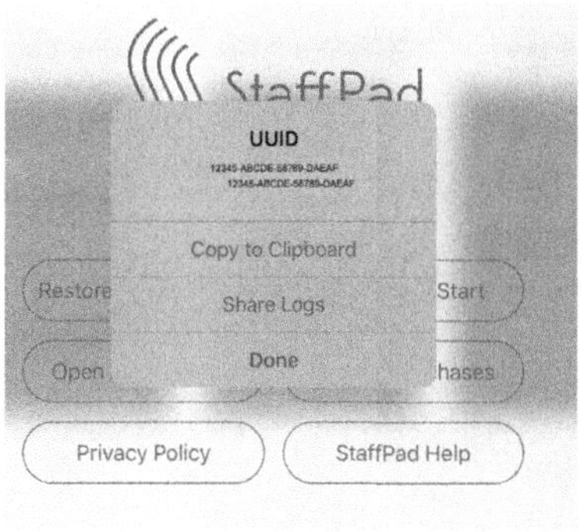

Saving

StaffPad automatically takes care of saving your work. You don't have to worry about saving it yourself. You can manually export the StaffPad file (with the extension .stf) to a location of your choosing. Refer to ***Chapter 11 - Sharing*** for details.

Apple devices will store your work in a StaffPad folder on iCloud. This is convenient since iOS would normally destroy all associated data whenever the app is removed from the device. Since the data is stored on iCloud, you can rest assured your work will always be available, even in the case of a catastrophe.

Microsoft users will be asked to select a folder on your device to store StaffPad data when the app is first installed. It is recommended that you choose a **OneDrive** folder to back up and easily restore later. This will ensure your work is backed up to the Microsoft Cloud when connected to the Internet, but still available when offline. You can always change the storage location in app settings by changing **Saved Score Location**. If you choose a cloud service like Dropbox, you need to ensure you have proper write and folder permissions for the folder you choose; and also that "prompts"/dialogs, like "are you sure you want to overwrite this file" are turned off. Otherwise, when the app tries to auto-save in the background, it will get blocked by Dropbox and the app will be unable to save.

Versions

Versions is a safe way to try things out in your score without irreversibly changing your original score. When you create a new version, it will be a copy of the current version you are editing.

While working in the score page, tap the Versions button from the Command Bar:

The Versions page will display a list of all the versions available for the current score:

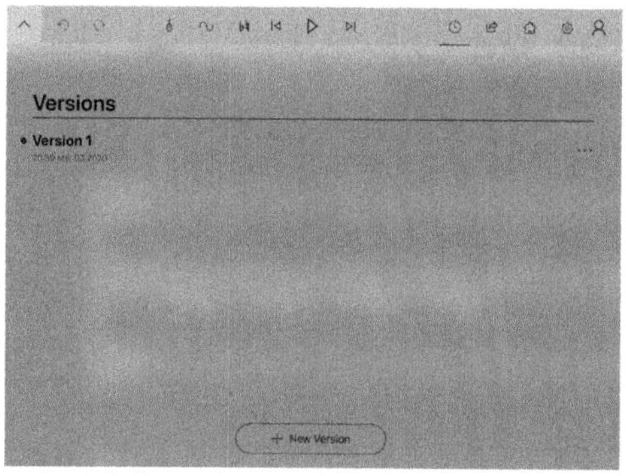

You can change the name of the version by tapping on the three dots on the far right of the version. It will reveal edit options. You can tap the pencil icon to change the name and description as well as delete the version.

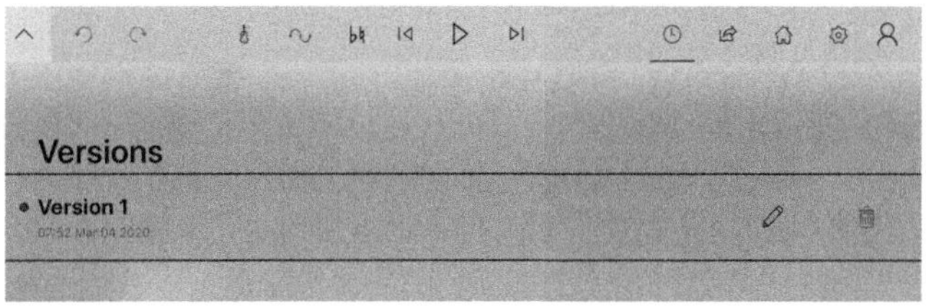

Tap the **+ New Version** button to add a new version based on the current version being edited.

A new version will be created with a default version number called **Name**. The pencil button will be highlighted indicating you can begin entering a new version name and description.

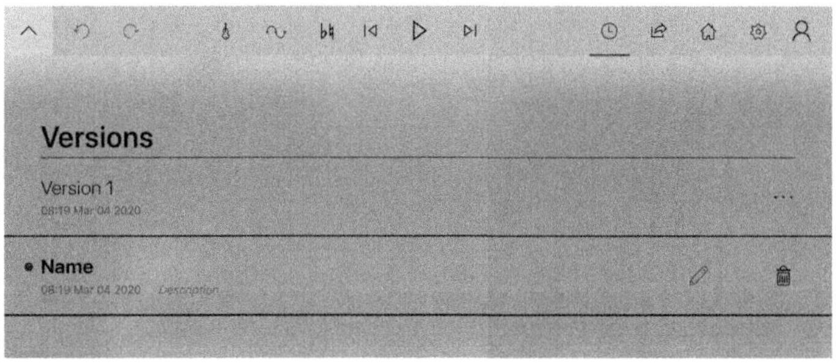

You cannot delete a version if it is the only one. You can only delete alternate versions.

Chapter 11
Sharing

Sharing encompasses the printing, exporting, and external saving of StaffPad scores in many different formats. From both the **Library** and **Collections** pages you can find the sharing option amongst other score management options by tapping the More button (three dots) on the far right of a score name:

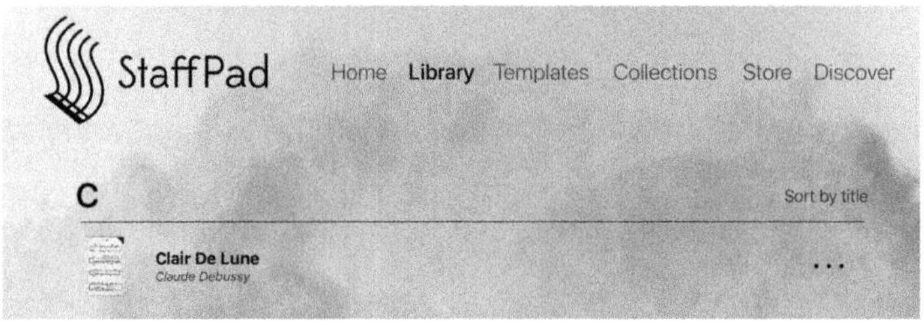

This reveals several options for score management:

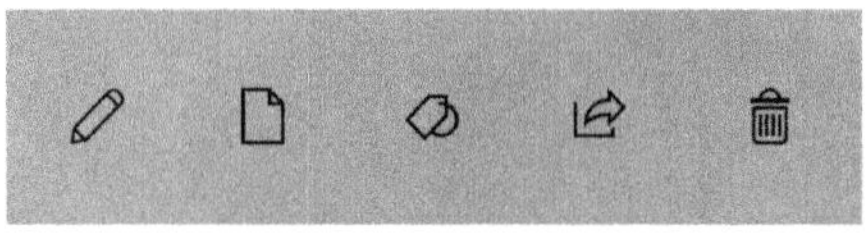

The same is true from the **Welcome Page** by tapping the More button (three dots) below a score's thumbnail image:

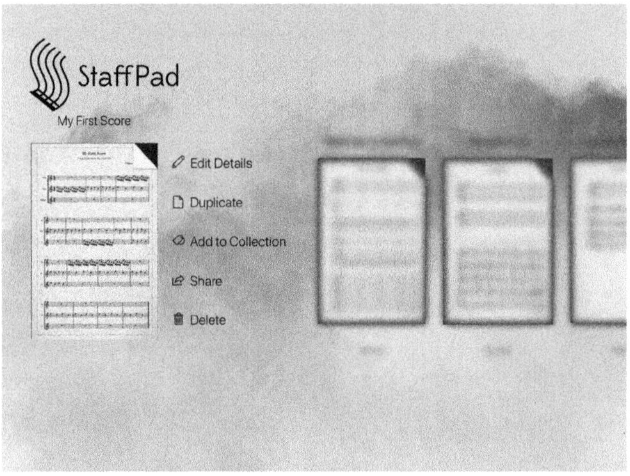

A share button is also accessible directly from within a score from the command bar:

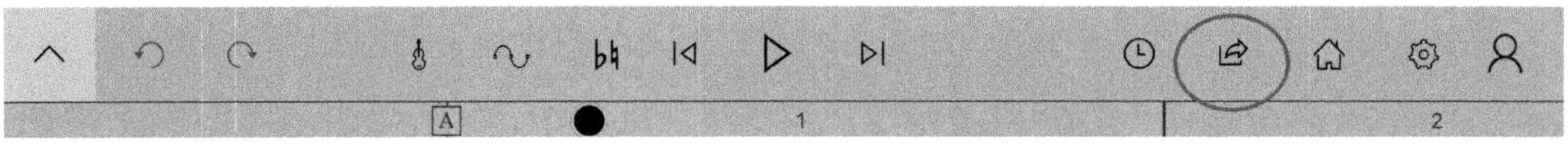

In each case, tap the **Share** button to open the share page. Your sharing options include:

- Printing the score and/or parts to a printer or as a PDF file
- Generate an audio file in AAC, WAV, MP3, or WAV stems
- Export the score as a MusicXML file
- Export the score as a MIDI file
- Save the score as a Template
- Save the score in the cloud in its native StaffPad file format

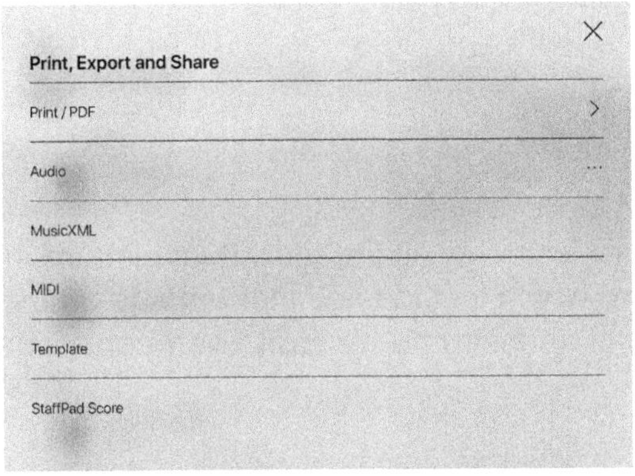

Print / PDF

You can choose to send the score to your Wi-Fi printer or to generate a PDF version. There are some differences in the setup page for printing between Microsoft and Apple devices.

For Microsoft devices, select the Print button from the Command bar.

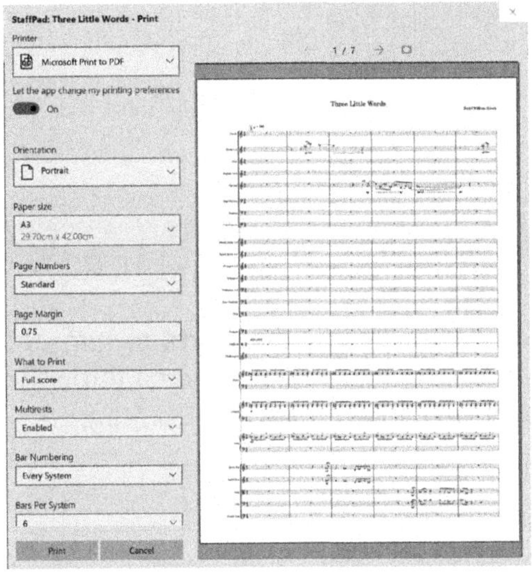

The options given for printing will depend on your printer's capabilities. You can select **More Settings** for additional printing options (also dependent on your printer's capabilities).

For Apple devices, select Print/PDF from the Print/Export/Share page. The following descriptions apply only for Apple devices.

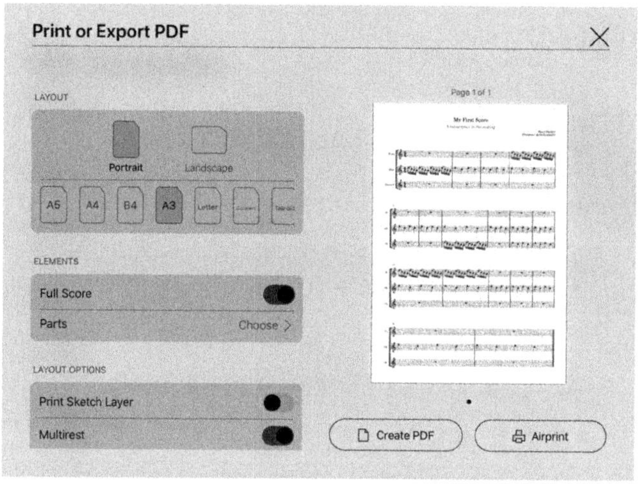

You can choose to print the full score, some or all the individual instrument parts, or both. Select the **Full Score** toggle to include the full score which includes all instruments on the page. The exception is when you have selected **Exclude from Parts** in an instrument's **Edit Staff** control panel. Please refer to ***Chapter 9 - Playback*** for more info.

Select the **Parts ... Choose >** option to select which individual parts to include:

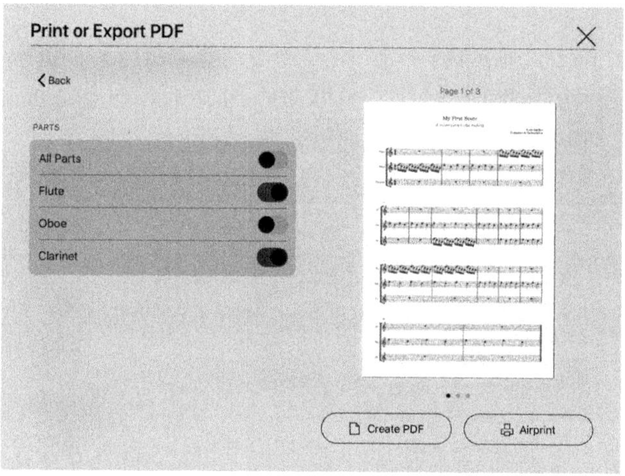

Select as many or as few parts as you'd like. Toggle **All Parts** to turn on the toggles for each part or to turn them all off. A print preview window to the right will let you scroll through all of the pages you have selected. When you are ready to print, tap the **Create PDF** or **Airprint** button:

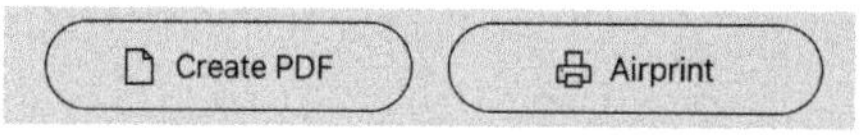

 Tapping the **Airprint** button will bring up a popup to select which Wi-Fi-connected printers are available along with additional printer-specific options.

Layout Options

You have quite a bit of flexibility when it comes to laying out your score. If you find that your score is still lacking in some of the finer layout capabilities of one of the desktop music engraving programs, you can always export your score as a MusicXML file to be optimized in one of those other programs.

You can choose between Portrait and Landscape printing, as well as several paper sizes: A5, A4, B4, A3 (default), Letter, Concert, and Tabloid.

The following is a list of layout options available in StaffPad:

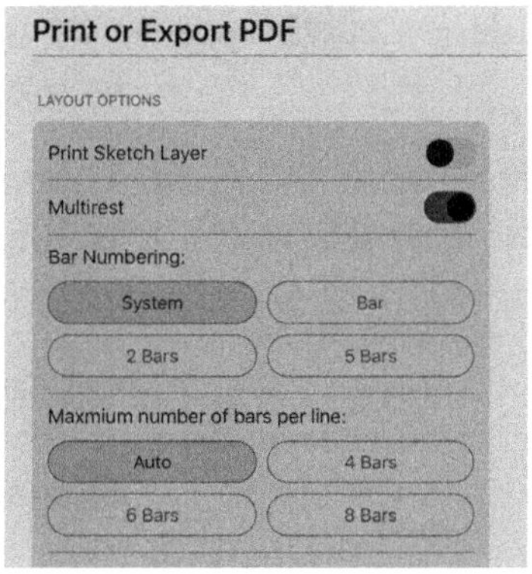

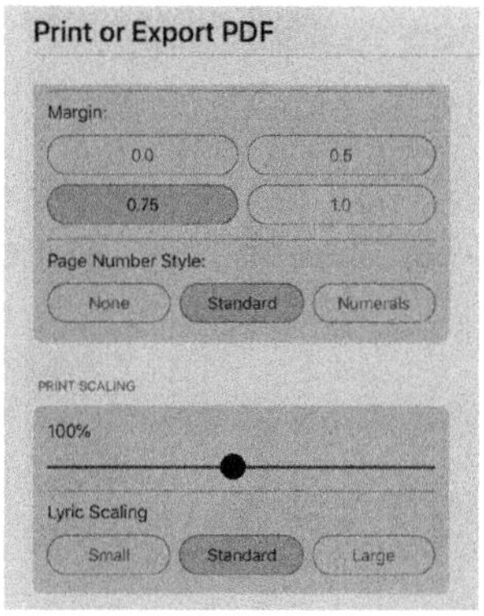

Print Sketch Layer - toggle to show or hide the sketch layer (markup) drawings and notes. Please refer to ***Chapter 4 - Music Input*** for more info on Markup.

Multirest - Enable (default) or disable multirests. When enabled, a multirest bar number (number of bars that contain consecutive whole measure rests) will be displayed over a single bar. Otherwise, every bar will be included. Multirests reduce the number of bars in a player's part.

With multirests

Without multirests

Bar Numbering - Choose how often bar numbers are displayed:

- System - Default. Displays a bar number at the beginning of each stave.
- Bar - Displays a bar number for every bar.
- 2 Bars - Displays a bar number every two bars.
- 5 Bars - Displays a bar number every five bars.

Maximum number of bars per line - StaffPad will attempt to layout bars on the page as efficiently as possible. When selecting **Auto** (default), the number of bars per line will vary depending how many notes and how dense each measure is. It will strive for maximum readability.

When choosing 4-, 6-, or 8-bars per line, StaffPad will display a maximum number of bars per line. It may also display fewer depending on how many notes and how dense each measure is.

Margin - You can decide how close to the left and right margins the music is printed on the page. At 0.0, it will stretch to the very edge. You can choose, in inches, from 0.5, 0.75 (default), and 1.0.

Page Number Style - Page numbers (if selected), will display at the upper left- and right- corners of pairs of pages. It is expected that the score will be laid out as a book with a left- and right-hand page. **Standard** style displays in common numbers (1, 2, 3, etc.). **Numerals** style will display as Roman numerals (i, ii, iii, iv, etc.).

Print Scaling - You can reduce or enlarge the size of the music to fit more or less on a page. You can scale from 10% to 200% of the original size. The larger sizes would be more suitable for children learning music. If you select a size that would be impossible to fit all the instruments on the page (full orchestra, for example), the percentage will be maxed out at the largest size that will fit.

Lyric Scaling - Adjust the size of the lyrics from small, standard, and large. This will only affect the printed output, not the size of the text while you're editing the music.

Audio

Your score can be rendered as an audio file in three formats: AAC (only), WAV, and MP3. WAV is a completely uncompressed format while both AAC and MP3 are compressed. MP3 renders at 192kbps, 48 kHz. WAV renders at 24-bit, 48 kHz. Stem export is also available.

Audio export on Apple devices is initiated by tapping the More button (three dots) to display the export options:

Microsoft devices will select the format in the Windows File Explorer dialog under **Save as**. Choose MP3 or WAV from the dropdown.

Exporting Stems

You may choose to edit your tracks in your DAW for finer control of mixing the audio for EQ, Pan, and Volume, plus selecting your own reverb settings and other audio plugins.

Choose **Export Stems**. Every instrument in your score will be rendered as WAV audio and wrapped up in a Zip file. As with other audio formats you will be given a choice where to send the file(s) to. The stems will also include a metronome track which may be useful for setting up a tempo map in your DAW.

Note: ALL instruments will be rendered as an audio stem even if the part is empty. To avoid this, remove unused instruments from the score before exporting stems.

MusicXML

MusicXML is "the standard open format for exchanging digital sheet music". As the creators of MusicXML describe it,

> *MusicXML was designed from the ground up for sharing sheet music files between applications, and for archiving sheet music files for use in the future. You can count on MusicXML files being readable and usable by a wide range of music notation applications, now and in the future.*

What does this mean for StaffPad? More flexibility. By being able to export your scores to be used by other programs, StaffPad is not the end-of-the-line when creating your musical masterpiece.

Export your score to be further modified by music engraving programs such as Finale and Sibelius to enhance your music notation with features only offered in these high-end music engraving programs.

Scores created in StaffPad can be imported into your favorite DAW to take advantage of virtual instrument sample libraries not available in StaffPad, as well as the ability of layering multiple sounds for each instrument as well as mixing and mastering capabilities only found in DAWs.

StaffPad supports both compressed and uncompressed MusicXML files.

When exporting in Microsoft, you will be given the option in the Windows File Explorer dialog to "**Save as**":

- MusicXML (compressed)
- MusicXML (uncompressed)

Visit www.MusicXML.com for more information.

MIDI

The MIDI file data format has been around since the mid-1980s. Although the MIDI 2.0 specification was finally ratified in early 2020, StaffPad will utilize the original MIDI 1.0 specification - at least for the time being.

Expression data - data that is created on the Automation Layer - is included in the MIDI file as CC 11 data, which is the common CC assignment for expression data. However, CC 1 - Modulation data - is *not* included in the MIDI file stream. This is significant because many sample libraries rely on CC 11/CC 1 combinations to breathe life into a MIDI performance.

The downside of only receiving CC 11 data alone is that you will be forced to add CC 1 data and it may not match the performance of the CC 11 data. CC 11 and CC 1 are frequently treated as exact copies of one another.

On the other hand, importing MusicXML data into your DAW instead of a MIDI file may be preferable as neither CC 11 nor CC 1 data is included. You are free to record your own performance of these controllers to suit the needs of the virtual instruments you assign to the MIDI tracks.

Template

Saving your score as a template is a time-saving device for creating predefined groupings of instruments. You are free to start with a blank score, add some instruments, then save it as a template. The next time you wish to start a score with these exact same instruments just select this template and off you go! Because it is a template, once you begin entering notes it will be saved as a new score. It will not overwrite your template.

As an example, let's say you are creating a series of pieces to be performed by an orchestra made up of one flute, one clarinet, one marimba, two violins, and a guitar. This is not your typical ensemble. Once you add this list of instruments to the score layout and save it as a template you will be able to recall this ensemble easily by selecting this template when you begin a new score.

Another example is when you have purchased one of the third-party sample library add-ons such as Berlin Strings. You could start with StaffPad's **Full Orchestra** template, replace the stock string instruments with the Berlin Strings version and save a *new* template called **Full Orchestra (with Berlin Strings)**.

When saving a template, you will be asked to name it and select a Category. The Category name can be anything you like. Before creating your own template categories, StaffPad provides a category called **StaffPad Templates**. You may name your category anything you like.

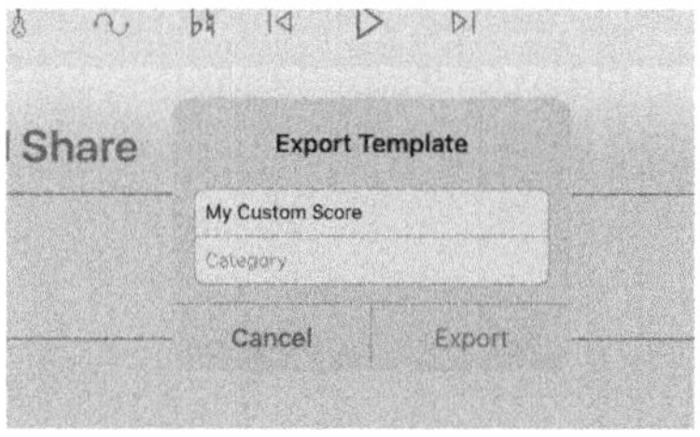

A handy tip for templates: Enter your name in the composer field to replace "Unknown Composer". This will save you time for every score.

StaffPad Score

Exporting your score as a "StaffPad Score" will save it in StaffPad's native file format. You may wish to save this file as a backup on the file system of your choice, or to share with other StaffPad users. You will be prompted for a location to save the file.

Chapter 12
Store

StaffPad has made playback of your score even more amazing by partnering with several sample library companies. From the Home page, tap the **Store** button at the top.

Custom versions of immensely popular sample libraries have been created specifically for StaffPad from *CineSamples*, *Orchestral Tools*, *Spitfire*, and others. For a complete detailed list of available libraries (at the time of this writing) see ***Appendix A - Add-on Sample Libraries***.

Products

The first thing you will see are the **Featured Today** products.

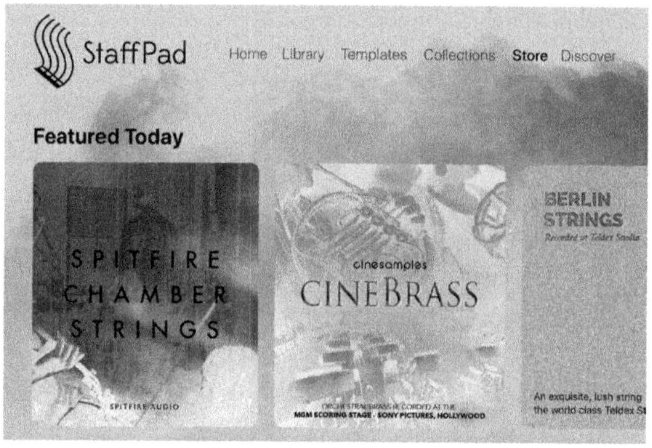

Each sample library company's products will be listed individually. There is also a category called **Essential Collection** including products by other companies, including StaffPad, that fall outside the category of orchestral instruments.

Select any product to see details and the purchase option.

If you've already purchased a library, you will see **Installed** instead of a purchase button.

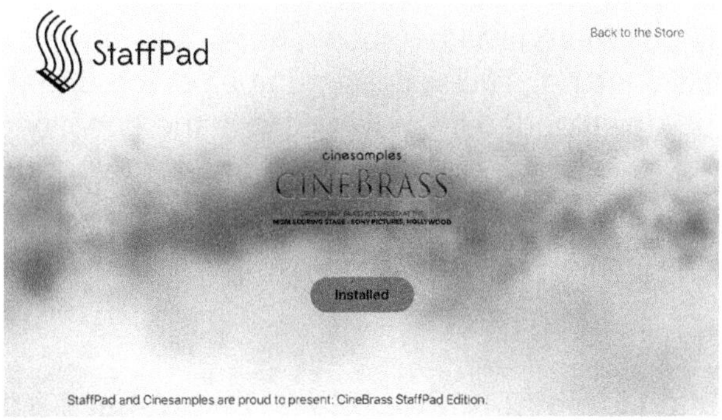

Occasionally a library will get updated. Instead of the usual **Installed** label you will see **Update** along with a version number. Tap on the **Update** button and the new version will be installed.

Downloads and Updates

At the bottom of the Store page is a button, **Downloads and Updates**, which manages your libraries.

All libraries that you have already purchased will be shown here. Any library with a pending update will show a down-arrow button for downloading. The version number of the update is displayed below the library name. The size of the library to be downloaded is shown next to the download button. Otherwise it will show INSTALLED and include a trash-can button to remove the library from your device.

Restore Purchases

At the bottom of the page is a button to **Restore Purchases**. Below that is an indicator of how much available space is left on your device so you'll know if you can install more libraries.

You can also find the **Restore Purchases** option from the **Home** page by tapping the StaffPad logo at the top.

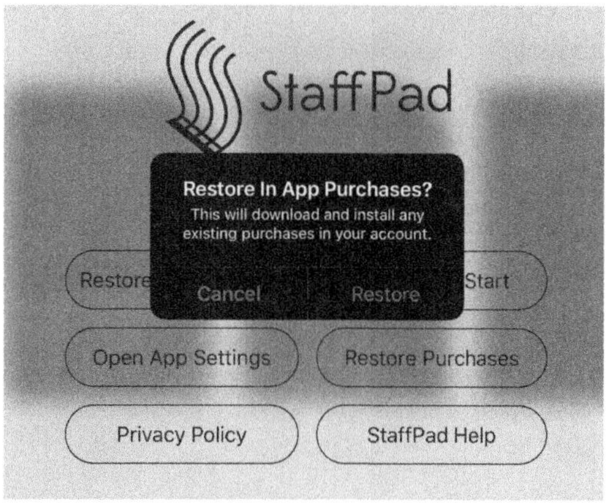

If at any time you need to redownload your purchase you may be asked to authorize the purchase. Don't worry, you won't be charged again! You will then be prompted with the message below. Tap OK. All is good!

Download Errors

A download error can occur for many reasons, usually related to your Wi-Fi connection, available bandwidth, etc. Fear not! If you see any error such as this, just keep re-trying, it will eventually sort itself out. If you continue having issues, you may need to reboot your modem and router or try later when Internet traffic is down.

Demos

Most libraries will include some demo audio and videos.

Demos

Snow Falling - Full CineOrch Demo   Copland - Fanfare   Walkthrough Video

You will see a complete list of included instruments...

Instruments

Solo Trumpet in Bb
2 Trumpets in Bb
Horn Solo
2 Horns
6 Horns
12 Horns
Trombone Solo
2 Trombones
Bass Trombone
Tuba

...and a list of features.

Features

True legato and espressivo legato interval sampling
Sustains with smooth dynamic morphing
True release samples to preserve the sound of the scoring stage
Speed controlled staccatos, spiccatos and staccatissimos
Marcato and Tenuto accent attacks
Recorded in a world-class scoring facility
Trills (semitone and whole tone)
Stopped/Muted sustains
Flutter/Rips
Natural release samples to preserve the sound of the scoring stage

Chapter 13
Writing Tips

Handwriting recognition in StaffPad is pretty darn good and continues to get better with each app update. Not only does it recognize shapes, it also considers *context*, i.e., it takes into consideration what else is being written - or has been written - in a bar before deciding on how to translate what you're writing.

You can still confuse StaffPad. It's not perfect. But you must do your part and give it the notation that it expects - or at least close to it. The following tips are designed to get you in the habit of translating what you know about writing music and what StaffPad understands. It's not that different from what you already know about writing music.

A doctor can scribble something unintelligible on a prescription pad and the pharmacist seems to be the only one who can decode it. That's because the pharmacist is looking for certain words (or letter combinations). The same goes for StaffPad: give it what it expects!

Practice Handwriting

Remember these? How many times did we need to practice these skills as children until our handwriting was neat and clear? If you're like me, probably a lot. And that's not even counting cursive practice! Wait, you don't know what cursive is? Go ask your grandparents.

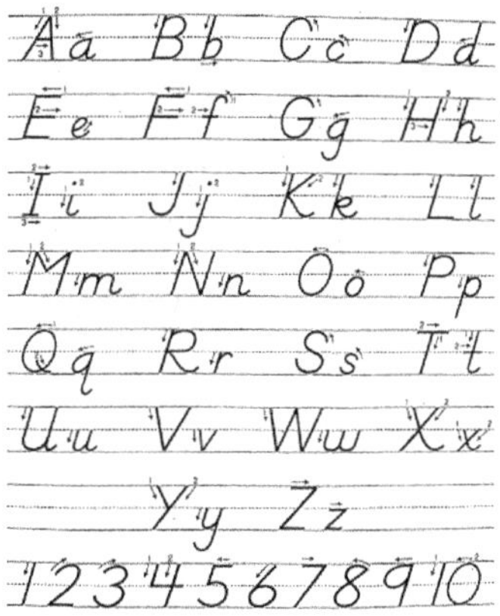

Spend time practicing writing music notation. Even though you've been writing music on paper for a while now, you may need to adjust your writing style so StaffPad can become your best friend.

Let's start with tips that will improve StaffPad's handwriting recognition.

Tips

Tip #1 - Size Matters

StaffPad expects note heads to be the proper size. What is the proper size? Looking at the example below, the first note, C, takes up the space between two lines. It should not extend beyond the line above it or the line below it.

With that as the benchmark, notes covering lines should be roughly the same size as notes filling in spaces. The first three notes below are acceptable, the fourth is not. The last note covers the D line (the intended note) but extends and touches the line above and the line below. This will confuse the recognition engine.

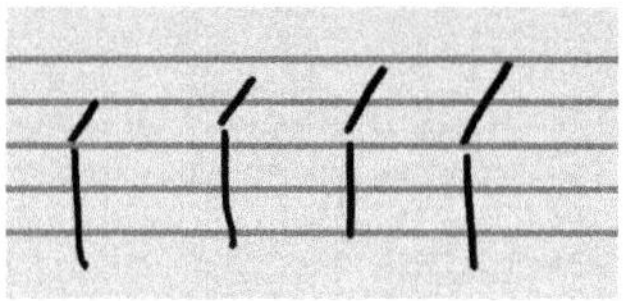

Tip #2 - Stem Distance to Note Head

Stems do not have to touch the note head. The first note below does touch the note head, but the next two notes do not. This is acceptable.

How far from the note head is okay? Believe it or not, the two examples below are perfectly acceptable! Why? Because the stem is a straight vertical line and it lines up with the left side of the note head.

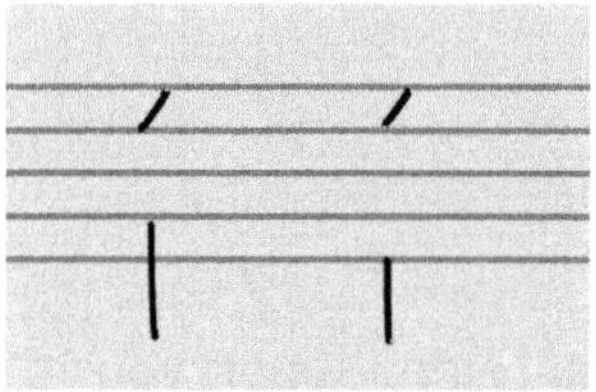

Tip #3 - Beaming Trouble

Two quarter notes can be turned into two eighth notes simply by beaming them together. Draw a line from the bottom of one stem to the bottom of the other. The only caveat is that both stems must be pointing in the same direction. The example below will not work.

The solution? Flip the stem direction of either one of the notes. Select one of the notes using the lasso and tap the **Swap Stem Direction** button. When you have completed drawing a beam, StaffPad will render the stem direction automatically according to music notation rules.

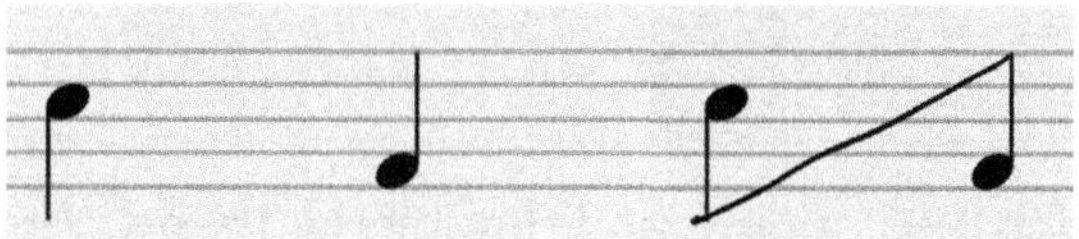

Tip #4 - Auditioning Articulations

What would a tenuto sound like on that note? How about a staccato? There are many different types of articulations available on any given instrument. How do you know which one sounds like what you had in mind? Does the sample library you have selected even support that articulation in the first place?

The simplest way to hear what will be performed is by tapping on a note and holding it, the same way you would hold a note to move it. As the pencil touches a note a sound will be heard. StaffPad will play that note with whatever articulation is associated with the note.

Tip #5 - Reducing Complexity

A passage like the one below is not overly complex, but there's enough information there to potentially confuse StaffPad if you attempt to write the entire phrase in one go. It only takes one badly written note to cause the entire bar not to render. But which note is the problem?

Break down complex lines into smaller pieces. In the example below, consider writing the first group of sixteenth notes, render it, write the next group of sixteenth notes, render it, and so on. Add the staccatos last. The same with the slur. Break it down into manageable chunks.

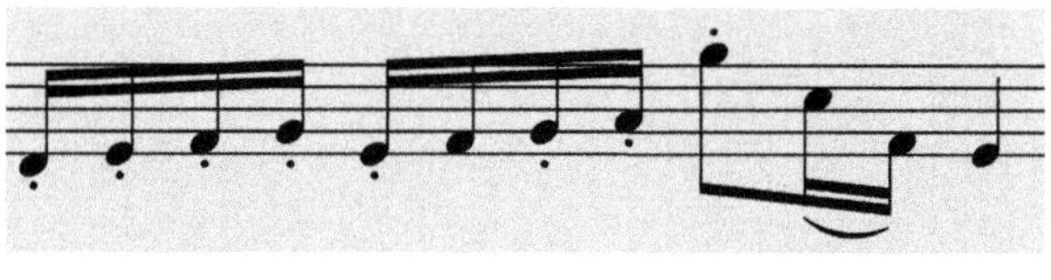

Tip #6 - Expand the Bar - Make Room to Write

Oops! I forgot to add that sixteenth note triplet followed by another pair of sixteenth notes.

This isn't going to end well. Scrunching up notes like this will only end in frustration because you haven't given yourself enough room to write clear notes.

Extend the bar width by grabbing the end barline and dragging it to the right. Now you'll have plenty of room to enter many more notes.

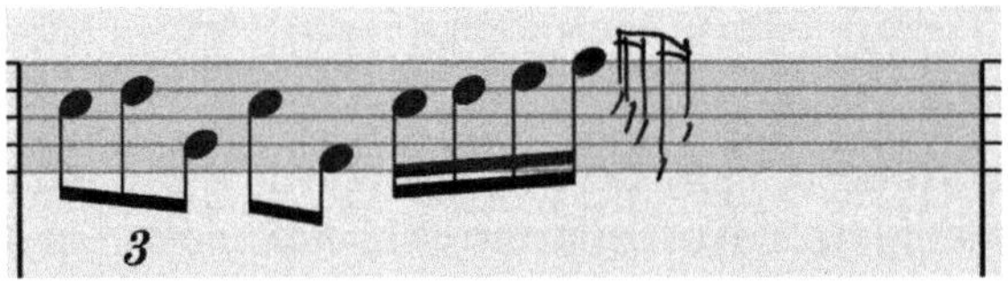

Tip #7 - Focus on the Rhythm

Related to Tip #5, lines with complex rhythms and many notes can lead to poorly written notes that will not render. If you have a complex bar with many sixteenth notes, for example, try writing *only* the rhythms.

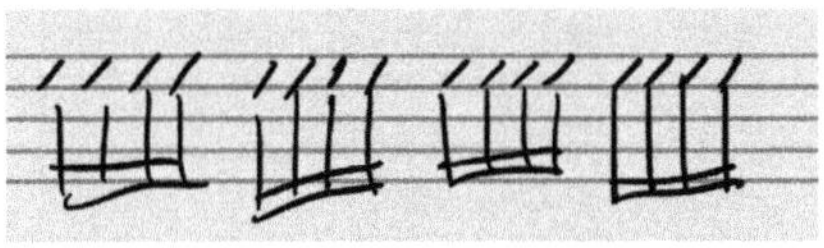

Render the notes:

Then move them to the correct pitch:

Tip #8 - Lasso That Sucker!

Related to Tip #7, if you find you have the same rhythmic value that will be repeated several times, write the rhythm (rhythm only, ignore the pitch) and copy it.

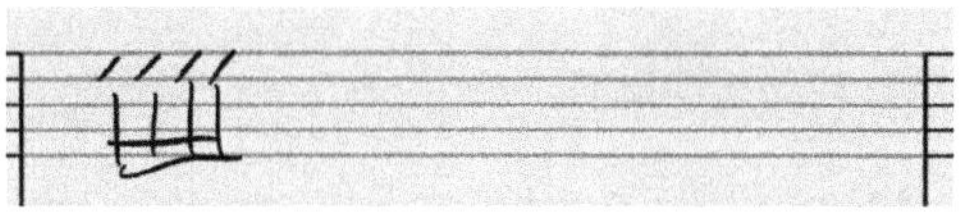

Render the notes:

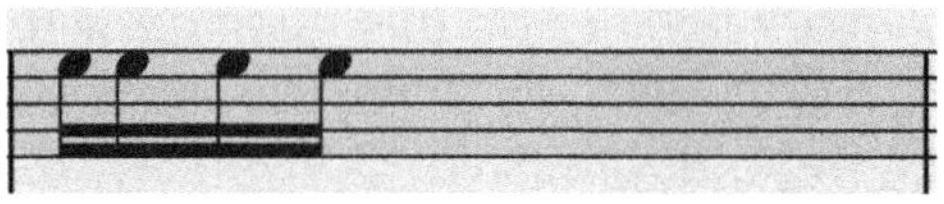

Lasso the notes. They will be automatically copied to the clipboard:

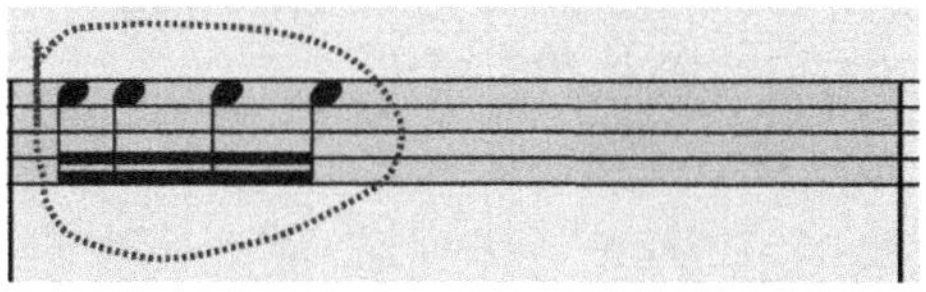

Tap the pencil as many times necessary where copies of this rhythm belong:

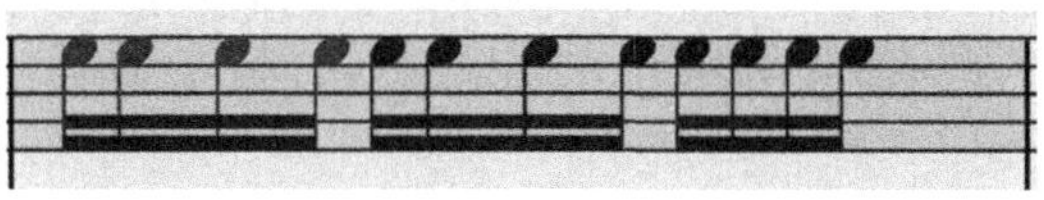

Then you can move the pitches to the correct values as noted in Tip #7.

Tip #9 - Clean Up Your Mess

Whenever you tap *away* from the bar you're working on, your bar of music will be rendered using handwriting recognition. But what you sometimes end up with is a different bar being littered with superfluous scribbles!

Whether you're a neat freak or not, these scribbles can be annoying to look at. Rather than turning on erase mode to remove these unwanted guests one at a time, double tap the bar to select it. Use the Selection Bar to *cut* the entire contents of the bar, then simply select the bar again (double-tap) and *paste* it back. Your original notes will be salvaged but the scribbles will disappear!

Tip #10 - Write Fast!

StaffPad is designed for a rapid workflow. That means writing quickly. StaffPad recommends that you work with the staff zoomed out as much as possible and work quickly. The closer you are zoomed in, the larger the notes must be, and this slows you down. You will find the optimal zoom level and writing speed after some practice.

Creator David William Hearn offers this explanation:

"It may interest you -- the engine predominantly analyses ink strokes, rather than the visual appearance of the ink itself (though it does do a visual pass and take that into account). As part of the ink analysis process it has to "thin out" the data points created by the Apple Pencil or the Windows Pen (they create thousands and thousands of individual points that come together to look like an ink stroke). Whilst it's a pretty robust process, it's actually harder than you might think to do this thinning without affecting key vector points that contain useful shape information. The slower you write, the more data points are generated by the pencil/pen, and thus the filtering has to be more aggressive. Conversely, the quicker you write, the fewer data points are generated and the less manipulation StaffPad has to do to the ink stroke itself...

Thus, StaffPad actually responds better the quicker you write -- it's a sort of a counterintuitive thing. The temptation upon seeing pending bars to slow down and draw things _really_ carefully actually exacerbates any recognition issues. Working fast and clean is the key!"

Tip #11 - Drawing Tools

Many composers and music copyists writing on paper have taken advantage of working with a *square triangle* drawing tool. The square triangle is primarily used in engineering and technical drawing professions but works wonders when writing music.

The small design of the triangle is optimal for holding in your non-writing hand to assist in drawing straight lines, beams, and stems. Draw along the long straight edge for beams and with one quick flip of the wrist the short straight edge can be used for drawing stems. The long edge is also great for drawing hairpins.

I've used this tool over the years on paper and found it can also be used on a tablet. And why not? If the tablet is flat on your table, you can easily use it just as you would on paper.

If you're having trouble drawing straight lines, give the square triangle a try. Without assistance, your beams may have too much of an arc and StaffPad will think you're trying to draw a slur. It can take some time to develop drawing skills on a tablet and a straight edge tool can be just the solution!

Tip #12 - Compose First, Details Last

To become an efficient composer, you need to break down tasks into categories in order to keep the creative flow moving. Make sure your harmony, melody, and counterpoint are correct before moving on. Do the important things first:

1. Write the notes
2. Add articulations to the notes
3. Add dynamics
4. Add tempo changes
5. Etc.

Tip #13 - Lasso Dynamics

Entering dynamics can be tedious when multiple staves will require the same marking on the same bar. Consider, for example, a string section where every instrument will be assigned a ***mf*** on the same bar.

Write the first dynamic (using the pencil or *Insert Text*). Using the lasso tool, copy that dynamic and simply tap to paste it again and again for the other instruments.

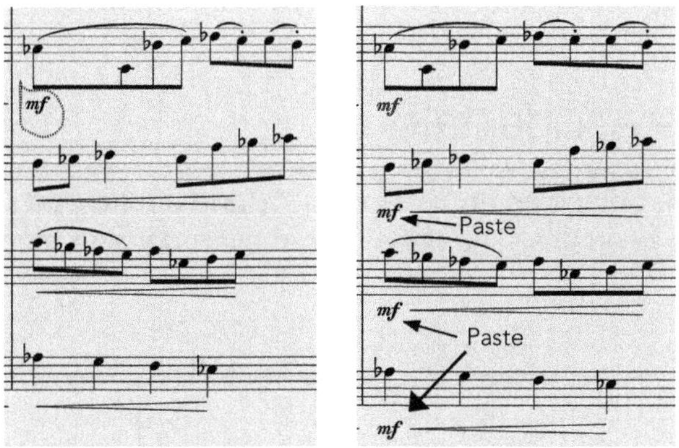

Tip #14 - Take Advantage of Versioning

If you feel like experimenting and don't want to risk losing any brilliant ideas in your current score, consider creating a new version. This is a quick way to make a duplicate of your current score. This alleviates the need to export your score as a backup while trying out some new ideas.

Tap the **Versions** button from the Toolbar and add as many versions as you like. Refer to ***Chapter 10 - Score Management*** for details.

Tip #15 - How to Write That Effing *f*!

Writing a forte symbol (***f***) tends to be somewhat difficult for many people. Writing a ***mf*** is less challenging. So why is the ***f*** symbol so difficult? Without knowing the logic behind the handwriting recognition engine, I have analyzed this problem and have come up with a solution of my own.

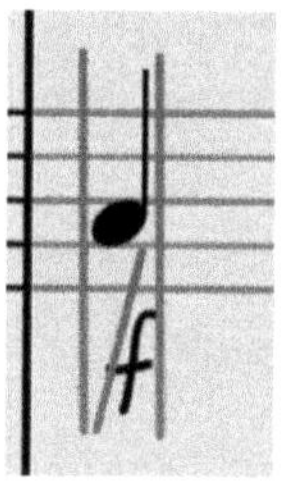

Consider the width of the note head. The first stroke is a slightly angled line with a little hook at the top. The angle should stretch across the width of the note head, but not exceed it. Placement under the note is crucial. The horizontal cross in the center of the ***f*** should also not exceed the width of the note head.

I have spent a great deal of time testing this. It is not without fail, however. It does take practice, and as we discuss at the beginning of this chapter, practice makes perfect.

A note about handwriting recognition and rendering: As the app becomes more mature, it's likely that writing the ***f*** symbol will become easier and more tolerant of your writing style.

Tip #16 - How to Write Accidentals

When writing the natural symbol, draw it as an "L" and a "7", one stroke each. Make sure the center of the symbol matches where the note head sits. The lines do not even need to touch.

With sharps, the lines should be more vertical and horizontal as in the first example. Think of a tic-tac-toe game. Even though when rendered a sharp symbol has a bit of an angle as is drawn in the second example, this won't render properly. Keep it simple with horizontal instead of angled lines.

Flats are the opposite of sharps in drawing with angles. A rendered flat symbol has a slight angle in the oval shape. This time it's preferred to have that 45-degree angle in the oval. A more rounded oval like a pure letter "b" will not render.

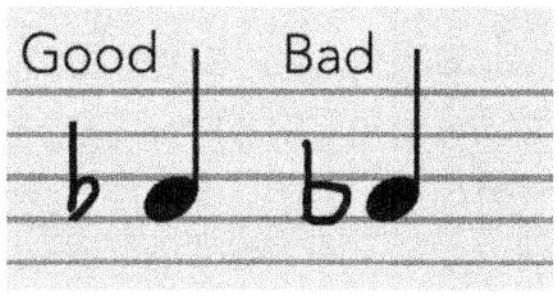

A note about handwriting recognition and rendering: As the app becomes more mature, it's likely that even the bad examples shown above will eventually render correctly.

Tip #17 - Export MusicXML or MIDI File?

Both types of files, MusicXML and MIDI, can be imported into your DAW program for further editing. This is helpful if you don't have any of the third-party add-on sample libraries in StaffPad and want to render your audio project using sample libraries that you may already have in your DAW.

The biggest difference between the two data formats is that the MIDI file will contain *all* of the automation layer data that you've customized in StaffPad. This includes Expression (CC 11), Volume (CC 7), and Pan (CC 10). The resulting data is demonstrated below after importing the MIDI file into a Cubase project.

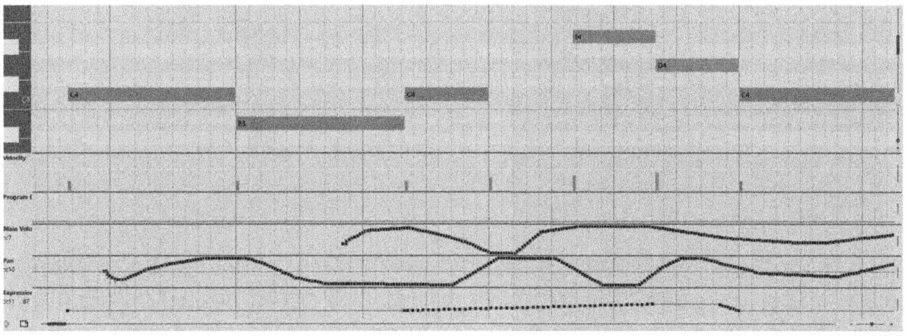

A MusicXML file, on the other hand, will not contain *any* of the automation layer data. One downside of the Expression data from the MIDI file is that the Expression layer will only represent CC 11 data. Many sample libraries often pair CC 11 and CC 1 (modulation) data to sculpt the instrument's performance. This means that you will need to add CC 1 data on your own.

Tip #18 - Voice Layer

When should you use voice layers?

The primary reason you would want to use voice layers is when you need to separate musical lines between players sharing the same staff (such as two flute players) but you are not utilizing a divisi staff. Using voice layers is the only way to have independent melodic lines with opposing stems.

Separate musical lines sharing a staff is common practice when writing for French Horns. The typical structure is placing Horns 1 and 2 on one staff and Horns 3 and 4 on a second staff (these are *not* divisi staffs).

The first example below has both parts playing the exact same rhythms. This would be acceptable, and you could expect two players to read their lines. The second example contains the exact same notes and rhythms as the first, but with opposing stem direction. This would help with sight reading but is not a requirement.

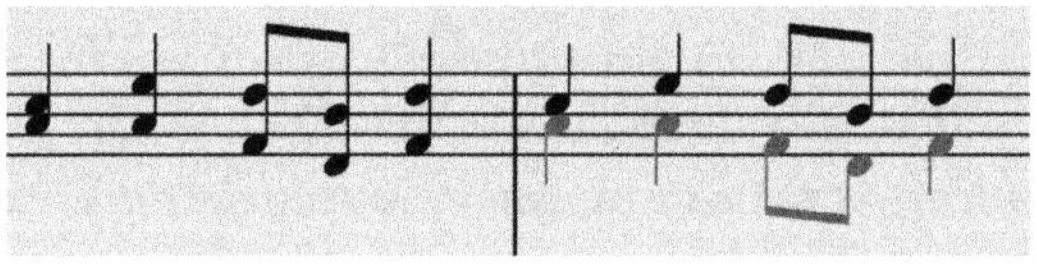

However, the next example has each part playing different rhythms. The proper way to notate this is by having each part notated with opposing stem direction.

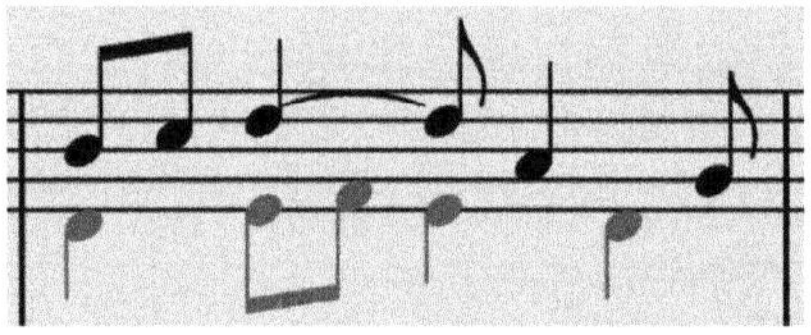

Another common usage is for duplicating parts an octave lower (or higher). Here is a piano part that needs help an octave lower. Use the lasso and select the group of notes. The notes will automatically be placed on the clipboard. Alternatively, tap on the entire bar to select all notes, and tap Copy to put the notes on the clipboard.

Next, switch to Voice Layer 2. Now, while the notes are still in the clipboard, tap on the bar below the original notes and the copied part will be added. The original notes in Voice Layer 1 have stems pointing up and the new notes in Voice Layer 2 have stems pointing down.

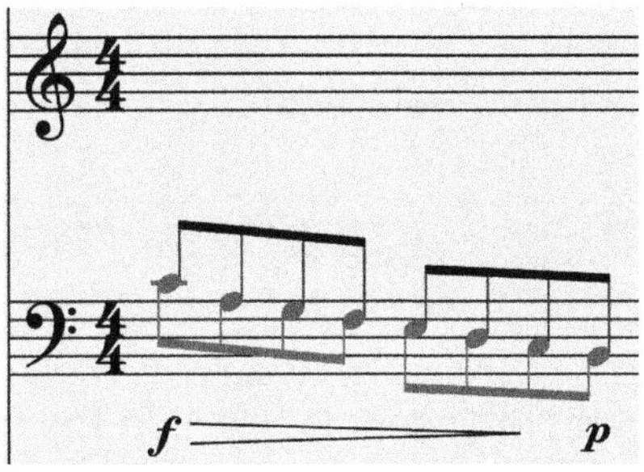

Next, lasso the notes in Voice Layer 2 and drag the notes as a group down to the lower octave.

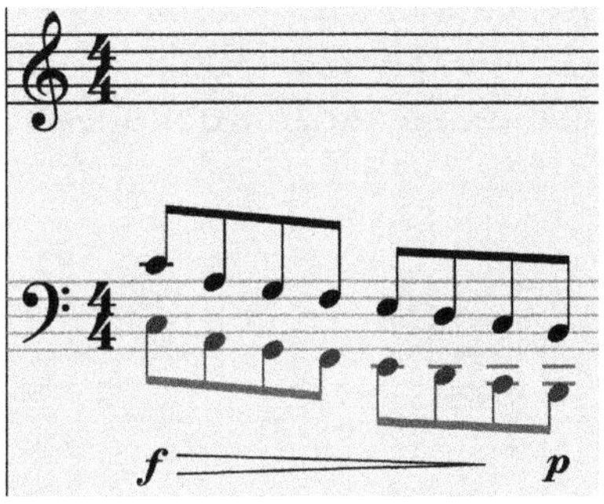

Add-On Libraries

The following tips may apply only to specific sample libraries.

Tip #19 - Bartok Pizz...It's a Snap!

Currently, StaffPad does not include a symbol for the Bartok Pizz articulation. That's the effect of a string player pulling on the string and letting it snap back onto the fingerboard. Spitfire Symphonic Strings, Berlin Strings, and CineStrings offer a Bartok Pizz articulation.

To achieve this effect, change the notehead to an X by selecting **X Notehead** from the symbols palette. Even though this is technically a pizzicato articulation, you do not have to add *pizz* above the note as technique text.

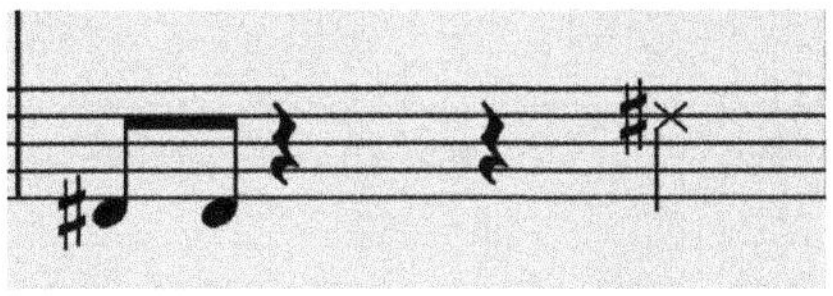

Tip #20 - Flutter and Rips

Flutter-tonguing is a wind instrument tonguing technique in which performers flutter their tongue to make a characteristic “FrrrrrFrrrrr” sound. CineBrass French Horns can achieve this effect by simply entering the text, “flutter” above the note. Note that in order to achieve this you must select the “4 Horns” patch. Any other French Horn patch will sound like a tremolo (repeated notes).

End the flutter effect by adding “normal” as text above the staff.

A horn “rip” is achieved by writing a very rapid ascending line. In the case of the CineBrass example, maintaining the flutter effect helps the effect of the rip. Without the “flutter” it will just sound like a fast scale. Also use the 4 Horns patch on this one.

Note that writing a grace note figure to achieve the rip effect is exactly as a real French Horn player would play it. While DAW-based sample libraries may have rips “built in”, mimicking that in StaffPad would result in a single note being notated. Maybe it would make sense from a DAW perspective, but not for a real player reading the score.

Alternatively, a rip can be notated by using the **scoop** symbol. In this case, the flutter articulation must *not* be used. Resume normal playing by designating either *normal*, *normale*, *norm*, or *ord*. These are all acceptable notations and StaffPad will understand any of them. Again, this requires the CineBrass 4-Horns instrument.

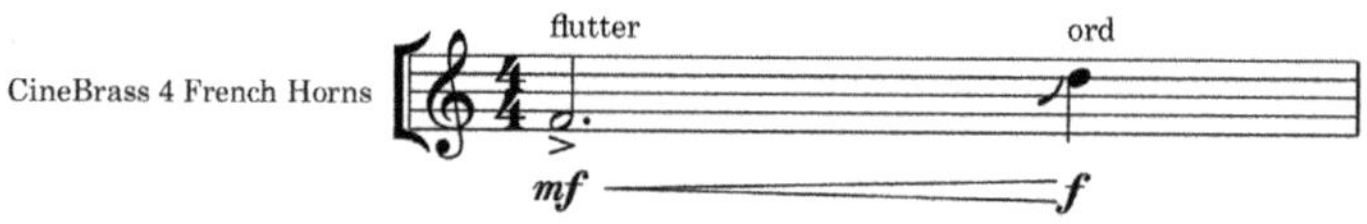

Tip #21 - Voxos Syllables

CineSamples Voxos gives you the ability to sing 30 different vowel type sounds. This feature only applies to the Voxos **Full Chorus** instrument. Full Chorus is displayed using a Grand Staff.

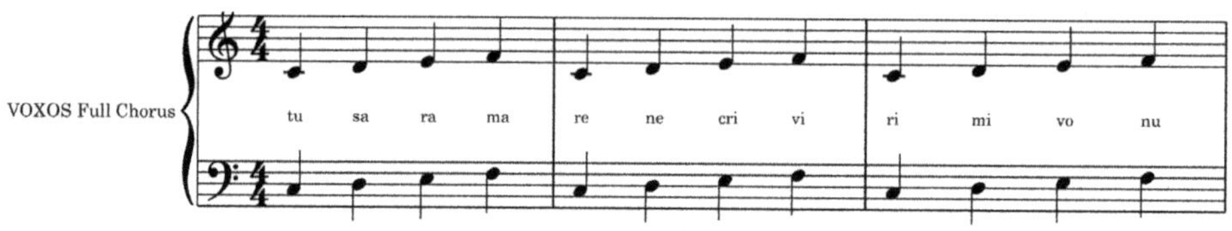

Voxos offers several other voices: Sopranos, Altos, Tenors, Basses, Boys Choir, Solo Soprano, and Solo Boy, but these will only voice ooh and ahh sounds.

The following chart lists the Full Chorus vowel sounds you can hear by entering them as lyrics:

A	E	I	O	U	Ca
Ta	Te	Di	Ky	Ti	Do
Tu	Sa	Ra	Ma	Re	Ne
Cri	Vi	Ri	Mi	Vo	Nu
Tis	Tus	Sact	Vos	Nus	Frayst

Tip #22 – Experiment with Pitches

It's not always obvious what is included with any given instrument. Case in point, CinePerc Monster Low Hits. Different drum sounds are included within the many octaves of the keyboard. Enter a note and slide it up and down to discover the range of notes available and what sounds are included.

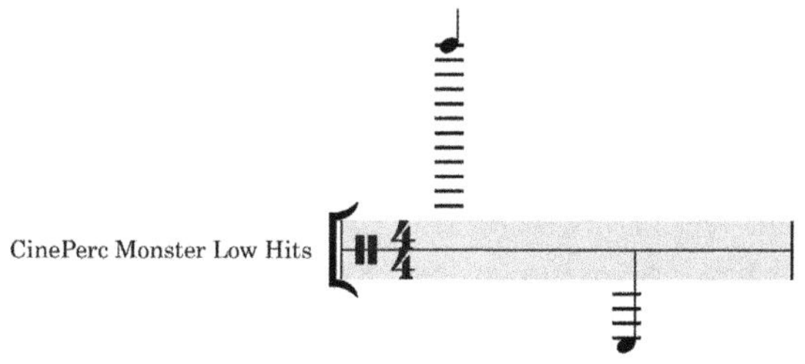

Chapter 14
StaffPad Reader

The StaffPad Reader app defines the future for performance and recording technology. Now, instead of reams of paper thrust upon each musician reading and performing the music, a digital tablet such as an iPad or Surface will sit on each player's music stand, turning pages for them, and updating notes right before their very eyes!

StaffPad Reader is a free app that runs on tablet devices (not phones). Each device will synchronize with the master score being run on one device hosting the StaffPad app. Each device must connect to the same Wi-Fi network that the StaffPad device is running on. The beauty of this setup is that an Internet connection is not required. In fact, it will work better if there is no interference from the Internet.

All that is required is a Wi-Fi router. A modem is not needed. As long as everyone logs into the same network, they can connect with StaffPad. The conductor (or whoever is running the session) will be viewing the master score on their StaffPad tablet.

Reader Menu

When you first start the Reader, you will see the Home page. It will instantly be searching for StaffPad to sync to. The "radar" icon in the center of the page will pulse to indicate that it is searching.

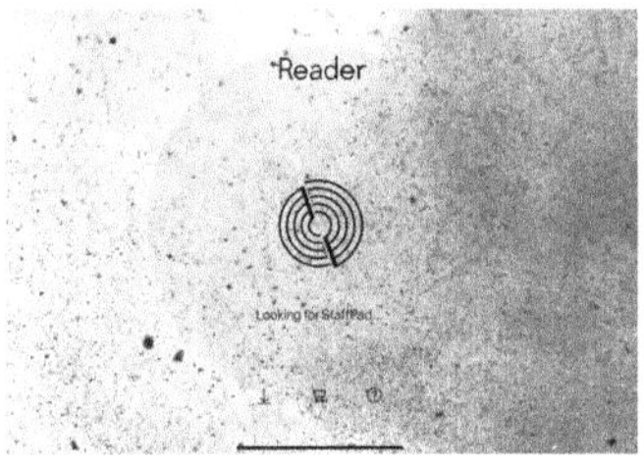

At the bottom of the Home page you will see three menu options.

Download, **Store**, and **Help**. Download allows you to view any score made available to you without the necessity of StaffPad to synchronize with. This way you are free to practice your part. The Toolbar will now include a Play button. The score will move along the bars in time. Turn on the metronome to hear a click. The Reader will not play any sounds (unless an In-App purchase is made. More info below).

Double-tap on a bar to begin playback from the beginning of that bar.

Main Toolbar

Once a score is opened, the Toolbar will contain the following buttons:

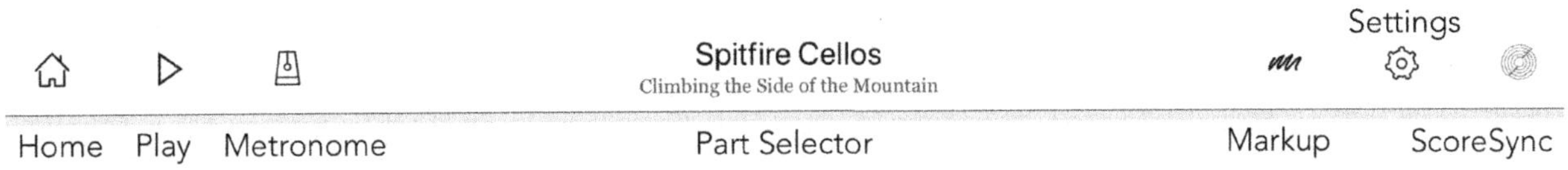

- **Home** - Returns to the Home page where you can download scores, access the Store, and get Help.
- **Play** - The play button will only be available when using imported scores. Scores synchronized with StaffPad will be controlled by StaffPad only.
- **Metronome** - Plays an audible click.
- **Part Selector** - Displays a list of parts available from the full score.
- **Markup** - Pens, private and public, for annotating the score.
- **Settings** - Configurable options for the app.
- **ScoreSync** - Will be highlighted once synchronized with StaffPad.

Annotation and the Ink Toolbar

Tap on the **Markup** button to access the pens. The toolbar will become an Ink Toolbar.

- **Close** - Dismisses the ink toolbar and returns to the main toolbar.
- **Undo** - Undoes the most recent inking actions.
- **Redo** - Redoes the previously undone actions.
- **Eraser** - Erases ink strokes.
- **Red pen** - This is the default pen and is private. Any annotations made with this pen are only seen by the Reader.
- **Gray pen** - This is a public pen. Any annotations made with this pen are visible on the StaffPad score and can be seen by anyone.
- **Yellow Highlighter** - This is also a private pen and can only be seen by the Reader.
- **Delete All** - Removes ALL markup. Use this carefully.

All annotations made on a part are saved with the Reader. The next time the same score is synchronized with the device the original annotations will be visible.

Start Your Engines

From the StaffPad app, tap the **ScoreSync** button on the Toolbar to activate synchronization for all Reader devices. When a Reader app starts it will immediately begin scanning for Staffpad's transmission.

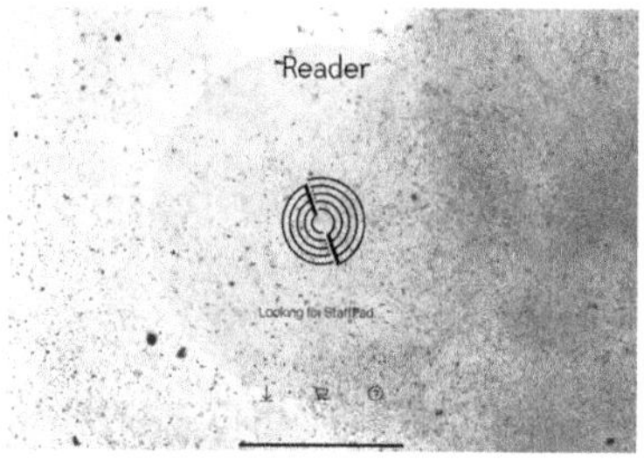

Once the signal is found it will begin to load the score and all its parts.

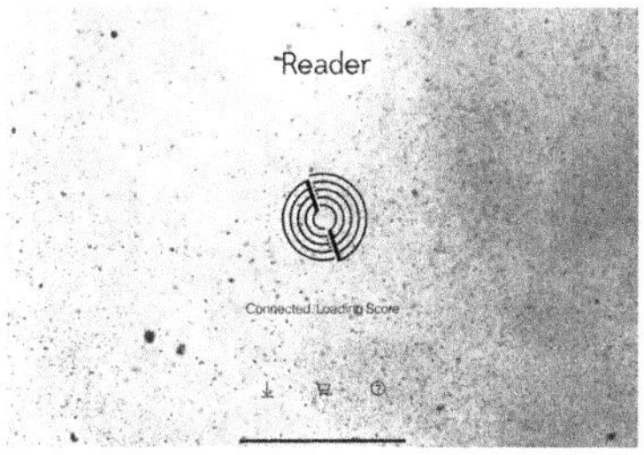

The name of the score will appear at the top of the screen. Below the title is the highlighted name of the default instrument. More on this in a minute. Below that is a scrollable list of other possible instrument parts to be chosen based on what is included in the score.

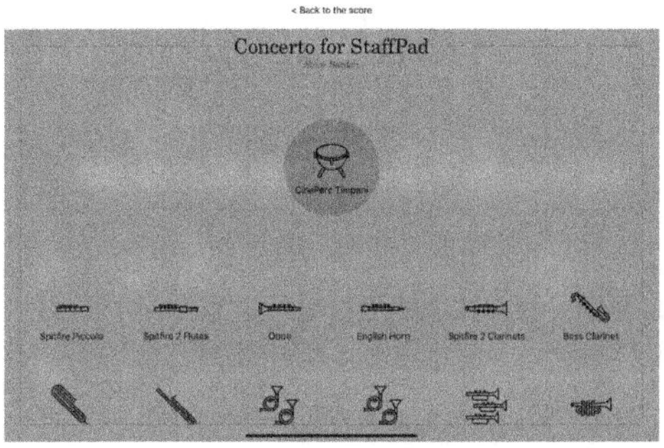

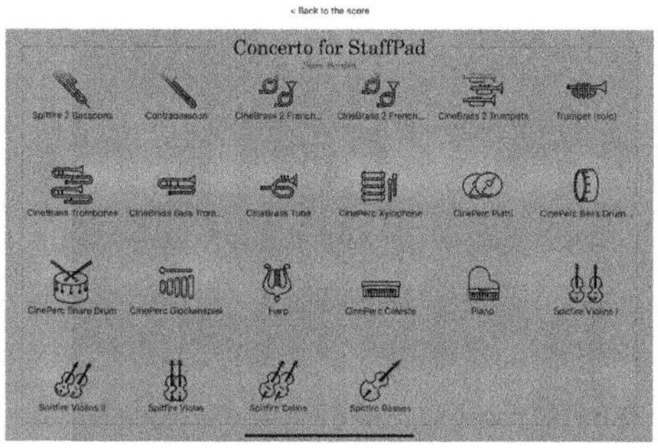

Select which instrument part to perform. Once you select an instrument it will become your default instrument and that instrument's part will open by default from now on. This can be changed in the Settings menu. More on this below.

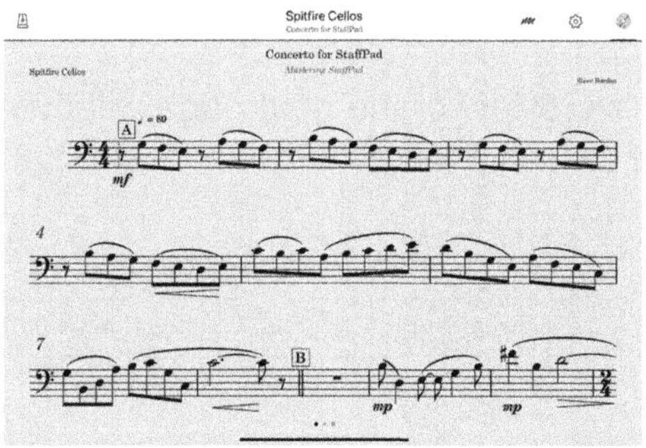

The first page of the part will display. The current instrument is displayed in the center of the Toolbar. Tapping on the instrument name will return you to the instrument selection page where you can choose a different instrument.

At the bottom of the page are dots indicating that there are additional pages in the score. You can manually swipe the screen to turn the pages, but during performance the pages will turn automatically! This feature can be disabled in Settings.

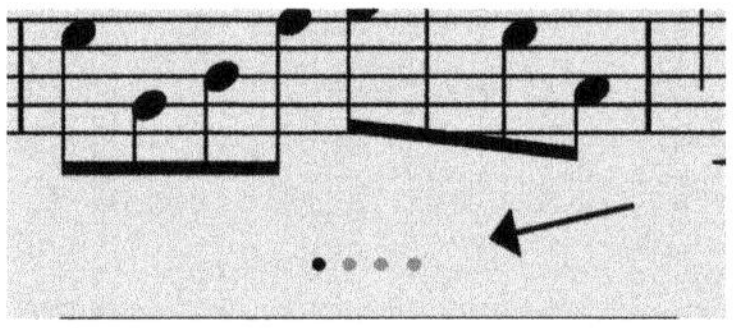

Ready, Set, Go!

When the conductor hits PLAY from StaffPad, the Reader's part will be synchronized. A shaded progress bar will move across the staff following the beat. As each new bar begins, the barline will highlight in blue. Although it may be difficult to see from this screenshot, bar 17 is highlighted and the shading of the measure has begun moving across beat 1.

As you reach the bottom of the page a preview of the next page will overlap at the top. In this next example, page 1 has reached the bottom stave (bar 7). Notice that bar 12 has appeared at the top.

Once bar 11 at the bottom concludes, the entirety of page 2 will be shown.

As soon as page 2 gets to the bottom stave (beginning with bar 24), page 3 will appear at the top (beginning with bar 28). The process will continue as long as there are additional pages to display.

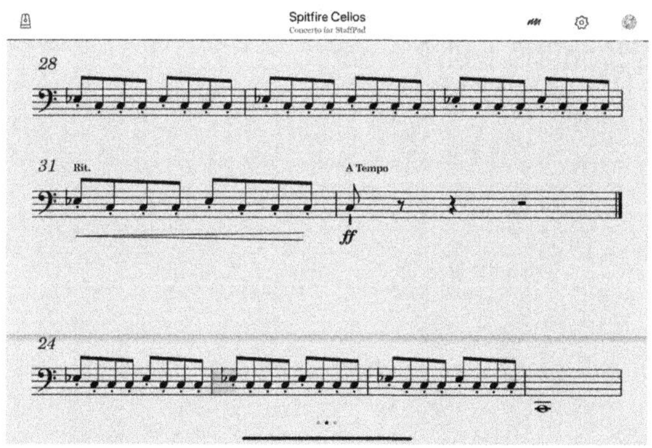

Keeping Time

Tap the metronome button in the Toolbar to hear a click. This will only sound when the conductor has begun playing the score. Even though you are visually able to see where you are, it's sometimes necessary to have an audible click track to follow. Your personal tablet's volume control will adjust the sound level.

Keeping the Lines of Communication Open

Any annotations the conductor writes on the score (public, not private) will be visible in the player's part.

Here's a scenario where the conductor has made an annotation on the cellist's part.

In real time, the annotation appears on the cellist's part.

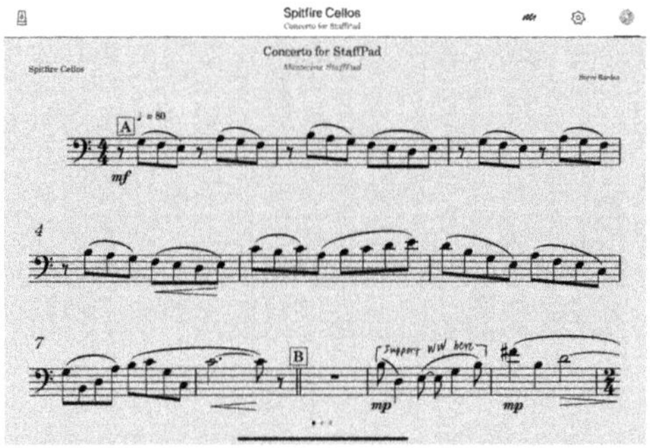

The cellist decides to correct the composer's suggested slurring in bar 5 by scribbling out the written slur and drawing a better version. She also offers a vote of confidence on bar 7 by commenting on the notes.

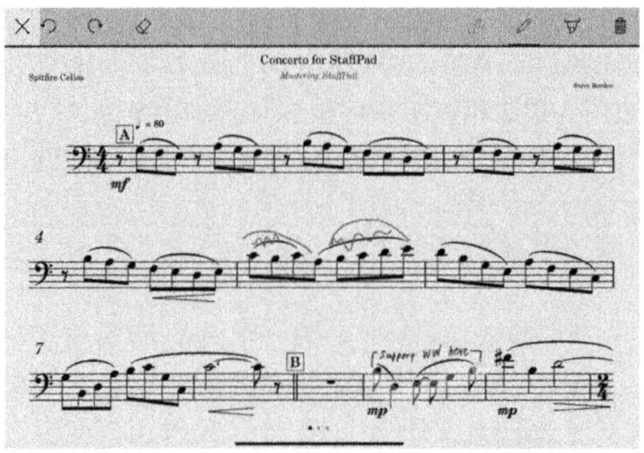

The player's annotations will appear in real time back on the conductor's score.

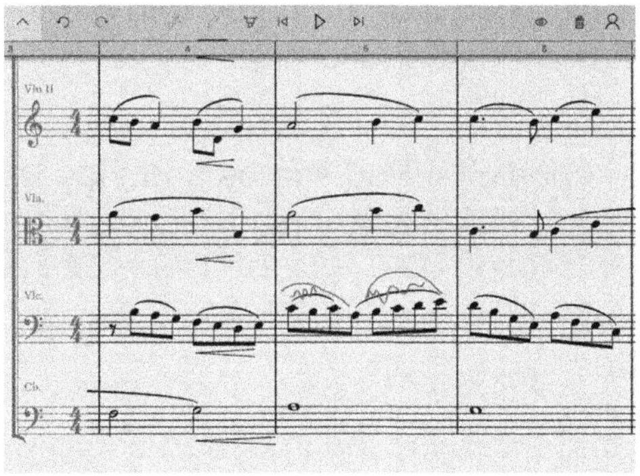

Viewing Options

Using pinch & zoom, there are three different scaling options for viewing the part. The zoom level is remembered between sessions.

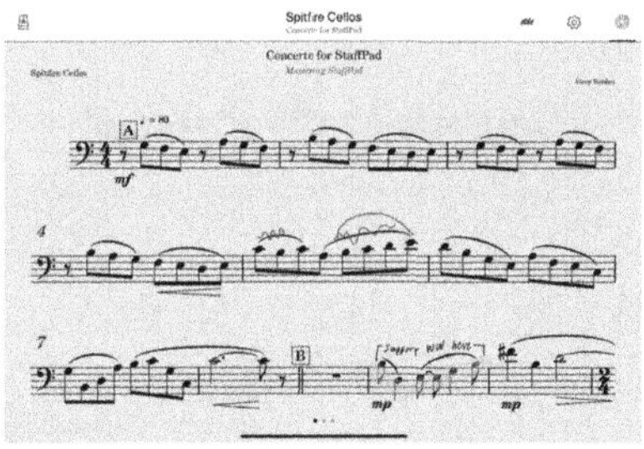

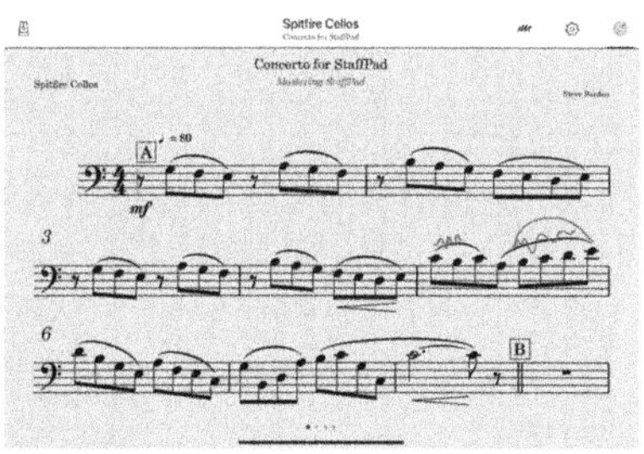

There is even a *dark mode* option for viewing in low light conditions. Dark mode is a feature only available as an In-App purchase (see below).

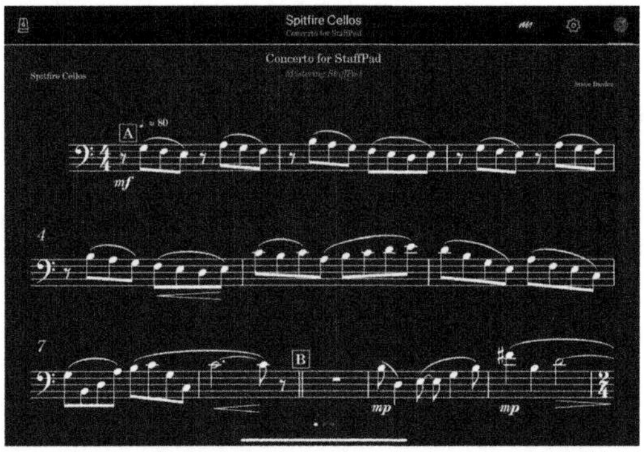

In-App Purchases

From the Home page, tap on the shopping cart icon at the bottom of the page to access the store. From here you can purchase a single upgrade that offers the following:

- **Full Playback** - allows you to import StaffPad scores and play them back with a collection of stock orchestral instruments, the same set of instruments included with the StaffPad app.
- **View the Full Score** - This gives you the ability to view the entire score, not just the individual parts.
- **ScoreSync** - This allows you to ScoreSync the imported score with other Readers without the need for StaffPad. Full synchronization between devices is possible.
- **Dark Mode** - Lets you invert the color from black-on-white to white-on-black for low light circumstances such as performing in a theatre.
- **Restore Purchases** - Completely restore the upgrade purchase. Useful when installing the app on a different device.

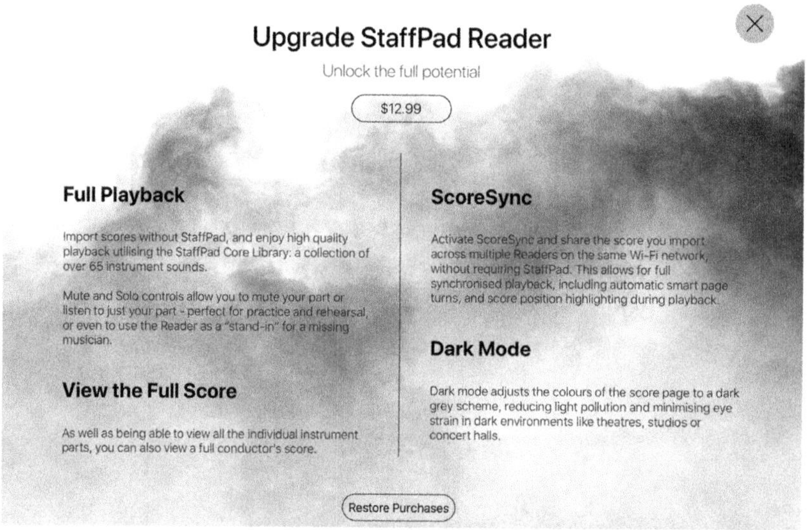

Settings

Tap on the gear icon on the Toolbar to open the Settings panel.

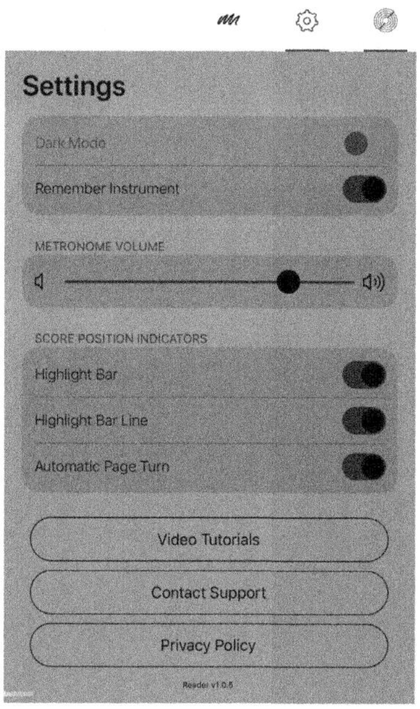

The following options are available:

- **Dark Mode** - Inverts the display from black-on-white to white-on-black for viewing in low light conditions (available only if purchased).

- **Remember Instrument** - The instrument you select will be remembered each time you use the Reader. You can always switch to a different instrument, but that will become the "remembered" instrument going forward.

- **Metronome Volume** - Adjusts the volume level of the metronome click for your device only.

- **Highlight Bar** - A "progress bar" will scroll across the currently playing bar as the music plays.

- **Highlight Bar Line** - As the music plays, a blue vertical barline will display in the currently playing bar.

- **Automatic Page Turn** - With this option turned on, a preview of the next page will overlap at the top of the page once the last stave on the page appears. If not activated, you must manually turn the page by swiping or connecting a Bluetooth page turning device.

In addition, there are three additional buttons:

- Video Tutorials - Displays useful videos about the Reader.
- Contact Support - Opens a browser window to contact StaffPad support.
- Privacy Policy - Opens a browser window displaying the company's privacy policy.

APPENDIX A

Add-on Sample Libraries

While it's entirely possible to work with only the included set of stock musical instruments in StaffPad, you may wish to enhance your soundset with professional sound libraries from some of the top virtual instrument companies in the world. While this list may be the available choices at the time of this writing, new libraries are expected to be added in the future.

CineSamples

CineBrass

Instruments

Solo Trumpet in Bb

2 Trumpets in Bb

Horn Solo

2 Horns

6 Horns

12 Horns

Trombone Solo

2 Trombones

Bass Trombone

Tuba

Features

True legato and espressivo legato interval sampling

Sustains with smooth dynamic morphing

True release samples to preserve the sound of the scoring stage

Speed controlled staccatos, spiccatos and staccatissimos

Marcato and Tenuto accent attacks

Recorded in a world-class scoring facility

Trills (semitone and whole tone)

Stopped/Muted sustains

Flutter/Rips

Natural release samples to preserve the sound of the scoring stage

CineWinds

Instruments

Piccolo

Flute

Alto Flute

Bass Flute

Oboe 1

Oboe 2

English Horn

Clarinet in Bb

Clarinet in Eb

Bass Clarinet

Contrabass Clarinet

Bassoon

Contrabassoon

Features

True Legato interval sampling

Re-bow samples for smooth connected repeated notes

Sustains with smooth dynamics morphing

Smooth dynamic morphing between multiple dynamic layers

Speed controlled Staccato/Staccatissimo

Tenuto/Marcato accents

Trills (Half Step and Whole Step)

Natural release samples to preserve the sound of the scoring stage

CineStrings

Instruments

1st Violins

2nd Violins

Violas

Cellos

Basses

Features

Vibrato and expressive sustains with up to 5 dynamic layers

Re-bow samples for smooth connected repeated notes

Natural true legato samples

True release samples to preserve the sound of the scoring stage

4x RR for staccato, staccatissimo, spiccato, accent, pizzicato and snap pizzicato

Tremolo

Trills (semitone and whole tone)

Pizzicato and Bartok (snap) Pizzicato

Col Legno

Harmonic sustains

CineStrings Solo

Instruments

Violin 1

Violin 2

Viola

Cello

Bass

Features

Sustains with multiple dynamic layers

Standard and expressive "seamless" true legatos

Speed controlled Spiccato/Staccatissimo

Marcato accents

Pizzicato

Bartok Pizzicato (Violin 2, Viola and Bass only)

Tremolos (Violins and Viola only)

CinePerc

Instruments

Timpani - Soft/Medium/Hard Mallets

Bass Drum 1 - 28in

Bass Drum 2 - 36in

Snare - Concert

Snare - Military

Snare - Piccolo

Snare - Tenor

Snare - Popcorn

Snare - Metal

Concert Toms

Concert Toms - Hits Only

Suspended Cymbals

Gongs + Tam Tam

Piatti Crash Cymbals

Orchestral Shakers

Orchestral Percussion Ensemble

Xylophone

Glockenspiel

Marimba

Crotales - Mallets

Crotales - Bowed

Vibraphone - Motor Off

Vibraphone - Motor On

Vibraphone - Bowed

Glass Marimba

Tubular Bells

Low Chimes

Celeste

Wood Blocks

Temple Blocks

Claves

Castanets

Guiro

Slapstick

Puili Sticks - Single

Puili Sticks - Group

Tickies

Anklungs

Apple Box

Hot Rods

Log Drum

Triangles

Mark Tree

Bell Tree

Sleigh Bells

Tambourines

Cow Bells

Ensemble Crashes

Ensemble Metal Hits

Single Metal Hits

Chain Hits

Cricket

Windchimes

Finger Cymbals

Circular Bells

Brake Drum

Suspended Cymbals - Scrapes

Suspended Cymbals - Bowed

Gongs + Tam Tam - Bowed and Scraped

Bongos

Congas

Doumbek + Darabuka

Bodhran

Frame Drums

Daff

Cajon

Timbales

Talking Drum

Udu

Whale Drum

Tongue Drum

Ocean Drum

Rain Sticks

Tambourika

Rikh

Bamboo Shaker

Plastic Pear + Turtle Shell Shakers

Cabasa

African Pod Shaker

Shakere

Jaw Bone

Small Metal Shaker

Vented Steel Orb Shaker

Caxixi

Ankle + Seed Rattle Shakers

Ganziro Shaker

Metal Shaker

Synthetic Shaker

Meinl Shaker

Agogo

Metal Bar Shaker

Monkey Stick

Asian Wooden Chimes

Small Flower Charm Chimes

Fish Bell Chimes

Samba Whistles

Cuica

Ensemble - Bass Drums + Crash

Ensemble - Mids + Highs

Ensemble - Mahler Hammers

Stomps

Taikos

Surdos

Roto Toms

Roto Toms - Hits Only

Octobans

Shime Daiko

Djembe

Gong Drum

Djun Djun

Oil Drum

Monster Low Hits

Monster Low Swooshes

Ratchet

Vibraslap

Sand Blocks

Waterphone - Dry

Waterphone - Water

Flexatone

Whistles

Typewriter

Keyboard + Mouse

Spring Drum

Lions Roar

Car Horn

Ensemble - Claps + Snaps

Bottle Caps + Lids

Washboard

Tines

Springs

Water Jugs

Prepared Piano + Bucket

Hammer Bolts + Nails

Buckets

Water Jars

Flower Pots

Glass Bottle Blows

Wooden Cricket

Features

Over 100 percussion instruments

Extensive use of StaffPad's unique Preset system

Various different mallets, sizes and techniques for each instrument

Recorded in a world-class scoring facility

Natural release samples to preserve the sound of the scoring stage

CineHarps

Instruments

Concert Harp 1

Harp 2

Harp 3

Features

Plucked Sustains (all harps)

Bisbigliando (tremolo) (Concert Harp)

Harmonics (Concert Harp)

Xylophonics (Concert Harp)

2 Additional Harp sizes and perspectives

CinePiano

Instruments

9 foot concert grand piano

Features

A huge recorded dynamic range, from intimate ppp to thundering fff

Additional mechanical noise layer for enhanced realism

A special “Cinematic” mix, featuring softer samples and more reverb - perfect for smaller moments

Recorded at the MGM Scoring Studios in Los Angeles by Dennis Sands

Natural release samples to preserve the sound of the scoring stage

Voxos

Instruments

Sopranos

Altos

Tenors

Basses

Full Choir Staff, including glissando, cluster and whisper FX

Boys Soprano (Treble)

Boys Alto

Boys Tenor

Boys Basses

Full Boys Choir Staff

Solo Female Soprano with Ah, Oo true legato and staccato

Solo Boy with Ahh legato

Features

True legato samples for connected “ooh” and “aah” vowel sustains

Ah and Oo vowels for all sections

Staccato and sustains for 30 vowel types (controlled via the lyrics feature within StaffPad)

Unpitched FX shouts and whispers (using X noteheads)

Full Choir and Full Boys Choir combined staff

Natural release samples to preserve the sound of the scoring stage

Orchestral Tools: The Berlin Series

Berlin Strings

Instruments

1st Violins (8 players)

2nd Violins (6 players)

Violas (5 players)

Celli (5 players)

Basses (4 players)

Features

Fluid true legato sampling, with repeated note legato, fast and slow transitions

Sustains with multiple dynamic layers and vibrato types

Multiple dynamic layers for every articulation

Trills (half step and whole step)

Speed controlled staccato, staccatissimo, spiccato

Marcato, portato and accented attacks

Harmonics (sustains and staccatos)

Pizzicato and Bartok Pizzicato

Col Legno

Fast run "blurred" articulations for increased realism for fast playing

Berlin Brass

Instruments

Horn 1

Horn 2

Horn 3

Horn 4

Horn Ensemble (a4)

Trumpet 1

Trumpet 2

Trumpet 3

Trumpet Ensemble (a3)

Trombone 1

Trombone 2

Bass Trombone

Trombone Ensemble (a2)

Tuba

Features

Adaptive Legato (Slurred Legato, Retongued Legato, Playable Runs)

Extensively sampled solo instruments for realistic voicings

Ensemble sections for Horns, Trumpets and Trombones

Multiple repetition samples

Speed controlled staccato and staccatissimo samples

Trills (semitone and whole tone)

"Zampano" Mariachi style playing for trumpets

Multiple dynamics layers

Recorded at Teldex Studios, Berlin

Berlin Woodwinds

Instruments

Piccolo Flute

Flute 1

Flute 2

Flute 3

Alto Flute

Oboe 1

Oboe 2

English Horn

Clarinet 1

Clarinet 2

Eb Clarinet

Bass Clarinet

Bassoon 1

Bassoon 2

Contrabassoon

Features

True Legato interval sampling

Re-tongue samples for smooth connected repeated notes

Multiple Round Robins for staccato, staccatissimo, spiccato and portato

Trills (half and whole tone)

Marcato accent attacks

Smooth dynamic morphing between multiple dynamic layers

Recorded at Teldex Studios, Berlin

Perfectly blends with Berlin Strings and Berlin Brass

Berlin Percussion

Instruments

Anvils and Brake Drums

Gran Casa (4 sizes)

Bell Trees (2 sizes)

Bird Call/Slide Whistle

Body Percussion

Bongos (2 sets)

Car Horns

Castanets

Celesta

Claves

Congas

Cow Bells

Crotales (including bowed)

Cuckoo whistle

Cymbals (4 sizes, multiple mallets)

Drum Sticks

Duck Call

Finger Cymbals

Fog Horn

Glockenspiel (multiple mallets)

Guiro

Headless Pop Tambourine

Mark Tree (2 sizes)

Piatti (3 sizes)

Railroad Crossing Bell

Rototoms (6 sizes)

Shaker (7 types)

Ships Bell

Sleigh Bells (3 sizes)

Snare Drums (7 sizes, wires on and off)

Tam Tams (4 sizes, multiple mallets)

Tambourines (2 sizes)

Temple Blocks (4 sets)

Thunder sheets (2 sizes)

Timbales (2 sizes)

Timpani (multiple mallets)

Toms (5 sizes)

Triangles (3 sizes)

Tubular Bells (multiple mallets)

Vibraphone (various mallets, rotor on/off)

Vibraslap (2 sizes)

Windmaker

Woodblocks

Xylophone

Features

Multiple repetition samples for all instruments

Different Mallets for respective instruments

Sizes and styles easily switchable through staff presets

Hits, rolls, muted hits, secco and many more articulations

Recorded at Teldex Studios, Berlin

Berlin Strings: First Chairs

Instruments

1st Violin

2nd Violin

Viola

Cello

Contrabass

Features

True Legato and Portamento interval sampling

Re-bow samples for smooth connected repeated notes

Trills (semitone and whole tone)

Tremolo

Pizzicato

Portato (short and long)

Accented sustains and legatos

Staccato and Spiccato (speed controlled)

Multiple Round Robins for staccato, staccatissimo, spiccato and portato

Smooth dynamic morphing between multiple dynamic layers

Recorded at Teldex Studio, Berlin

Perfectly blends with Berlin Strings

Berlin Symphonic Harps

Instruments

Harp 1

Harp 2

Features

Sustain, and damped sustain (secco)

True staccato with repetition samples

Harmonics

Bisbigliando (tremolo)

Glissandi

"Pres De La Table" (near the fingerboard)

Recorded at Teldex Studios, Berlin

The Orchestral Grand

Instruments

Steinway D

Steinway B

Sustaining "Intimate" Grand

Features

Three deep-sampled pianos with a unique sound character

Mechanical noises layer for extra realism

Multiple repetition samples for sustains and staccatos

Up to 8 dynamic layers

Recorded at Teldex Studios, Berlin

Spitfire

Spitfire Symphonic Strings

Instruments

Violins 1 (16)

Violins 2 (14)

Violas (10)

Cellos (8)

Basses (6)

Features

Sustains with multiple dynamic layers, with sul tasto, sul ponticello, and con sordino variants

True legato and portamento interval samples

Staccato/Staccatissimo/Spiccato short notes

Pizzicato and Bartok (snap) Pizzicato

Marcato and Tenuto attack

Tremolo

Trills (minor and major 2nd)

Harmonics, sustain and staccato

Spitfire Symphonic Woodwinds

Instruments

Piccolo

Flute

Flutes a2

Alto Flute

Bass Flute

Oboe

Oboes a2

Clarinet in Bb

Clarinets a2

Bass Clarinet

Contrabass Clarinet

Bassoon

Bassoons a2

Contrabassoon

Features

Sustains with multiple dynamic layers

True legato interval samples for increased realism

Flutter tongue sustains

Trills (semitone and whole tone)

Tenuto and Marcato accent attack

Harmonics for flutes

Spitfire Symphonic Brass

Instruments

Horn Solo

2 Horns (a2)

6 Horns (a6)

Trumpet Solo

2 Trumpets (a2)

6 Trumpets (a6)

Trombone Solo

2 Trombones (a2)

6 Trombones (a6)

Bass Trombone Solo

2 Bass Trombones (a2)

Contrabass Trombone Solo

Tuba Solo

Contrabass Tuba Solo

Cimbasso Solo

2 Cimbassi (a2)

Features

Sustains with multiple dynamic layers

True legato interval samples for Horns, Trumpets, and Tuba

Speed controlled Staccato/Staccatissimo

Tenuto and Marcato Accents

Rips and falls for most instruments

Trills (horns, trumpets only)

Flutter/Buzz (trombones and trumpets only)

Spitfire Symphonic Percussion

Instruments

Agogo

Anvils

Bass Drum

Bongos

Cabasa

Castanets

Celeste

Claves

Congas

Cowbells

Crotales

Suspended Cymbals

Desk Bells

Field Drums

Gankogui

Glockenspiel

Gong Drum

Guiro

Jawbone

Marimba

Mark Tree

Piatti

Rain Sheet

Ratchet

Rivet Cymbal

Rototoms

Shakers

Ships Bell

Sleigh Bells

Snare Drums

Tam Tam

Tambourines

Temple Blocks

Timbales

Timpani

Toms

Trash Metals

Triangles

Tubular Bells

Vibraphone

Wind Gong

Woodblocks

Xylophone

Features

A huge collection of 43 percussion instruments

Extensive use of StaffPad Presets for instrument mallet, size or technique choice

Up to 8 repetition samples and 8 dynamic layers per instrument

Beautiful and magical celeste and vibraphone

Recorded through a pristine signal path in The Hall at AIR Studios

Spitfire Chamber Strings

Instruments

Violins 1 (4)

Violins 2 (3)

Violas (3)

Cellos (3)

Basses (3)

Features

Fluid true legato sampling, with repeated note legato, fast and slow transitions

Multiple dynamic layers for every articulation

Steel Drums

Instruments

Steel drums

Features

Beautiful soft layers to searing metallic bites

Blends with Spitfire Audio's orchestral libraries

Union Chapel Organ

Instruments

Legendary London Organ

Features

Each manual and pedal stop combination is presented as separate presets

Originals: Felt Piano

Instruments

Upright piano with soft felt placed between the hammers and the strings

Features

Performed by jazz legend and Mercury Prize nominee Gwilym Simcock. Includes 4 Staff Presets; main piano; short staccato; reverse staccato and an ambient pad

StaffPad Ltd

Toy Glockenspiel

Instruments

Toy Glockenspiel

Features

Recorded in gorgeously wide stereo

2 repetition samples and 2 dynamics per note

Guitars, Vol. 1

Instruments

Fingerpicked nylon guitar

Mandolin

Ukulele

Charango

Clean electric Les Paul guitar

Features

Contains two dynamic layers

Separate staccato and tremolo articulation samples where appropriate

Accordion

Instruments

Musette Accordion

Features

A classic musette style accordion

Retro Keyboards

Instruments

Fender Rhodes

Wurlitzer A200

Hammond

Challen Upright

Features

Electric pianos recorded through a crunchy Watkins amp

A Hammond drawbar and tonewheel organ with switchable vibrato

Challen upright piano with honky-tonk sound

Antique Keys

Instruments

Dyson & Sons Dulcitone, 1910

German Celeste, 1960

English Spinet, 1718

Italian Harpsichord, 1579

Grand Piano, Erard

English Harpsichord, 1766

Dutch Harpsichord, 1628

Early Pianoforte, 1793

Pianoforte, 1848

English Spinet II, 1705

The German Lautenwerck

Italian Harpsichord II

French Harpsichord

The Orphica Piano

Italian Harpsichord III

German Theorbo-Harpsichord

Austrian Harpsichord

German Harpsichord, 1741

German Harpsichord, 1738

Features

Vast dynamic range - sampled with up to 32 dynamic layers per note

Recorded with vintage Neumann™ TLM170® microphones with Crane Song™ preamps and Universal Audio™ 2192® converters

Up to 8 release samples per key

Uniquely presented in the original tuning and ranges

Multiple presets per instrument for various stop and buffer configurations

Audioollie

Scoring Synths

Instruments

Bass Pluck

Bass Pluck Solo

Bass Solo

Bass Synth

Noise Drums

Hi Hats

Kick Drums

High Pads

Low Pads

Synth SFX

Stabs

Sub Exciters, Fillers and Drops

Swells

Synth Plucks

Synth Noise Taps

Tonal Percussion

Features

100 presets

Two iconic analogue synths

Worldised with amazing analog gear, in a great studio space

Recorded by Oliver Codd and Nick Spezia

Multiple presets per instrument for easy sound switching

APPENDIX B

Glossary

Common Musical Terms Used in Conjunction With Digital Music Production and Music Notation

A Tempo	Resume normal speed. This marking is used after a change of tempo, often a rallentando or a ritenuto, to indicate that a performer should return to the main tempo.
AAC	Advanced Audio Coding is an audio coding standard for lossy digital audio compression. Designed to be the successor of the MP3 format, AAC generally achieves higher sound quality than MP3 at the same bit rate. AAC has been standardized by ISO and IEC, as part of the MPEG-2 and MPEG-4 specifications.
Accelerando	accelerando (often abbreviated accel.) is an indication to gradually increase the tempo of a song until otherwise noted. The marking is often used in combination with a dotted line to indicate the length of passage over which it should occur. It may also be used in combination with the marking poco or molto: poco accelerando means 'get a little faster', while molto accelerando means 'get much faster'. Often an accelerando will lead to a new tempo.
Accidentals	An accidental is a note of a pitch (or pitch class) that is not a member of the scale or mode indicated by the most recently applied key signature. In musical notation, the sharp (♯), flat (♭), and natural (♮) symbols, among others, mark such notes—and those symbols are also called accidentals.
Adagietto	Fairly slow - usually means a slow tempo marking between Largo and Andante, but slightly faster than Adagio.
Adagio	A slow tempo marking between Largo and Andante. A composition written in a slow tempo, frequently the second movement of sonatas, symphonies, etc. Italian. A slow tempo. (1) played slowly, but not as slowly as largo (2) indication of tempo and is sometimes used to describe a slow movement, even when the indication of speed at the start of the movement may be different. The diminutive form adagietto is a little faster than adagio.
Algorithm	A process or set of rules to be followed in calculations or other problem-solving operations, especially by a computer.
Algorithmic Composition	Algorithmic composition is the technique of using algorithms to create music. Algorithms (or, at the very least, formal sets of rules) have been used to compose music for centuries; the procedures used to plot voice-leading in Western counterpoint, for example, can often be reduced to algorithmic determinacy.

Allegretto	In a moderately quick tempo, usually considered to be slightly slower than allegro but faster than andante.
Allegrissimo	A very fast tempo marking between Presto and Vivacissimo. Very fast, though slower than presto.
Allegro	*Fast, lively; also - cheerfully, joyfully, with joy.* Originally understood in the Baroque period as 'joyfully, cheerfully', the term has changed over the years and now generally relates to tempo - fast and lively.
Andante	An Italian word that means "walking", andante is a moderate tempo marking between Largo and Moderato. This tempo is typically between 76 and 108 beats per minute.
Andante moderato	Andante moderato has between 72-78 beats per minute.
Andantino	An indication to play in a relaxed, moderate tempo that is slightly faster than andante. Andantino is sometimes defined as slightly slower than andante, in which case its BPM is between 64-72.
Arpeggio	An arpeggio is a type of broken chord, in which the notes that spell a chord are played in a rising or descending order.
Arranger	A music arranger is someone who arranges a piece of music for a music director, music producer, conductor, a group of performers or a single performer. Most music arrangers know how to read and write music, have a good knowledge of music theory and know how to play several instruments.
Articulation	Articulation is a fundamental musical parameter that determines how a single note or other discrete event is sounded. Articulations primarily structure an event's start and end, determining the length of its sound and the shape of its attack and decay. They can also modify an event's timbre, dynamics, and pitch.
Artificial Intelligence	The theory and development of computer systems able to perform tasks that normally require human intelligence, such as visual perception, speech recognition, decision-making, and translation between languages.
Audio Bus	A mixing path allowing audio signals to be combined into a single sound source to create 'sub mixes'.
Automation	Automatically perform tasks over time, particularly moving knobs, faders, and switches for you. The most popular use of automation in mixing is to adjust the volume of a track.

Bar	A bar or measure is used in writing music. It is a way of organizing the written music in small sections. Each bar is a small amount of time. Most music has a regular beat (or pulse) which can be felt.
Bar Line	A bar line (or barline) is a single vertical line used to divide a musical staff into measures. In piano music – or any music in which a grand staff is used – bar lines connect both staves throughout the composition; these are called "systemic barlines."
Bar Number	Bars (or measures) are numbered in a sequence starting with bar 1. The exception is with pickup bars which are considered bar 0. The first full measure is bar 1.
Bass Trap	Bass traps are acoustic energy absorbers which are designed to damp low frequency sound energy with the goal of attaining a flatter low frequency (LF) room response by reducing LF resonances in rooms.
Beam	In musical notation, a beam is a horizontal or diagonal line used to connect multiple consecutive notes (and occasionally rests) to indicate rhythmic grouping. Only eighth notes (quavers) or shorter can be beamed. The number of beams is equal to the number of flags that would be present on an unbeamed note.
Bowing	A bow is a stick which is strung with hair. It is used to pull across the strings of a string instrument such as a violin, viola, cello or double bass.
BPM	Beats per minute (bpm) is a unit typically used as a measure of tempo in music and heart rate. The bpm tempo of a piece of music is conventionally shown in its score as a metronome mark.
Brass	A brass instrument is a musical instrument that produces sound by sympathetic vibration of air in a tubular resonator in sympathy with the vibration of the player's lips. Brass instruments are also called labrosones, literally meaning "lip-vibrated instruments."
Broadcast Quality	Indicates the level of musical audio quality meeting the expectations of the television broadcast industry.
CC Controller	In MIDI terms, a continuous controller (CC) is a MIDI message capable of transmitting a range of values, usually 0-127. ... CC's are commonly used for things like MIDI controlling volume (#7), pan (#10), data slider position (#6), mod wheel (#1) and other variable parameters.
Chord	Any harmonic set of pitches consisting of multiple notes that are heard as if sounding simultaneously. For many practical and theoretical purposes, arpeggios and broken chords, or sequences of chord tones, may also be considered as chords.

Chorus	A distinct section in a musical composition that is repeated multiple times. The chorus complements the other sections including the verse and bridge.
Clef	A musical clef is a symbol that is placed at the left-hand end of a staff, indicating the pitch of the notes written on it. It is essential for a musician to be able to read the music in front of them, as it tells them which lines or spaces represent each note. There are many types of clefs, but the four that are regularly used in modern music are Treble, Bass, Alto, and Tenor.
Click Book	A tool used by film composers, a click book contains tables of timings with each page in the book showing timings for one particular tempo, calibrated in film frames divided into eighths of a frame. The first click book was assembled by music editor Carroll Knudson in 1965.
Cloud Storage	Cloud storage is a cloud computing model in which data is stored on remote servers accessed from the Internet, or "cloud." It is maintained, operated and managed by a cloud storage service provider on storage servers that are built on virtualization techniques.
Coda	A passage that brings a piece to an end. Technically, it is an expanded cadence. It may be as simple as a few measures, or as complex as an entire section.
Common Time	Common time, also known as time, is a meter with four quarter-note beats per measure. It's often symbolized by the common-time symbol.
Compression	Compression is the process of lessening the dynamic range between the loudest and quietest parts of an audio signal. This is done by boosting the quieter signals and attenuating the louder signals.
Continuous Controller	See *CC Controller*.
Convolution Reverb	In audio signal processing, convolution reverb is a process used for digitally simulating the reverberation of a physical or virtual space through the use of software profiles; a piece of software (or algorithm) that creates a simulation of an audio environment.
Copyright	The exclusive legal right, given to an originator or an assignee to print, publish, perform, film, or record literary, artistic, or musical material, and to authorize others to do the same.
Counter Melody	A subordinate melody accompanying a principal one. See also *Counterpoint*.
Counterpoint	The art or technique of setting, writing, or playing a melody or melodies in conjunction with another, according to fixed rules.

Crescendo	The Italian musical term crescendo (abbreviated cresc.) is an indication to gradually increase the volume of a song until otherwise noted. A crescendo is marked by a horizontal, opening angle which may be followed by another dynamics command. It is the opposite of diminuendo and, of course, decrescendo.
Cue	Originating in theatre, a music cue is a visual or aural signal for an action to occur, either by an actor or stage hand, or for an actor to deliver a line. In film and production music, the piece of music being used is referred to as a 'cue'.
Cue Sheets	Cue sheets are the primary means by which performing rights organizations track the use of music in films and TV. Without cue sheets, it would be nearly impossible for such composers and publishers to be compensated for their work. An accurately filled out cue sheet is a log of all the music used in a production.
Cut Time	Alla breve – also known as cut time or cut common time – is a musical meter notated by the time signature symbol (¢), which is the equivalent of ($^2/_2$). The term is Italian for "on the breve", originally meaning that the beat was counted on the breve. Alla breve is a "simple-duple meter with a half-note pulse".
Dal Segno	Italian for "from the sign," refers to a symbol or navigation marker that instructs a musician to repeat a passage starting from the sign. In word form, it is most often abbreviated D.S. in musical notation or just called a segno in English.
DAW	A digital audio workstation (DAW) is a computer that is specially equipped with a high-quality sound card and programming for editing and processing digital audio at a professional level. Digital audio workstations can range from a simple two-channel editor to a complete digital recording studio suite.
Decrescendo	Decrescendo (abbreviated decresc.) is an indication to gradually decrease the volume of the music. The musical symbol for decrescendo is a narrowing angle, often followed by another dynamics command. It is the opposite of crescendo. Also known as: diminuendo (Italian).
Denominator	The Numerator in the time signature indicates the number of beats in a measure. It is the type of note which equals 1 beat. For example, in 3/2, there are 3 beats per measure and a half note (2) represents one beat. The Denominator indicates which type of note receives one beat. See also *Numerator.*
Digital Audio	In sound recording and reproduction systems, digital audio refers to a digital representation of the audio waveform for processing, storage or transmission. When analog sound waves are stored in digital form, each digital audio file can be decomposed into a series of samples.
Digital Samples	A sample is a digital representation of an analog signal. Both digital video and digital audio files are created using samples.

Diminuendo	Diminuendo (abbreviated dim.) literally means "diminishing," and is an indication to gradually decrease the volume of the music. The musical symbol for diminuendo is a closing angle, often followed by another dynamics command. Opposite of crescendo.
Divisi	Used as a direction in music for orchestral players reading the same musical staff to divide into two or more voice parts. Abbreviation div.
Doits, Falls, Plops and Scoops	Jazz articulations to direct the musician to scoop into or away or drop into or away from a note. Funny names but cool because it's jazz.
Double Flat	A double-flat is the equivalent of two flats and lowers a note's pitch by two half steps. The double-flat symbol (𝄫) is placed before a note like other accidentals.
Double Sharp	A double-sharp is an accidental for a note that has two sharps, meaning the original note is raised by two half-steps (also called semitones). The double-sharp symbol resembles a bold letter "x" and is placed before a notehead, similar to other accidentals.
Dynamics	The dynamics of a piece is the variation in loudness between notes or phrases. Dynamics are indicated by specific musical notation, often in some detail.
Edit Points	A musically logical place where a music editor can cut the cue to fit within the context of the visuals.
EDM	Electronic Dance Music (EDM) is popular music intended for dancing to in clubs, typically having a repetitive beat and a synthesized backing track.
Eighth note	An eighth note, also called a quaver is a note played for one eighth the duration of a whole note (semibreve). It lasts a quarter of the duration of a half note (minim) and half of the duration of a quarter note (crotchet). In 4/4 time a whole note lasts for four beats. An eighth note lasts for half a beat.
Endings	The ending is the conclusion of a composition and may take the form of a coda or outro. Pieces using sonata form typically use the recapitulation to conclude a piece, providing closure through the repetition of thematic material from the exposition in the tonic key.
Expression	Musical expression is the art of playing or singing with a personal response to the music. At a practical level, this means making appropriate use of dynamics, phrasing, timbre and articulation to bring the music to life. In the world of digital MIDI music, expression is represented by CC 11.
Fermata	A fermata (Italian: "from fermare, to stay, or stop"); also known as a hold, pause, colloquially a birdseye or cyclops eye, or as a grand pause when placed on a note or a rest is a symbol of musical notation indicating that the note should be prolonged beyond the normal duration its note value would indicate.

Film Composer	The composer assigned to create an original piece of music to accompany a film. See also *Music Score.*
Fingerprint	Digital fingerprinting is the identification of large data files or structures using truncated information. A fingerprinting algorithm is one that reduces a larger data set to a very small data set, sometimes called a bit string, to promote efficient identification and search protocols.
Flag	The mark added to a note stem to indicate the beat division of that note. A flag added to any note will cut the duration of that note in half. For example a quarter note with a flag added to it is one half the duration of the quarter note (i.e., eighth note). If adjacent pitches contain flags, they can be connected by beams for better legibility. One flag denotes an eighth note, two flags equals a sixteenth note, three flags equals a thirty-second note, four flags equals a sixty-fourth note, and five flags equals a one hundred twenty-eighth note.
Flat	Flat means "lower in pitch by one semitone (half step)", notated using the symbol ♭ which is derived from a stylised lowercase 'b'.
Form	Musical form (or musical architecture) refers to the overall structure or plan of a piece of music, and it describes the layout of a composition as divided into sections.
Forte	A musical dynamic meaning "loudly" or "strong".
Fortisissimo	Fortississimo is an indication to play as loudly as possible; louder than fortissimo.
Fortissimo	Fortissimo is a dynamic marking that indicates a VERY LOUD volume. It is one step up from forte, which means loud.
Genre	A music genre is a conventional category that identifies some pieces of music as belonging to a shared tradition or set of conventions. It is to be distinguished from musical form and musical style, although in practice these terms are sometimes used interchangeably.
Glissando	A glissando (Italian: [glisˈsando]; plural: glissandi, abbreviated gliss.) is a glide from one pitch to another. It is an Italianized musical term derived from the French glisser, "to glide". In some contexts, it is distinguished from the continuous portamento.
Grace note	A grace note is a kind of music notation denoting several kinds of musical ornaments. It is usually printed smaller to indicate that it is melodically and harmonically nonessential.
Grave	The slowest tempo in music. A directive to perform a certain passage of a composition in a solemn, grave, or slow manner. An extremely low pitch. Heavy, slow, ponderous in movement.

Hairpin	The terms crescendo, and diminuendo (or sometimes decrescendo), mean a gradual getting louder or softer. They can also be shown by signs known as "hair-pins". A hairpin opening out is a crescendo, one which closes is a diminuendo.
Half note	A half note (American) or minim (British) is a note played for half the duration of a whole note (or semibreve) and twice the duration of a quarter note (or crotchet).
Handwriting Recognition	Handwriting recognition (HWR), also known as Handwritten Text Recognition (HTR), is the ability of a computer to receive and interpret intelligible handwritten input from sources such as paper documents, photographs, touchscreens and other devices.
Harmon Mute	The Wah-wah mute (also known by the brand name Harmon) is a hollow, bulbous mute in two parts. Unlike the more common straight or cup mutes, the Harmon mute has a solid ring of cork that completely blocks the air leaving the bell, forcing all of it into the mute.
Harmonic Note	A note based on the overtone series, ie, a sequence of frequencies in which each frequency is a multiple of the fundamental pitch. On guitar, for example, harmon-ics can be achieved by lightly touching the string above the 7th or 12th fret.
Harmony	Harmony is the process by which the composition of individual sounds, or super-positions of sounds, is analyzed by hearing. Usually, this means simultaneously occurring frequencies, pitches, or chords.
Hybrid	A mixture of traditional orchestral instruments and contemporary synthesized instrument sounds.
Improvise	Musical improvisation (also known as musical extemporization) is the creative activity of immediate ("in the moment") musical composition, which combines per-formance with communication of emotions and instrumental technique as well as spontaneous response to other musicians.
In the Box	The ability to produce music entirely within the confines of a computer without any extra-neous outboard sound processing.
Instrumentation	The particular instruments used in a piece of music; the manner in which a piece is arranged for instruments.
Interval	An interval is the difference in pitch between two sounds. An interval may be described as horizontal, linear, or melodic if it refers to successively sounding tones, such as two adjacent pitches in a melody, and vertical or harmonic if it per-tains to simultaneously sounding tones, such as in a chord.
Key Signature	Any of several combinations of sharps or flats after the clef at the beginning of each stave indicating the key of a composition.

Keyswitches	Specific notes assigned on a musical keyboard to trigger alternate sounds and articulations of a sample library instrument.
Larghetto	A tempo not quite as slow as largo. Larghetto is between 60 and 66 beats per minute. Somewhat slowly, not as slow as largo.
Larghissimo	An extremely slow tempo, slower than largo. Larghissimo is 40 beats per minute or less.
Largo	A very slow tempo. In Italian, the word means broad. Large, broad, slow and stately.
Lasso	A lasso is a metaphor for the technique for selecting a group of things such as musical notes to be edited.
Legato	Legato ([le'ga:to]; Italian for "tied together"; French lié; German gebunden) indicates that musical notes are played or sung smoothly and connected. That is, the player makes a transition from note to note with no intervening silence. Legato technique is required for slurred performance, but unlike slurring (as that term is interpreted for wind instruments), legato does not forbid rearticulation.
Lento	At a slow tempo.
Loops	A short piece of music, often one to four measures in length, that is repeated continuously.
Major Key	A key signature whose harmony is based on the major scale.
Marcato	Marcato (short form: Marc.; Italian for marked) is a musical instruction indicating a note, chord, or passage is to be played louder or more forcefully than the surrounding music. The instruction may involve the word marcato itself written above or below the staff or it may take the form of the symbol ʌ, an open vertical wedge. The marcato is essentially a louder version of the regular accent > (an open horizontal wedge).
Marcia moderato	Moderately, in the style of a march (83–85 BPM).
Martellato	Indicates that the note is strongly accented, or hammered out, as to bowed string instruments and the piano.
Mastering	A form of audio post production, mastering is the process of preparing and transferring recorded audio from a source containing the final mix to a data storage device (the master); the source from which all copies will be produced (via methods such as pressing, duplication or replication).
Measure	See *Bar*.

Melody	A melody, also tune, voice or line, is a linear succession of musical tones that the listener perceives as a single entity. In its most literal sense, a melody is a combination of pitch and rhythm, while more figuratively, the term can include successions of other musical elements such as tonal color.
Metronome	A device that produces an audible click or other sound at a regular interval that can be set by the user, typically in beats per minute (BPM). Musicians use the device to practice playing to a regular pulse.
Mezzo Forte	Moderately loud. Louder than mezzo piano (mp) and softer than forte (f).
Mezzo Piano	Moderately soft. Louder than piano (p) and softer than mezzo forte (mf).
Microphone	An instrument for converting sound waves into electrical energy variations, which may then be amplified, transmitted, or recorded.
Middle C	Middle C is the name given to the musical note C which is in the middle of the piano keyboard. It is not actually quite the middle note of the keyboard, but very nearly, and of all the Cs on the piano it is the one nearest to the middle.
MIDI	MIDI (Musical Instrument Digital Interface) is a technical standard that describes a protocol, digital interface and connectors and allows a wide variety of electronic musical instruments, computers and other related devices to connect and communicate with one another.
MIDI Keyboard	A piano-style user interface keyboard device used for sending MIDI signals or commands over a USB or MIDI cable to other devices connected and operating on the same MIDI protocol interface.
Minor Key	A key signature whose harmony is based on a minor scale. Minor scales are natural minor, melodic minor, and harmonic minor.
Mixing	The process of blending all the individual tracks in a recording to create a version of the song that sounds as good as possible – the "mix". The process can include: balancing the levels of the tracks that have been recorded. Fine-tuning the sound of each instrument or voice using equalization (EQ).
Moderato	A moderate tempo that is slower than allegretto but faster than andante.
Modulation	The process of changing from one key (tonic, or tonal center) to another. This may or may not be accompanied by a change in key signature. Modulations articulate or create the structure or form of many pieces, as well as add interest.

Molto accelerando	It may also be used in combination with the marking poco or molto: poco accelerando means 'get a little faster', while molto accelerando means 'get much faster'. Often an accelerando will lead to a new tempo. For example, a piece may begin adagio and an accelerando will lead seamlessly to a new tempo such as allegro.
Molto rallentando	A rallentando is a gradual slowdown in tempo. Molto means 'very much'. Molto Rallentando is a dramatic decrease in tempo or slowing down.
Molto ritardando	Slow down a lot.
Mood	A temporary state of mind or feeling that occurs from hearing a particular piece of music.
Mordent	A mordent is an ornament indicating that the note is to be played with a single rapid alternation with the note above or below. Like trills, they can be chromatically modified by a small flat, sharp or natural accidental.
MP3	Stands for "MPEG Audio Layer-3." MP3 is a compressed audio file format developed by the Moving Picture Experts Group (MPEG). A typical MP3 file sounds similar to the original recording but requires significantly less disk space. MP3 files are often about one tenth the size of an uncompressed WAV or AIFF file, which have the same audio quality as a CD.
Music Composition	Musical composition can refer to an original piece of music, either a song or an instrumental music piece, the structure of a musical piece, or the process of creating or writing a new song or piece of music. People who create new compositions are called composers.
Music Copyist	Those who are employed by the music industry to produce neat copies from a composer's or arranger's manuscript.
Music Cue	The common term for a piece of music that is used in a television show or film. Also referred to as 'music track'.
Music Editor	A type of sound editor in film or other multimedia productions (e.g. video or games) responsible for compiling, editing, and syncing music during the production of a soundtrack.
Music Engraving	Music engraving is the art of drawing music notation at high quality for the purpose of mechanical reproduction. The term music copying is almost equivalent—though music engraving implies a higher degree of skill and quality, usually for publication.
Music Score	A music score (also sometimes called background score, background music, movie soundtrack, film music or incidental music) is original music written specifically to accompany a film by a music composer.

MusicXML	MusicXML is an XML-based file format for representing Western musical notation. The format is open, fully documented, and can be freely used under the W3C Community Final Specification Agreement.
Musical Palette	A sonic palette that identifies a set of musical instruments whose combination defines the sound, or "color" of the music.
Mute	A mute is a device fitted to a musical instrument to alter the sound produced: by affecting the timbre, reducing the volume, or most commonly both. The use of a mute is usually indicated in musical notation by the Italian direction con sordino and removed with the direction senza sordino or via sordino.
Natural	In music theory, a natural is an accidental which cancels previous accidentals and represents the unaltered pitch of a note. A note is natural when it is neither flat or sharp. Natural notes are the notes A, B, C, D, E, F, and G represented by the white keys on the keyboard of a piano or organ.
Note Head	A notehead is the part of a note, usually elliptical in shape, whose placement on the staff indicates the pitch, to which modifications are made that indicate duration. Noteheads may be the same shape but colored completely black or white, indicating the note value.
Numerator	Top Number/Numerator: Number of beats per measure. Bottom Number/Denominator: Type of note which equals 1 beat. The Numerator in the time signature indicates the number of beats in a measure. For example, in 3/2, there are 3 beats per measure and a half note (2) represents one beat. The Denominator indicates which type of note receives one beat. See also *Denominator*.
Octave	An octave or perfect octave is the interval between one musical pitch and another with double its frequency. The octave relationship is a natural phenomenon that has been referred to as the "basic miracle of music", the use of which is "common in most musical systems".
Orchestration	The arrangement or scoring of music for orchestral performance. See also *Instrumentation*.
Orchestrator	An orchestrator is a trained musical professional who assigns instruments from an orchestra or other musical ensemble to a piece of music written by a composer, or who adapts music composed for another medium for an orchestra.
Ostinato	An ostinato is a motif or phrase that persistently repeats in the same musical voice, frequently in the same pitch.
Pan; Panning	Panning is when you alter the volume of one or the other so that the sound is more prominent on one side or another. For example, if you record drums with two overhead mics it is common to pan the signal from the left mic to only the left speaker and the signal from the right mic to the right speaker.

Pedals and Retakes	A sustain pedal or sustaining pedal (also called damper pedal, loud pedal, or open pedal) is the most commonly used pedal in a modern piano. It is typically the rightmost of two or three pedals. When pressed, the sustain pedal "sustains" all the damped strings on the piano by moving all the dampers away from the strings and allowing them to vibrate freely. All notes played will continue to sound until the vibration naturally ceases, or until the pedal is released. The pedal release is notated as a "retake".
Percussion	A percussion instrument is a musical instrument that is sounded by being struck or scraped by a beater including attached or enclosed beaters or rattles struck, scraped or rubbed by hand or struck against another similar instrument.
Pianisissimo	(ppp) Very, very soft. Softer than pianissimo.
Pianissimo	(pp) Very softly; softer than piano, but louder than pianississimo.
Piano (dynamic)	(p) Soft. Louder than pianissimo (pp) but softer than mezzo piano (mp).
Pickup	An anacrusis (also known as a pickup, or fractional pickup) is a note or sequence of notes, a motif, which precedes the first downbeat in a bar in a musical phrase.
Pitch	Pitch is a perceptual property of sounds that allows their ordering on a frequency-related scale, or more commonly, pitch is the quality that makes it possible to judge sounds as "higher" and "lower" in the sense associated with musical melodies.
Plugin	An audio plugin, in computer software, is a plugin that can add or enhance audio-related functionality in a computer program. Such functionality may include digital signal processing or sound synthesis.
Poco accelerando	Get a little faster.
Poco rallentando	Perform a certain passage of a composition with a gradual slowing of the tempo.
Poco ritardando	Slow down a little.
Poco stringendo	Progressively quickening in tempo a little.
Portamento	Portamento (plural: portamenti, from old Italian: portamento, meaning "carriage" or "carrying") is a pitch sliding from one note to another.
Prestissimo	A directive to perform a certain passage of a composition very, very fast; as fast as possible; faster than presto.
Presto	Perform the indicated passage of a composition very quickly. Faster than allegro.

Production Music	Production music (also known as stock music or library music) is the name given to recorded music that can be licensed to customers for use in film, television, radio and other media. Oftentimes, the music is produced and owned by production music libraries.
Public Domain	The status of a literary work or an invention whose copyright or patent has expired or that never had such protection.
Publisher	A music publisher (or publishing company) is responsible for ensuring the songwriters and composers receive payment when their compositions are used commercially.
Quarter note	A quarter note or crotchet is a note played for one quarter of the duration of a whole note. Often, musicians will say that a crotchet is one beat, but this is not always correct, as the beat is indicated by the time signature of the music; a quarter note may or may not be the beat.
Rallentando	A direction to reduce tempo, often abbreviated to *rall*. In the 18th century the form lentando was common. Rallentando itself is of relatively recent usage, being scarcely encountered in scores before the 19th century; now it is perhaps the most common of such terms, though ritardando and ritenuto both occur frequently.
Recording Interface	An audio interface is a piece of hardware that expands and improves the sonic capabilities of a computer. Some audio interfaces give you the ability to connect professional microphones, instruments and other kinds of signals to a computer, and output a variety of signals as well.
Rehearsal mark	Rehearsal marks consist of one or more letters and/or numbers, and appear in sequence in the score—e.g. A, B, C..., or 1, 2, 3... etc. Alternatively, they may display measure numbers (usually larger than standard measure numbers, boldface and/or enclosed in boxes).
Repeat	A repeat sign is a sign that indicates a section should be repeated. If the piece has one repeat sign alone, then that means to repeat from the beginning, and then continue on (or stop, if the sign appears at the end of the piece). A corresponding sign facing the other way indicates where the repeat is to begin. These are similar to the instructions *da capo* and *dal segno*.
Reverb	Reverb occurs when a sound hits any hard surface and reflects back to the listener at varying times and amplitudes to create a complex echo, which carries information about that physical space. Reverb pedals or effects simulate or exaggerate natural reverberations.
Rhythm	Rhythm is the pattern of regular or irregular pulses caused in music by the occurrence of strong and weak melodic and harmonic beats.

Ritardando	Ritardando (or rit.) is an indication to gradually decrease the tempo of the music (opposite of accelerando). The length of a ritardando is extended by a dashed, horizontal line; and, if applicable, the previous tempo may be restored with the commands *tempo primo* or *a tempo*.
Sample Library	A sample library is a collection of digital sound recordings, known as samples, for use by composers, arrangers, performers, and producers of music. The sound files are loaded into a sampler—either hardware or software-based—which is then used to create music.
Sample Player	A sample player ("sampler") is an electronic or digital musical instrument similar in some respects to a synthesizer, but instead of generating new sounds with filters and oscillators, it uses sound recordings (or "samples") of real instrument sounds (e.g., a piano, violin or trumpet), excerpts from recorded songs or other sounds. The samples are loaded or recorded by the user or by a manufacturer. These sounds are then played back by means of the sampler program itself, a MIDI keyboard, sequencer or another triggering device to perform or compose music. A single sample may often be pitch-shifted to different pitches to produce musical scales and chords.
Sample Rate	Sample rate is the number of samples of audio carried per second, measured in Hz or kHz (one kHz being 1,000 Hz). For example, 44,100 samples per second can be expressed as either 44,100 Hz, or 44.1 kHz. Bandwidth is the difference between the highest and lowest frequencies carried in an audio stream.
Scale	In music theory, a scale is any set of musical notes ordered by fundamental frequency or pitch. A scale ordered by increasing pitch is an ascending scale, and a scale ordered by decreasing pitch is a descending scale.
Scoring	The job of composing music to visuals, such as film and television. See also *Music Score.*
Section	See *Form*.
Segno	The musical term dal segno, which is Italian for "from the sign," refers to a symbol or navigation marker that instructs a musician to repeat a passage starting from the sign. In word form, it is most often abbreviated D.S. in musical notation or just called a segno in English.
Sforzando	Sforzando (sfz) is an indication to make a strong, sudden accent on a note or chord. Sforzando literally means subito forzando (fz), which translates to "suddenly with force."
Sharp	Sharp means higher in pitch. More specifically, in musical notation, sharp means "higher in pitch by one semitone". Sharp is the opposite of flat, which is a lowering of pitch. An associated sharp symbol that resembles the number sign "#" occurs in key signatures or as an accidental.

Sheet Music	Sheet music is a handwritten or printed form of musical notation that uses musical symbols to indicate the pitches, rhythms or chords of a song or instrumental musical piece.
Shuffle	Shuffle rhythm is a specific 8th note rhythmic feel. It is based on triplet subdivisions of the beat rather than on dividing each beat perfectly in half (a.k.a. straight 8th notes).
Sixteenth note	A sixteenth note (American) or semiquaver (British) is a note played for half the duration of an eighth note (quaver), hence the names.
Slur	A slur is a symbol indicating that the notes it embraces are to be played without separation. A slur is denoted with a curved line generally placed over the notes if the stems point downward, and under them if the stems point upwards.
Solo	A solo is a piece or a section of a piece played or sung featuring a single performer, who may be performing completely alone or supported by an accompanying instrument such as a piano or organ, a continuo group, or the rest of a choir, orchestra, band, or other ensemble.
Sound Processing	Audio signal processing or audio processing is the intentional alteration of audio signals often through an audio effect or effects unit. As audio signals may be electronically represented in either digital or analog format, signal processing may occur in either domain.
Sound Treatment	Acoustic foam is an open-celled foam used for acoustic treatment. It attenuates airborne sound waves by increasing air resistance, thus reducing the amplitude of the waves. The energy is dissipated as heat.
Soundproofing	Soundproofing is any means of reducing the sound pressure with respect to a specified sound source and receptor. There are several basic approaches to reducing sound: increasing the distance between source and receiver, using noise barriers to reflect or absorb the energy of the sound waves, using damping structures such as sound baffles, or using active anti-noise sound generators.
Staccatissimo	A style of playing notes in a detached, separated, distinct manner that shortens the notated duration of the note in a more exaggerated way than normal staccato.
Staccato	Staccato ([stakˈkaːto]; Italian for “detached”) is a form of musical articulation. In modern notation, it signifies a note of shortened duration, separated from the note that may follow by silence
Staff	In Western musical notation, the staff or stave is a set of five horizontal lines and four spaces that each represent a different musical pitch or in the case of a percussion staff, different percussion instruments.
Stave	See *Staff*.

Stem (mixing)	Stem-mixing is a method of mixing audio material based on creating groups of audio tracks and processing them separately prior to combining them into a final master mix. Stems are also sometimes referred to as submixes, subgroups, or busses.
Stock Music	Stock music (also known as production music or library music) is the name given to recorded music that can be licensed to customers for use in film, television, radio and other media. Oftentimes, the music is produced and owned by production music libraries.
Straight	Straight timing is where the beat is split into equal subdivisions (a ratio of 1:1) for playing notes. Swing timing is where the beat is split into two-third plus one-third subdivisions (a ratio of 2:1).
Straight Mute	A variety of mutes have been used on brass instruments, most of which either squeeze inside the bell of the instrument or are hung or clipped to the outside of the bell. The most common type is the straight mute, a hollow, cone-shaped mute that fits into the bell of the instrument.
Stringendo	With a pressing forward or acceleration of the tempo.
Strings	A string is the vibrating element that produces sound in string instruments such as the guitar, harp, piano (piano wire), and members of the violin family. Strings are lengths of a flexible material that a musical instrument holds under tension so that they can vibrate freely, but controllably.
Structure	Song structure or the musical forms of songs in traditional music and music are typically sectional, repeating forms used in songs, such as strophic form and is a part of the songwriting process. Other common forms include thirty-two-bar form, verse-chorus form, and the twelve-bar blues.
Style	An artistic form of auditory communication incorporating instrumental or vocal tones in a structured and continuous manner.
Swing	The name swing came from the 'swing feel' where the emphasis is on the off–beat or weaker pulse in the music.
Swung	See *Swing*.
Synthesizer	An electronic musical instrument, typically operated by a keyboard, producing a wide variety of sounds by generating and combining signals of different frequencies.
Template	DAW projects utilize templates - predefined projects containing tracks already configured with instruments, plugins, and mixing settings to speed up the composing process. See also *DAW*.

Tempo	Tempo can be defined as the pace or speed at which a section of music is played. Tempos, or tempi, help the composer to convey a feeling of either intensity or relaxation. We can think of the tempo as the speedometer of the music. Typically, the speed of the music is measured in beats per minute, or BPM.
Tempo Map	A tempo map is a part of a MIDI file. Musical events occur as a succession of events in time, whose speed is tempo. Music also organizes these according to a framework called meter, by partitioning time into patterns of "strong" and "weak" beats.
Tenuto	Tenuto (Italian, past participle of tenere, "to hold") is a durational direction used in musical notation which means to hold or sustain a note for its full length.
Tie	A tie is a curved line connecting the heads of two notes of the same pitch, indicating that they are to be played as a single note with a duration equal to the sum of the individual notes' values.
Time Signature	An indication of rhythm following a clef, generally expressed as a fraction with the denominator defining the beat as a division of a whole note and the numerator giving the number of beats in each bar.
Transpose	Transposition refers to the process or operation of moving a collection of notes up or down in pitch by a constant interval.
Tremolo	The word 'tremolo' is an Italian word that actually means 'trembling.' In musical notation, a tremolo indicates that a musician should repeat a specific note or notes as rapidly as possible to produce the quivering effect.
Trill	The trill is a musical ornament consisting of a rapid alternation between two adjacent notes, usually a semitone or tone apart, which can be identified with the context of the trill. It is sometimes referred to by the German Triller, the Italian trillo, the French trille or the Spanish trino.
Tuplets	A tuplet is "any rhythm that involves dividing the beat into a different number of equal subdivisions from that usually permitted by the time-signature". This is indicated by a number, indicating the fraction involved. The notes involved are also often grouped with a bracket or a slur.
Turn	A turn is a flourish of added notes, similar to a trill. However, instead of alternating notes, like in a trill, a turn is a specific pattern that is played by first playing the note above the one that is written, then the written note, a note below the written note, then the written note again. The symbol for a turn is an S laying on its side and is placed above the bar either directly over a note, or between them. The exact speed and performance of a turn is usually determined by its context within the composition, and the style of the piece. A turn, trill, mordent, appoggiatura, acciaccatura, glissando and schleifer are all a class of musical embellishments called "ornaments".

Verse	In popular music, a verse roughly corresponds to a poetic stanza because it consists of rhyming lyrics most often with an AABB or ABAB rhyme scheme. When two or more sections of the song have almost identical music and different lyrics, each section is considered one verse.
Vivace	Lively, quick. Spirited, bright, rapid, equaling or exceeding allegro a musical direction to play fast.
Vivacissimo	In a very lively or vivacious manner.
Volume	Musically speaking, volume can be defined as the loudness of a sound, as measured in decibels. A common, non-technical term meaning sound pressure level, and meaning audio voltage level.
WAV	WAV files are lossless uncompressed broadcast CD quality music files.
Whole note	A whole note or semibreve is a kind of note used in music notation. It has a time duration of four beats in time.
Woodwinds	A woodwind is a type of musical instrument that you play by blowing into its mouthpiece. Flutes, clarinets, and oboes are all woodwinds.

APPENDIX C

Common Musical Terms in Italian, German, and French

Italian is the most common language used in music - even more so than English. Just peruse any classical music score and you'll see nothing but Italian, German, and French. So many words that we've come to take for granted you may not realize are Italian words: tempo, violin, forte, crescendo, piano, pizzicato, the list goes on.

Here for your reference you'll find lists of common music terms in Italian (most used), German (second most used), and French (third most used).

Italian Terms

Italian Word / Phrase	Translation / Meaning / Usage
a	*"at; to; by; for; in"* eg: a tempo = in time (back to the previous speed)
a capella	*"unaccompanied"* Usually in choral music
a piacere	*"at pleasure"* The performer is not bound to follow the given rhythm exactly.
accelerando (accel)	*"gradually getting faster"* An increase in the speed of the music
accento	*"accented; emphasised"*
ad libitum (ad lib)	*"at choice; freely"* 1) A passage may be performed freely. 2) An instrument in a score may be omitted.
adagietto	*"rather slow"* Usually a little faster than adagio
adagio	*"slowly"* Often indicates a speed somewhere between andante and largo
affabile	*"friendly"*
affettuoso	*"tenderly"*
affrettando	*"hurrying"*
agitato	*"agitated; restless"*

al; alla	*"in the manner of"* eg: alla marcia = in the style of a march
alla breve	*"with a minim beat"*
allargando	*"broadening"*
allegretto	*"fairly quick"* Faster than andante and usually slower than allegro
allegro	*"fast"*
alt	*"high"* "in alt" is used in vocal music to refer to notes in the octave above the treble stave
amabile	*"amiable; pleasant"*
amore	*"love"*
andante	*"walking speed"* Moderately slow
andantino	*"like walking speed"* This can mean either slightly slower or slightly faster than andante. It is ambiguous
anima	*"soul; spirit"* eg: con anima = with spirit
animando	*"becoming more lively"*
animato	*"animated; lively"*
appassionato	*"with passion"*
arco	*"with the bow"* An instruction to string players to use the bow
arioso	*"like an aria"* Play in the style of an aria (singing)
assai	*"very"* eg: allegro assai = very fast
attacca	*"go straight on"* Indicates an immediate move to the next section of music
ben	*"well"*
bis	*"twice"* Indicates the repetition of a short passage
bravura	*"skill; brilliance"*
brio	*"vigour"* With vigour

calando	*"getting softer; dying away"* Usually includes slowing down
cantabile	*"in a singing style"*
cantando	*"singing"*
capriccioso	*"in a whimsical or fanciful style"*
col; colla; colle	*"with"* eg: colla voce = with the voice
come	*"as; similar to"* eg: come prima = as before
comodo	*"convenient"* eg: tempo comodo = at a comfortable speed
con	*"with"* eg: con moto = with movement
crescendo (cresc)	*"gradually getting louder"*
da capo (D.C.)	*"from the beginning"* An instruction to repeat the music from the beginning
dal segno (D.S.)	*"from the sign"* An instruction to repeat the music from the sign
deciso	*"with determination"*
decrescendo (decresc)	*"gradually getting softer"*
delicato	*"delicate"*
diminuendo (dim)	*"gradually getting softer"*
dolce	*"sweetly"* eg: dolcissimo = as sweet as possible
dolente	*"sad; mournful"*
dolore	*"grief"* eg: doloroso = sorrowful
doloroso	*"sorrowful"*
doppio movimento	*"twice as fast"*
e; ed	*"and"*
energico	*"energetic"*
espressivo (espr)	*"expressive"*
estinto	*"as soft as possible"*
facile	*"easy"*
felice	*"happy"*
fermata	*"pause"*

feroce	*"fierce"*
fine	*"the end"* Often used in conjunction with "da capo" or "dal segno" to indicate where to end the piece after repeating. eg: al fine = to the end
flessibile	*"flexible"*
forte (f)	*"loud; strong"*
fortepiano (fp)	*"loud then immediately soft"*
fortissimo (ff)	*"very loud"*
forza	*"force"* eg: forzando (fz) = strongly accented
fretta	*"haste"*
fuoco	*"fire"*
furioso	*"furious"*
giocoso	*"playful; humorous"*
giojoso	*"joyful; merry"*
giusto	*"proper; exact"*
grandioso	*"grandly"*
grave	*"very slow; solemn"*
grazioso	*"graceful"*
impetuoso	*"impetuous"*
incalzando	*"getting quicker"*
inquieto	*"restless"*
in relievo	*"prominent"* A direction to make the melody stand out
lacrimoso	*"sad"*
largamente	*"broadly"*
larghetto	*"rather slow"* Slightly faster than largo
largo	*"rather slow; stately"*
legato	*"smoothly"* Indicates no break between notes
leggiero	*"light; nimble"*
lento	*"slow"*
liberamente	*"freely"*
l'istesso	*"the same"* eg: l'istesso tempo = at the same speed

loco	*"at the normal pitch"* Used to cancel an 8va direction. Also used to confirm that 8va is not intended
lugubre	*"mournful"*
lunga	*"long"* eg: lunga pausa = long pause
lusingando	*"coaxing"*
ma	*"but"* eg: allegro ma non troppo = quick but not too quick
maestoso	*"majestic"*
mancando	*"fading away"*
marcato (marc)	*"emphatic; accented"*
marziale	*"in a military style"*
meno	*"less"* eg: meno forte = less loud
mesto	*"sad"*
mezzoforte (mf)	*"moderately loud"*
mezzo piano (mp)	*"moderately soft"*
misterioso	*"mysterious"*
misura	*"measure"* eg: alla misura = in strict time; senza misura = in free time
moderato	*"moderate speed"* eg: allegro moderato = moderately fast
molto	*"very; much"* eg: allegro molto = very fast
morendo	*"dying away"*
mosso	*"movement"*
moto	*"movement"*
niente	*"nothing"*
nobilmente	*"nobly"*
non	*"not"*
nuovo	*"new"* e.g. di nuovo = again
obbligato	*"obligatory"* Indicates that an instrument has a special role and is essential
ossia	*"or; alternatively"* Often used to indicate a simpler version of a difficult passage

ostinato	*"persistent"* Generally refers to a persistently repeated rhythmic or melodic figure
parlando	*"speaking"* A direction for a singer to sing in a conversational style
patetico	*"with deep feeling"*
pausa	*"pause"*
per	*"by; for; to"*
perdendosi	*"dying away"*
pesante	*"heavy"*
piacevole	*"pleasant"*
piangevole	*"plaintive"*
pianissimo (pp)	*"very soft"*
piano (p)	*"soft"*
più	*"more"* e.g. più forte = louder
pizzicato	*"plucked"* An instruction to string players to pluck the strings, rather than bow them
placido	*"calm; peaceful"*
pochettino (poch)	*"rather little"*
poco	*"a little"* e.g. poco a poco = little by little
possible	*"possible"* e.g. presto possible = as fast as possible
precipitando	*"rushing; headlong"*
presto	*"very fast"*
prima	*"first"* (Prima; Primo) e.g. prima volta = first time; tempo primo = revert to the speed at the beginning of the piece of music
quasi	*"as if; resembling"* e.g. quasi recitativo = like a recitative
rallentando (rall)	*"gradually getting slower"*
rigoroso	*"strict"*
rinforzando (rf; rfz)	*"reinforcing"*
risoluto	*"bold; strong"*
ritardando (rit)	*"gradually getting slower"*
ritenuto (rit)	*"held back"*
ritmico	*"rhythmically"*

rubato	*"with some freedom of time"*
scherzando	*"playful; joking"* Also scherzoso
scherzo	*"joke; jest"* A movement in a piece, generally light and humorous in nature
seconda	*"second"* (Seconda; secondo)
semplice	*"simple; plain"*
sempre	*"always"* e.g. sempre staccato = always detached
senza	*"without"* e.g. senza misura = freely (not in time)
segue	*"go straight on"*
sforzando (sf; sfz)	*"forced; accented"*
simile (sim)	*"in the same way"*
slargando	*"getting slower"*
slancio	*"enthusiasm"*
smorzando (smorz)	*"dying away"* Both tone and speed
soave	*"gentle; smooth"*
solenne	*"solemn; grave"*
sonoro	*"resonant; with rich tone"*
sopra	*"above"*
sospirando	*"sighing"*
sostenuto	*"sustained"*
sotto	*"below"* eg: sotto voce = in an undertone
spirito	*"spirited"*
spiritoso	*"spirited"*
staccato	*"detached"*
strepitoso	*"noisy; boisterous"*
stretto	*"quickening the speed"* Also means overlapping entries of a fugue subject
stringendo	*"gradually getting faster"*
subito	*"suddenly"*

tacet	*"silent"* A direction that a particular part has nothing to play in a section of music
tanto	*"so much"*
tempo	*"speed"* eg: a tempo = return to the previous speed, after a slowing down or speeding up.
teneramente	*"tenderly"*
tenuto	*"held"*
tosto	*"swift; rapid"*
tranquillo	*"calm"*
trionfale	*"triumphant"*
triste	*"sad; sorrowful"*
troppo	*"too much"* eg: allegro ma non troppo = fast, but not too fast
tutti	*"all; everyone"*
veloce	*"swift"*
vigoroso	*"vigorous; strong"*
vivace	*"lively"*
vivo	*"lively"*
voce	*"voice"*
volante	*"flying; fast"*
volta	*"time"* e.g. prima volta = first time
volti subito (V.S.)	*"turn the page at once"*

German Terms

German Word / Phrase	**Translation / Meaning / Usage**
aber	*"but"*
als	*"than"*
ausdruck	*"expression"*
bestimmt	*"with decision"*
bewegt	*"with movement; agitated"*
breit	*"broad; expansive"*
doch	*"however; yet"*
ein	*"a; one"*
einfach	*"simple"*
empfindung	*"emotion; feeling"*

etwas	*"somewhat; rather"* e.g. etwas schneller = somewhat faster
feurig	*"fiery"*
fliessend	*"flowing"*
frei	*"free"*
frisch	*"vigorous"*
fröhlich	*"cheerful; joyful"*
gebunden	*"joined"*
gehend	*"at a steady speed"*
gesangvoll	*"in a singing style"*
geschwind	*"quick"*
generalpause (G.P.)	*"everyone is silent"* An indication to an individual player that all players are silent
immer	*"always"* e.g. immer langsam = always slowly
innig	*"heartfelt; sincere"*
kräftig	*"strong"*
langsam	*"slow"*
lebhaft	*"lively"*
leicht	*"light; nimble"*
leidenschaft	*"passion"*
leise	*"soft; gentle"*
soft; gentle	*"lovely"*
lustig	*"cheerful"*
mässig	*"at a moderate speed"*
mit	*"with"*
munter	*"lively"*
nach und nach	*"gradually"*
nicht	*"not"*
ohne	*"without"*
rasch	*"quick"*
ruhig	*"peaceful"*
schleppen	*"dragging"*
schnell	*"fast"*
schwach	*"weak"*
sehr	*"very"* e.g. sehr ruhig = very calm
stark	*"strong"*

süss	*"sweet"*
traurig	*"sad"*
und	*"and"*
viel	*"much"*
voll	*"full"*
vorgetragen	*"brought out; prominent"*
wenig	*"little"*
wieder	*"again"*
zart	*"tender; delicate"*
ziemlich	*"moderately"*
zu	*"to; too"*

French Terms

French Word / Phrase	**Translation / Meaning / Usage**
à	*"at; to"* e.g. peu à peu = little by little
amour	*"love"*
animé	*"animated; lively"*
apaisé	*"calmed"*
assez	*"enough; sufficiently"*
avec	*"with"*
cédez	*"yield; relax the speed"*
come	*"as; similar to"* e.g. come prima = as before
douce	*"sweetly"* Also doux
emporté	*"fiery; impetuous"*
en animant	*"becoming more lively"*
en cédant	*"yielding"*
en dehors	*"prominent"* A direction to make the melody stand out
en mesure	*"in time"*
en pressant	*"hurrying on"*
en retenant	*"holding back"*
en serrant	*"becoming quicker"*
et	*"and"*

flottant	*"floating"*
gracieux	*"graceful"*
joyeux	*"joyful"*
légèrement	*"light"*
lent	*"slow"*
librement	*"freely"*
lointain	*"distant"*
lourd	*"heavy"*
mais	*"but"*
modéré	*"at a moderate speed"*
moins	*"less"*
peu	*"little"*
plus	*"more"*
presser	*"hurry"*
ralentir	*"slow down"*
retenu	*"held back"*
sans	*"without"* e.g. sans ralentir = without slowing down
sautillé	*"springing"*
sec	*"crisp; dry"* Suppress the sound as quickly as possible - do not allow it to reverberate
seul	*"alone"*
serrer	*"hurry; quicken"*
sonore	*"resonant; with rich tone"*
sous	*"under"*
très	*"very"*
un	*"one"*
vif	*"lively"*
vite	*"quick"*
vivement	*"lively"*

APPENDIX D

Musical Instrument Names in Italian, German, and French

English	Italian	German	French
Voice	Voce	Stimme	Voix
Strings	**Archi**	**Streich-instrumente**	**Cordes**
Violin(s)	Violino(-i)	Violine(n), Geige(n)	Violon(s)
Viola(s)	Viola, Viole	Bratsche(n)	Alto(s)
Cello(s)	Violoncello(-i)	Violoncello(-e)	Violoncelle(s)
Double Bass(es)	Contrabbasso(-i)	Kontrabass(-bässe)	Contrebasse(s)
Harp(s)	Arpa, Arpe	Harfe(n)	Harpe(s)
Woodwinds	**Legni/Fiati**	**Holzbläser**	**Bois**
Piccolo	Flauto piccolo, Ottavino	Kleine Flöte, Pikkoloflöte	Petite Flûte
Flute(s)	Flauto(-i)	Flöte(n)	Flûte(s)
Alto flute	Flauto contralto	Altflöte	Flûte alto en sol
Bass flute	Flauto basso	Baßflöte	Flûte basse
Oboe(s)	Oboe, Oboi	Oboe, Hoboe, Oboen	Hautbois
English horn	Corno inglese	Englisch Horn	Cor anglais
Oboe d'amore in A	Oboe d'amore	Liebesoboe	Hautbois d'amour
Eb Clarinet	Clarinetto piccolo in mib	Es Klarinette	Clarinette en mib
Clarinet(s)	Clarinetto(-i)	Klarinette(n)	Clarinette(s)
Bass clarinet	Clarione, Clarinetto basso	Bassklarinette	Clarinette basse
English	**Italian**	**German**	**French**
Bassoon(s)	Fagotto(-i)	Fagott(e)	Basson(s)
Contrabassoon(s)	Contrafagotto(-i)	Kontrafagott(e)	Contre-basson(s)
Saxophone(s)	Sassofono(-i)	Saxophon(e)	Saxophone(s)
Harmonica	Armonica a bocca	Mundharmonika	Harmonica à bouche
Brass	**Ottoni**	**Blech-instrumente**	**Cuivres**
French Horn(s)	Corno(-i)	Horn, Hörner	Cor(s)
Trumpet(s)	Tromba, Trombe	Trompete(n)	Trompette(s)
Cornet(s)	Cornetto(-i)	Kornett(e)	Cornet(s)
Flugelhorn	Flicorno	Flügelhorn	Bugle a pistons
Trombone(s)	Trombone(-i)	Posaune(n)	Trombone(s)
Bass trombone	Trombone basso	Baßposaune	Trombone basse
Tuba(s)	Tuba	Tuba	Tuba(s)

Baritone Horn(s), Euphonium(s)	Bombarda, Flicorno basso	Euphonion, Baryton	Baryton, Euphonium, Euphonion, Saxhorn tuba, Tuba ténor
Percussion	**Percussione / Batteria**	**Schlagzeug**	**Batterie**
Marimba	Marimba	Marimba, Marimbaphon	Marimba
Xylophone	Silofono, Xilofono, Gigelira	Xylophon, Strohfiedel	Xylophone, Claquebois
Glockenspiel, Orchestral Bells	Campanelli	Glockenspiel	Jeu de timbres, Carillon
Vibraphone	Vibrafono	Vibraphon	Vibraphone
Tubular Bells, (Bell) Chimes	Campani tubulari	Glocken, Röhrenglocken	(Tubes de) Cloches
Celesta	Celesta, Celeste	Celesta	Célesta

English	Italian	German	French
Antique Cymbals, Crotales	Crotali, cimbali	(Antike) Zimbeln, Crotales, Antike Cymbeln	Cymbales antiques, crotales
Handbells	Campanella a mano	Handglocken	Clochettes à mains
Almglocken	Campane da pastore	Almglocken	Sonnailles de troupeau
Timpani (pl), Kettle drums	Timpano(-i)	Pauke(n)	Timbale(s)
Woodblock	Cassetina, Blocco di legno (cinese)	Holzblock	Wood bloc, Bloc de bois
Temple blocks	Blocchi di legno coreani, Blocchi cinesi	Tempelblöcke	Temple-blocs
Cymbals (pl)	Piatti (pl)	Becken (pl)	Cymbales (pl)
Crash cymbals	Piatti, cinelli	Becken-Paar, Becken gewönlich	Cymbales
Suspended cymbal	Piatto sospeso	Hängendes Becken, Becken freihängend	Cymbale suspendue
Tam-tam	Tamtam	Tamtam	Tam-tam
Gong	Gong	Gong	Gong
Snare drum, Side drum	Tamburo, Piccolo Cassa, Tamburo piccolo	(Kleine) Trommel	Tambour, Caisse claire
Bass Drum (upright/on side)	(Gran) Cassa, Tamburone, Tamburo grande (orizzontale)	Grosse Trommel (aufrecht/liegend)	Grosse Caisse (verticale/à plat)
Pianoforte, Piano	Pianoforte, Piano	Pianoforte, Piano, Klavier	Pianoforte, Piano
Harpsichord	Cembalo, Clavicembalo, Arpicordo	Cembalo, Clavicembalo, Arpicordo	Clavecin
Organ	Organo	Orgel	Orgue

Acknowledgements

There are several individuals that must be thanked for helping to make this book possible.

First and foremost, a big thanks to David William Hearn, for without your vision StaffPad would not exist and I would not have a reason to write this book in the first place! For being supportive of my effort to write this book, and finally, for creating StaffPad in the first place! You've made writing music fun again.

A special thanks to my publisher Ron Middlebrook for encouraging me to write another book even when I insisted that I could not think of anything new to write about. Also, for letting me see your amazing guitar collection.

There are quite a few members of the Facebook StaffPad User Group that have been helpful, inspirational, and supportive of one another as we've become StaffPad users. In no particular order I'd like to thank John MacKay, David Coscina, Marshall Shaw, Juliana Sousa Santos, Gary Atkins, Steve Locks, Gert-Jan Maas, Ole Jørgensen, Tigtig Cuaian, Nickie Katharina, Fønshauge, Lennart Bäckblom, Keith Walls, TP Shimmons, James Claude, Chris Piorkowski, Fred Selden, Adam Cohen, David Sandberg, David Tobin, Annika Böttcher, Carlos Oliveira, Siegfried Schüßler, George Bogatko, Bill Reed, and Jacob Moss.

If I missed anyone from the group, I apologize, but your contributions are noted and greatly appreciated.

And lastly, I need to thank my wife, Leanne, for supporting my efforts to get this book done in a timely fashion.

About the Author

Steve Barden is a production music composer for film and television. His music can be heard on television somewhere in the world on a daily basis. His music has aired on ABC, CBS, NBC, FOX, CW, ABC Family, A&E, American Heroes Channel, Animal Planet, Biography Channel, Bravo, The Cooking Channel, Discovery Channel, E!, Food Network, Game Show Network, HGTV, Investigation Discovery, Lifetime, MTV, National Geographic Channel, Oprah Winfrey Network, Outdoor Channel, Oxygen, PBS, Science Channel, Style Channel, SyFy Channel, TLC, Travel Channel, truTV, Univision, and VH1.

Steve is a multi-instrumentalist playing guitar, piano, and violin. He has studied guitar at the Guitar Institute of Technology in Hollywood (currently Musician's Institute) and studied film scoring at UCLA. He has scored animated television series *Tic Tac Toons, Journey to the Heart of the World*, and *Button Nose.* He also scored the award winning animated short, *The Baseball Card Shop*, originally produced by Nickelodeon. He has also written jingles and theme songs for Los Angeles radio personalities, *Mark & Brian*, and also *Kevin & Bean*.

Steve is a husband, father, grandfather, and cat guardian. He lives in Lakewood, California with his wife, Leanne, and an undisclosed number of cats.

You can find Steve Barden online at his website, www.stevebarden.com.